PITTSBURGH LIVES

MEN AND WOMEN WHO SHAPED OUR CITY

Pittsburgh Post-Gazette

EDITED BY

DAVID M. SHRIBMAN AND ANGELIKA KANE

TRIUMPH
B O O K S
Chicago

Library of Congress Cataloging-in-Publication Data

Pittsburgh lives : men and women who shaped our city / Pittsburgh Post-Gazette ; edited by David M. Shribman and Angelika Kane.
    p. cm.
  ISBN-13: 978-1-57243-900-9
  ISBN-10: 1-57243-900-9
    1. Pittsburgh (Pa.)—Biography. 2. Obituaries—Pennsylvania—Pittsburgh. I. Shribman, David M. II. Kane, Angelika.
  F159.P653A273 2006
  920'.074886—dc22

                                                                    2006023740

This book is available in quantity at special discounts for your group or organization. For further information, contact:

Triumph Books
542 S. Dearborn St.
Suite 750
Chicago, IL 60605
(312) 939-3330
Fax (312) 663-3557

Printed in U.S.A.
ISBN-13: 978-1-57243-900-9
ISBN-10: 1-57243-900-9
Design by Chris Mulligan
Cover design by Paul Petrowsky

Contents

Acknowledgments

The *Pittsburgh Post-Gazette* would like to thank the following people for their assistance with this project: Allison Alexander, Kyra Brogden, John Butler, Doreen Boyce, Gene Collier, Cindy Denman, Bill Green, Sy Holzer, Bob Hoover, Stephen Karlinchak, Robert Lockwood, Frank Lucchino, Anne Madarasz, Susan Mannella, Andy Masich, John McGinley, Christopher Rawson, Larry Roberts, Jim Roddey, Clarke Thomas, Lillian Thomas, Lauren Uhl, Marylynn Uricchio, Larry Walsh, Allan Walton, and Sylvia Wilson.

Introduction

ootfalls. Always you can hear them in our town. They crop up late at night when the air is still and the skies are dark. They echo sometimes in the early morning when the air is fresh. They hit the pavement Downtown—where the steel barons once trod—and up in Oakland, where the early medical pioneers once toiled. Here in Pittsburgh, city of steel and the Steelers, of rivers and the Three Rivers Arts Festival, of jazz masters and symphony maestros, we never walk the streets alone. The footfalls are always there.

They are the footfalls of Billy Eckstine and Stanley Turrentine, who had beats all their own. They are the footfalls of Jonas Salk and Herbert Simon, who beat science and medicine's narrow expectations. They are the footsteps of Marshall Goldberg and Lloyd Waner, who beat almost everyone.

Our skyline may be new—look at our hospitals and our high-tech centers—but our streets and byways are not. And others walked them before us. They built the bridges that spanned the rivers. They built the plants that made America mobile, and they built the engines that kept America free. But they built something else, too—something that endures along with the bridges and the skyscrapers. They built a city and a tradition and a spirit that soars. They built Pittsburgh, and in building it they built a great American

city that has what some of the newer American cities lack: a center. A heart. A soul. And memories—lots and lots of memories.

Memories here are oil paintings, not misty watercolors. They are memories of the big men and strong women of the industrial age and the musicians who heard the rhythms of city life in the golden age of jazz. They are memories of great Steelers past—long may their legacy endure.

Because many of the giants who made Pittsburgh great are no longer with us, we've turned to the library of the city's great newspaper, the *Pittsburgh Post-Gazette*, to unearth the stories of their lives. *Pittsburgh Lives* is a collection of the best of the peculiar newspaper art form called the obituary. In this volume we are sharing some of the treasure that has been buried, in some cases for decades, within our own walls.

No collection like this can be complete. Some extraordinary lives are necessarily omitted when the collection is assembled by ordinary people. Some extraordinary lives escaped the attention of the newspaper's reporters and editors, and thus never were assigned. But there are other reasons why some of the most extraordinary residents of this town—among them the writer Willa Cather, the musician Victor Herbert, the activist Mother Jones, and the soldier-statesman George C. Marshall—are omitted. In the days in which these figures died, the *Post-Gazette* didn't always write its own obituaries. All of those obits were written by wire services and thus are not included in this volume. And others—of the journalist Jane Swisshelm, the artist Mary Cassatt, the general George B. McClellan, and the attorney general Philander C. Knox—we simply could not find, very likely because they never ran in the *Post-Gazette* or its predecessor newspapers.

But this is not an occasion to dwell on what we do not have. It is, instead, an occasion to marvel at what is included. Here is a remarkable obituary of the playwright August Wilson and one on the writer Gertrude Stein. In these pages you will read of Pie Traynor and Roberto Clemente, of Cardinal John Wright, of Andrew Carnegie and Jock Yablonski. And Stephen Foster and Perry Como and Fred Rogers. Plus David L. Lawrence, Richard S. Caliguiri, Pete Flaherty, and Josh Gibson and Honus Wagner. Pittsburghers all, and all in this book.

Most of the figures in this volume are famous—or were famous in their time. Their stories, taken together with the stories of those who were less well-known, provide a portrait of Pittsburgh that tells the history of this city and region: Pittsburgh, Allegheny County, and Southwestern Pennsylvania. These people gave Pittsburgh its character and plotted its course. And for that reason,

along with Molly Yard's obituary is the story of John Minadeo, the 15-year-old crossing guard who pushed children out of the way of the speeding car that killed him in 1954 and whose name graces an elementary school in Squirrel Hill. And along with the obituary of Andy Warhol is the obituary of Joey Diven, street fighter and Good Samaritan of legend and lore. This volume would not be complete without accounts of those who fled their hometowns and who abandoned most of society's conventions. For that reason we have included Gary Rotstein's tribute to his brother Wayne, whose life was fuller than most of the mysteries of life itself.

These obituaries tell us about the time they were written and the time in which we live today. By looking back, we can see how our world was shaped by theirs. These are profiles in courage, creativity, and vision. They are sketched in the blue skies of airy dreams and etched in the concrete of gritty reality. They are a look back, to be sure, but they are much, much more than that. They are also a way to look at our own lives. These stories instruct, and they inspire. Taken as a whole, these lives provide us with the ultimate lesson: these lives from another age teach us how to live in our own age.

—David M. Shribman
Pittsburgh Post-Gazette
executive editor

SECTION

I

Academia, Health, and Medicine

In postmodern Pittsburgh it is commonplace to say that the city's strength is its academic and medical power. But in an age when we believe that universities, hospitals, and research laboratories constitute the metaphorical steel mills of the 21st century, it is easy to forget that academic and medical power have been part of Pittsburgh's landscape and personality for half a century or more. The vitality of today's Pittsburgh, to be sure, is in this sector. But the roots of that vitality were planted in the past.

SATURDAY, JUNE 24, 1995

Jonas Salk, 80
Developed Polio Vaccine
By Douglas Heuck, *Pittsburgh Post-Gazette*

At a press conference Dr. Jonas Salk presents the polio vaccine he created. *Photo by Morris Berman.*

D r. Jonas Salk, hailed as the savior of children the world over for wiping out one of the most dreaded diseases of the 20th century, has died.

Salk, who conquered polio with his development of an effective vaccine in Pittsburgh, died yesterday afternoon of heart failure at Green Hospital of Scripps Clinic in La Jolla, California, where he had been hospitalized earlier in the day complaining of shortness of breath. He was 80 years old.

"I would say he was at peace," said his assistant, Kathleen Murray. "He had had some angioplasty on his legs (recently) and was looking forward to having more energy and continuing his work on his autobiography and the (HIV) vaccine." Angioplasty is a procedure to eliminate blockages in arteries.

In January, Salk, through the Immune Response Corp., was the first to get U.S. Food and Drug Administration approval for large-scale trials of a vaccine for people already infected with HIV, the virus that causes AIDS.

"They broke the mold when Jonas was made," said longtime friend Robert Aldrich of Seattle, Washington. "It's a shock. I've known many famous people, but Salk stands out. I just spent time with him 10 days ago, and he was talking about how to improve the human condition. My only regret with Jonas is that he didn't win the Nobel Prize—he earned it."

At the time of his death, Salk was married to the artist Francoise Gilot. With his first wife, Donna, Salk had three sons, each of whom is a doctor. He also leaves five grandchildren.

Aside from his work on polio and AIDS, his Salk Institute, founded in 1960, has become one of the world's preeminent facilities for basic research in biology.

Salk also was one of four primary people who helped establish the John D. and Catherine T. MacArthur Foundation, which is best known for the "genius" grants it makes to support the arts, sciences, and humanities across the country. The awards, each worth hundreds of thousands of dollars, annually go to about 30 people who are chosen by any of 100 anonymous nominators for their ability to contribute to humanity.

His Work in Pittsburgh

Salk arrived in Pittsburgh in 1947.

When he entered the old Municipal Hospital, later renamed Salk Hall at the University of Pittsburgh, the hospital floors above him were scenes of horror as young victims of polio, crippled by the mysterious and sometimes deadly disease, arrived one after the other. For many, the best help available was the coffin-like iron lung. Parents across the nation were panicked, fearing their children would come down with the disease and be paralyzed for life.

Through a $200,000 grant from the National Foundation for Infantile Paralysis, which became the March of Dimes, Salk began the task of classifying the different kinds of polio viruses in 1949.

Salk assembled a team of researchers and designed a lab in intricate detail. In classifying the various types of polio virus, he would be the administrator, dealing with the foundation, eminent research scientists across the land, and vendors across the world who would send him more than 17,500 monkeys for the research.

When Salk and his staff found innovative ways to do the job more quickly and less expensively, however, they ran into roadblocks from the scientific community.

And when Salk questioned the conventional methods at a meeting in New York, he tasted the ire of another leading polio researcher, Dr. Albert Sabin, for the first time. "Now, Dr. Salk, you should know better than to ask a question like that," Sabin scolded during one exchange. Theirs would become a bitter rivalry that would last until Sabin's death in 1993.

Still, Salk was on a fast track to developing a vaccine. He took discoveries he had made about influenza in the late 1930s and applied them to polio with a vaccine made of a killed version of the polio virus.

Against Prevailing Wisdom

Scientific orthodoxy at the time insisted that you could induce lasting immunity to a viral infection only by first provoking a weak infection. And a weakened, live virus put into a vaccine would do just that. It also could cause an acute infection, however.

Salk's killed-virus influenza vaccine challenged the prevailing wisdom and, by extension, would show that the careers of many scientists had been based on faulty conclusions.

"The question was, namely, can we improve upon nature?" Salk said in a *Post-Gazette* interview in October 1994. "Can we, in fact induce an immune response without the risk of disease? Having succeeded and learned how to do it for influenza, the logical next question was to work with polio viruses and see if the same thing could be true. Well, having found that it could be done, it was done."

On June 12, 1952, Salk took blood from 45 polio-afflicted children at D.T. Watson Home to test their levels of antibodies to the virus. On July 2 he inoculated the children to test whether the vaccine elevated their antibody counts.

"When you inoculate children with a polio vaccine," he later said, "you don't sleep well for two or three months."

When he saw that the vaccine boosted the number of antibodies in those who already had polio and that the vaccine created a level of antibodies necessary to kill the virus in those who weren't infected, Salk experienced what he would later call "the thrill of my life."

"Compared to the feeling I got seeing those results under the microscope, everything that followed was anticlimactic."

It would take another three years and a field trial involving 2 million children before his vaccine would be declared safe and reliable.

More than 100 million Americans helped finance the polio effort through the March of Dimes. More than 7 million had participated as foundation volunteers, committee workers, fundraisers, or as Polio Pioneers—as those inoculated in the trials were called. It was the biggest clinical experiment in medical history.

Trial Results Announced

April 12, 1955, was the day the results of the trials were to be announced. Dr. Alan Gregg, vice president of the Rockefeller Institute, told Salk that morning: "You must make a conscious decision. You must decide whether to spend the rest of your days enjoying your fame or working. You will be unable to do both. You can spend your life traveling, reading papers, accepting awards, and being comfortable. Or you can have the courage to turn aside publicity, the courage to resume your work, the courage to face the possibility that you may never again be able to do a piece of work as important as the work which brings us here today."

Salk chose the path of work. It fit well with his personality.

"Jonas was essentially a rather shy, self-effacing person when this press conference was called in 1955 to announce the effectiveness of polio vaccine," said Al Rosenfeld, a longtime science editor for *Life* magazine and Salk's friend.

"Naturally, polio was the most feared disease. Even more than AIDS is now. AIDS, you know what causes it. Back then nobody knew what caused all these kids to be paralyzed and end up in an iron lung. Every summer was polio season, and people were terrified. It was a foregone conclusion that whoever made the discovery would be on the front pages. There were polls taken years back in the *Saturday Review*, when the only two medical scientists anyone could think of were Louis Pasteur and Jonas Salk. He would rather, I think, have preferred not to have gotten the recognition," Rosenfeld said. "The irony was that he was idolized by the public, and only a minority of his peers ever publicly recognized what he had done.

"Jonas was the kind of free-thinking, creative guy who didn't do things by the rules, scientifically speaking. He wasn't accepted in the mainstream. He was never elected to the National Academy of Sciences. That's the biggest honor for an American scientist.

"People always said 'Well, what's he done lately?' Or 'How innovative was what he did? It was mechanical.' Well, it really was innovative."

The Sabin Rivalry

The most famous of those who didn't think much of Salk was Sabin, the University of Cincinnati researcher who lost the race to cure polio to Salk, but whose live-virus vaccine replaced Salk's in the United States. In retrospect, Salk said in October, part of the reason his vaccine was replaced was that the scientific world wasn't ready for his breakthrough.

Sabin, who did gain election to the National Academy of Sciences, once disparaged Salk's vaccine as "pure kitchen chemistry" and said, "Salk didn't discover anything."

Of Sabin, Salk said: "We just saw things differently. He was a virologist and I an immunologist. There's nothing much to say other than it's a pattern in all other human affairs, whether people see eye to eye or whether they don't. It acts itself out. That's what wars are all about. In the field of science, though, these things should be worked out."

After his momentous conquest of polio in 1955, the challenge for Salk, then 40, was what to do for an encore. By 1957 he was a treasured commodity at the University of Pittsburgh, where his title became commonwealth professor of experimental medicine.

Philanthropists bought Municipal Hospital on Terrace Street for $1.4 million, renamed it Salk Hall, and gave it to the university for Salk to use. He conceived of the facility as the home for his new vision, the Institute for Experimental Medicine. He envisioned it as being independent of the university but close enough to allow researchers to move back and forth.

The Move West

However, after continuous disagreements with Edward H. Litchfield, Pitt's new chancellor, Salk decided to try the West Coast instead.

He chose La Jolla for his institute. When the nonprofit institute began in 1963, its board members were among the most distinguished thinkers in the world.

Though it has not become all Salk hoped it would, last year the institute was named the world's top institution in molecular biology and genetics. In February it was ranked first in the world in neuroscience. Nine of its faculty have been elected to the National Academy of Sciences and seven are Nobel winners. Three more Nobel winners were trained at the institute.

Following his breakthrough on polio, Salk worked on many human ailments, including cancer, multiple sclerosis, and the nature of autoimmune diseases such as arthritis.

But perhaps more fitting for Salk than the title biologist, vaccinologist, or immunologist would be the term evolutionist. Salk wrote that there is no guarantee that our species will survive.

As he said, "Many more species have become extinct than have survived."

The difference for humankind is that we are capable of understanding nature's dictates and making conscious choices to go along with them. But if humanity doesn't go along with nature," Salk wrote, "nature can be expected to take an 'active hand' in correcting the 'errors.'"

Faith in the Future

Above all, say those who knew him, Salk was an optimist about the future of humankind. "I feel there is an inevitability about all this over the long term," he said. "Each generation that comes along has the challenge and opportunity to correct the errors of the past. We can create a better world and overcome the problems. That's what some people devote their lives to doing. Not everybody does, clearly. Unfortu-nately, there are many who do not have purposes in life. They're the unfortunate ones. So we have these two sets of forces going: problem solvers and problem creators. Well, that's what the problem solvers are here for."

Asked in October what awaited him at the end of his life, Salk gave an answer without hesitation: "Continuity. Through whatever you've contributed to influence the process of evolution. I'll be here forevermore through what I've been able to contribute, influencing the minds of others, hopefully for the better."

SATURDAY, FEBRUARY 10, 2001

Herbert A. Simon, 84
Nobel Prize Winner

By Byron Spice, *Pittsburgh Post-Gazette*

Nobel Prize–winner Dr. Herbert Simon in his office at Carnegie Mellon University, March 16, 1986. The computer expert was recognized for advancing the science of artificial intelligence. *Photo by Jim Fetters.*

Herbert A. Simon, whose curiosity about how people make decisions helped lay the groundwork for such fields as artificial intelligence and cognitive psychology and won him the 1978 Nobel Prize in economics, died yesterday at age 84.

Until just a few weeks ago, Dr. Simon had been in good health, continuing to pursue his research at Carnegie Mellon University, publishing papers, and seeing students. But in mid-January, he underwent surgery at UPMC Presbyterian to remove a cancerous tumor from his abdomen. The surgery was successful and the care he received was exquisite, said his daughter, Katherine Simon Frank, but he then suffered a series of what turned out to be fatal complications.

"Obviously, we're all talking a lot about him today around here," said psychology professor Kenneth Kotovsky. "One of the joys of my existence...has been that his office is right down the hall from me. Running into him in the hall would often lead to an amazing intellectual discussion. You could talk to him about anything."

Dr. Simon had been a fixture for 52 years at Carnegie Mellon, a university that he helped transform and make famous. He and the late Allen Newell gained renown in the mid-1950s when they created the first "thinking machine" and launched the field of artificial intelligence. Both also were central figures during the cognitive revolution in psychology in the 1960s as scientists began to use computer models to study human thought processes.

As a scientist and later a university trustee, Dr. Simon played key roles in creating the computer science department and the Robotics Institute and founding the cognitive science group within the psychology department. The Graduate School of Industrial Administration and the departments of social and decision sciences, philosophy, statistics, and physics all bear his imprint.

"Few, if any, scientists and scholars in the world have had as great an influence as has Herb across so many fields— economics, computer science, psychology, and artificial intelligence among them," said university president Jared L. Cohon.

Dr. Simon's presence attracted scores of other researchers and untold numbers of students to the university, making him arguably one of the most powerful figures on the campus. His influence was so great, suggested psychology professor David Klahr, "it should be named Carnegie Mellon Simon University."

Born in Milwaukee in 1916, Simon's father was an electrical engineer–turned–patent attorney; his mother was an accomplished pianist.

"I like to think that since I was about 19, I have studied human decision-making and problem-solving," Dr. Simon said in a *Post-Gazette* interview last fall. He earned a doctorate in political science at the University of Chicago in 1943 and took teaching positions at the Illinois Institute of Technology and the University of California at Berkeley before joining the newly established industrial administration school at the Carnegie Institute of Technology.

He had hoped to use mathematics to give the social sciences the same rigor as such hard sciences as physics and chemistry, but found that to be a frustrating experience; even with the new machine called a computer that was available at Carnegie Tech, it seemed that something was always missing when human factors were translated into numbers.

In the mid-1950s, however, he came to realize that computers weren't just number-crunchers but could be used to study patterns of any type. "I realized that you could formulate theories about human and social phenomena in language and pictures and whatever you wanted on the computer, and you didn't have to go through this straitjacket adding a lot of numbers," he said in his *Post-Gazette* interview.

During Christmas break in 1955, Simon, Newell, and programmer J.C. Shaw made that vision a reality by creating Logic Theorist, a computer program that could discover proofs of geometric theorems. It was the first computer program capable of thinking and marked the beginning of what would become known as artificial intelligence.

In 1957 Dr. Simon became convinced that computers not only could think, but that a computer would be able to beat the world's best chess player within 10 years. It was a prediction that would later come back to haunt him; it was actually 40 years before IBM's Deep Blue would win the chess championship from Garry Kasparov. But Raj Reddy, former dean of computer science, said that prediction really wasn't so far off. "It was a doable thing in 10 years," he said. "But it was like putting a man on the moon. You had to devote resources to it, and no one did then."

Dr. Simon's infatuation with human decision-making would lead him across other academic disciplines. He and Newell developed a theory that the human mind manipulates symbols in much the same way that a computer does. They were at the core of the cognitive revolution in the 1960s, when psychologists began to use computers to study how the thinking process works. Most notably, his quest to understand decision-making led him to develop his economic theory of bounded rationality, for which he was awarded the 1978 Nobel in economics.

Classical economists had argued that people make rational choices to obtain the best commodity at the best price. Dr. Simon said that was impossible—too many choices and too little time to analyze them cause people to choose the first option that is good enough to meet their needs.

Dr. Simon once wrote that the best choice he ever made was to convince Dorothea Pye to marry him on Christmas Day 1937.

In his 1991 autobiography, *Models of My Life*, Dr. Simon said he feared that his dedication to his work, which often entailed 60- to 80-hour weeks, had made him a less-than-perfect father. But his daughter, Katherine, didn't see it that way. "I respected the fact that he was so devoted to his work. I always viewed him as a model to be followed." She remembers that the family always had meals together, despite her father's long hours, and that he always led them in lively conversations. Adding to the conversational milieu were her father's graduate students, who were often invited to dinner.

One of those students in the early 1960s was Klahr, who remembers his mentor as both brilliant and intimidating. "He always assumed that the people he was talking to knew as much as he did—and they rarely did." And Simon seemed to know everything, conversing as easily about astrophysics as his own field of cognitive psychology.

Kotovsky, another former graduate student, said Dr. Simon loved to argue. When he would preface a statement with the words, "Look, friend...," that was a signal that he was about to put the kibosh on his opponent's argument. You had to be sure your head was attached when he used the word *friend*," said Kotovsky. He recalled the first time Dr. Simon directed "Look, friend" his way: "That was the moment I passed into adulthood."

Dr. Simon enjoyed playing the piano and, particularly in recent years, used to gather with friends who played violin, viola, and other instruments.

In addition to the Nobel, Dr. Simon was the recipient of virtually every top award in every scientific field he pursued: the A.M. Turing Award in computer science, the American Psychological Association Award for Outstanding Lifetime Contributions to Psychology, induction into the Automation Hall of Fame, the American Society of Public Administration's Dwight Waldo Award, and the National Medal of Science, among them.

He was always appreciative of such honors but maintained they were no big deal. "The thing that he really cherished was doing his job as a professor," Kotovsky said. One night, for instance, Kotovsky had invited the Nobel laureate to speak to a group of freshmen at one of the residence halls. After Dr. Simon spoke, everyone sat on the floor eating submarine sandwiches while the students huddled around him. The conversation continued for hours until Kotovsky, worried that Dr. Simon might be getting impatient and tired, sidled up and asked, "Will you be ready to leave soon?"

"No, you go on," Dr. Simon replied. "I'll be fine here."

"That," Kotovsky added, "was who he was."

Dr. Simon is survived by his wife, Dorothea; two daughters, Katherine Simon Frank of Minneapolis, Minnesota, and Barbara M. Simon of Wilder, Vermont; and a son, Peter Simon of Bryan, Texas.

SECTION

II

Authors, Activists, and Artists

Deep in the heart of the American civilization are thoughts that will not die, movements that will not expire, intellectual impulses that cannot be repressed. Some of them were written in Pittsburgh, nurtured by Pittsburgh, inspired by Pittsburgh. Gertrude Stein and Molly Yard changed the way Americans look at themselves. Stefan Lorant changed the way Pittsburgh looks at itself. Andy Warhol changed the way people look at art. Mary Roberts Rinehart wrote stories that endure. Through their contributions, the men and women of this chapter are still alive in Pittsburgh and in its character.

MONDAY, JULY 29, 1946

Gertrude Stein, 72
"A Rose Is a Rose Is a Rose"
By the *Pittsburgh Post-Gazette*

Gertrude Stein, age 72, the Pittsburgh-born writer whose weird syntax taxed the critical faculties of two generations of literary critics, died Saturday in Neuilly, France, after a European residence of 40 years.

Although born in 1874 amidst the industrial smoke of old Allegheny, Miss Stein's most famous quotation was addressed to the field of horticulture, in which she apostrophized the rose: "A rose is a rose is a rose."

The daughter of Daniel and Amelia Keyser Stein, Gertrude was taken to France by her family a year after she was born. She subsequently returned to the United States to study at Radcliffe Institute and Johns Hopkins School of Medicine, but in 1906 she took up permanent residence in Paris, where she became a symbol of "modernism" in literature.

An intimate friend of James Joyce, Pablo Picasso, and other giants of the literary and art worlds, her home at 5 Rue Christine, Paris, became a shrine of GIs who visited her after the liberation of Paris. While her puzzling literary style raised the eyebrows of most readers, her homely courtesy charmed the soldiers of the United States Seventh Army.

Among the books written by Miss Stein were: *Four Saints in Three Acts, The Autobiography of Alice B. Toklas, Picasso, The World Is Round,* and *Wars I Have Seen.* She never married.

TUESDAY, SEPTEMBER 23, 1958

Mary Roberts Rinehart, 82
Successful Novelist
By the *Pittsburgh Post-Gazette*

Mary Roberts Rinehart, one of America's best-known and most successful novelists, died last night in her home in New York City.

Death came to the 82-year-old writer about 10:00 while she was asleep. A native Pittsburgher, Mrs. Rinehart began her career as an author while living here, and her most famous novel, *The Circular Staircase,* has as its locale the Rineharts' rambling old mansion in Sewickley, Pennsylvania.

Wanted to Be Nurse

Mrs. Rinehart was born here August 12, 1876, and her early ambition was to be a nurse. It was while she was studying at the Pittsburgh Training School for Nurses that she met her husband, the late Dr. Stanley M. Rinehart.

The young couple, the parents of three sons, met with financial misfortune during a stock market crash in 1903, which not only wiped out their savings but left them heavily in debt. That misfortune served to spur Mrs. Rinehart in her early efforts at writing, which she first began while recovering from diphtheria.

Novel's Sales Soared

Then 27 years old, Mrs. Rinehart turned out 45 short stories and novelettes in her first year as an author, and in 1908 she wrote the novel that was to make her nationally famous—*The Circular Staircase.*

That novel alone—the first of 60 she was to produce—sold a million and a quarter copies. It was the first of the series of gripping novels which put her in the forefront of mystery writers.

But despite her rigid writing schedule, Mrs. Rinehart found time to he a devoted wife to her husband, who died in 1932, and mother to her sons: Stanley Jr., Frederick, and Alan. All three sons engaged in the book-publishing business in later life.

Her life was marked by tragedy and illness. Her father, an unsuccessful inventor, committed suicide, and her mother was accidentally scalded to death in her bath. Mrs. Rinehart herself underwent 15 operations, one of them for cancer, and suffered four coronary attacks. Despite her many illnesses, Mrs. Rinehart—who did all her writing

Mary Roberts Rinehart. *Photo courtesy of the Pittsburgh Post-Gazette.*

in longhand—continued writing until two years ago, when she contracted writer's cramp.

Mrs. Rinehart was active in many civic and philanthropic enterprises. She was an early advocate of women's suffrage, aided the government in defense work during World War I, and served with the American forces in France under special assignment by the War Department. In the last-named role she visited many Army camps, hospitals, and dispensaries.

In addition to novels, she also wrote a number of plays, and it was estimated that her millions of readers have spent around $27,000,000 to read her books or see her plays.

Mary Roberts Rinehart. *Photo courtesy of the Pittsburgh Post-Gazette.*

In the early 1920s the Rineharts moved to Washington, D.C., when Dr. Rinehart was appointed as a consultant in tuberculosis for the Veterans Administration. Following Dr. Rinehart's death, Mrs. Rinehart continued to live in Washington until 1935, when she moved to New York. She also maintained a home at Bar Harbor, Maine, and there she was involved in a real-life drama in 1947.

Her 65-year-old Filipino chef, who had been with her for 25 years, suddenly fired a shot at her and then attempted to slash her with knives. Other servants rescued her from the chef, who committed suicide in his cell the following day.

In addition to her Sewickley home, Mrs. Rinehart found inspiration or background for many of her works in her early life in old Allegheny and her career as a nurse. Aside from their literary interest, her works have had more-than-usual sentimental appeal to residents of this area.

MONDAY, FEBRUARY 23, 1987

Andy Warhol, 58
Prince of Pop Art
By David Guo, *Pittsburgh Post-Gazette*

Andy Warhol, an artist who grew up in Pittsburgh and who came of age by setting pop culture loose in Uptown Manhattan, died yesterday of a heart attack. He was 58.

The son of Slovak immigrants who came to Pittsburgh's Soho district at the turn of the century, Mr. Warhol died in his sleep at 6:31 AM in New York Hospital. He had undergone gall bladder surgery on Saturday, but according to hospital spokeswoman Diane Goldin, no complications had surfaced. The artist's death, she said, was "clearly unexpected." He had been admitted to the hospital Friday, Goldin said, and "his postoperative condition was stable."

Mr. Warhol's death shocked family members in the Pittsburgh area, including brothers Paul Warhola of Elizabeth, Pennsylvania, and John Warhola of the North Side.

Every Sunday morning for the past 20 years, Paul Warhola said, he would make a phone call to his brother, Andy. Yesterday was different. "I called this morning, and for the first time in 20 years, someone else answered the phone. It was my brother's publicist. He said, 'John, Andy died.'"

"I looked at him as my brother, not a famous man," added John Warhola, a manager at a local Sears, Roebuck and Co. store. "He was the kindest, nicest brother you could have."

Paul Warhola said his brother's public flamboyance belied his gentle nature. "People got the idea that he was a wild character, but he was the nicest person in the world," said Paul Warhola, the eldest brother.

As one of the most influential artists of his day, Mr. Warhol gained his place in art history by turning routine glimpses of pop culture into critically acclaimed paintings and drawings. To his eye, chic was anything from a row of Campbell's soup cans to a candy-colored portrait of Marilyn Monroe.

Indeed, the artist's often splashy, free-flung work was in contrast to his signature appearance—thin, pale, and withdrawn, with hair as bright as talcum powder.

"He made his own lifestyle a work of art," Richard Oldenburg, director of the Museum of Modern Art, told the Associated Press. "He was one of the first people to really become a star as an artist, and, once celebrity came, he certainly enjoyed it."

Here in Pittsburgh, friends and family said that Warhol's time spent at Schenley High School and at Carnegie Institute of Technology seldom gave a clear sign of pending brilliance. Neither did young Andy's first paying job, family members said. He sold fruit in the Strip District while a student at Schenley in the early 1940s. Even as an art student at Carnegie Institute of Technology, the troublesome young artist did not distinguish himself as part of the class of 1949—a group that included renowned artists Philip Pearlstein, Harry Schwalb, and sculptor Henry Bursztynowicz.

Robert Lepper, a professor emeritus of art at Carnegie Mellon University, recalled that Andy Warhola—he didn't change his name until moving to New York in 1949—faced expulsion several times. Each time, the panel of 10 faculty members would weigh his lack of discipline against his potential. Each time, they would allow young Warhola to stay—though sometimes, recalled Lepper, the vote was close. "Andy was in difficulty his first two years, and the faculty had a nice time quarreling whether to let him stay," Lepper said.

"I'd like to say I gave him an *A*," Lepper added, "But I probably gave him a *B*, probably because he didn't come to class." Instead, he was probably Downtown in a display window at Horne's department store where, Lepper said, Warhol worked part time dressing mannequins.

"If anybody would have asked me who was least likely to succeed, I would've said Andy Warhola. What a guesser I am," Lepper said from his home in Shadyside.

Mary A. McKibbin, a retired director of art for Pittsburgh schools, recalled teaching Mr. Warhol in 1943. "He never used color much in his class. I didn't force myself on him because he was a very talented person. Color was there if he wanted it, but he preferred drawings in those days."

Born August 6, 1928, Andy Warhola was the third and youngest son of immigrants Ondrej and Julia Warhola. The Warholas came to Pittsburgh at the turn of the century and settled on Orr Street in the Soho district, near what is now the Lithuanian Hall.

Andy Warhola was six years old when the family moved across town to a brick rowhouse on Dawson Street in South Oakland.

As a child, family members said, young Andy was housebound and sickly. He had frequent bouts of St. Vitus dance, a disease that causes uncontrollable, seizure-like shaking. Instead of playing outside, family members recall, he stayed in his bedroom, filling up coloring books and drawing comic strips.

After graduating from Schenley in 1945, where his favorite classes involved art design and illustration, the young Mr. Warhola won a scholarship to Carnegie Institute. Even then, Mr. Warhola cast a wallflower-like image yet stood out in classes full of older army veterans of World War II. But Lepper said the older classmates "looked after him, particularly the women. He always got along with the women." Warhol, long rumored to be a homosexual, said he actually was uninterested in sex.

Despite his academic difficulties, Lepper said, Warhol's talent often shone through.

After graduating, he became Andy Warhol and moved to New York. His first job was illustraing advertisements for a shoe company.

By the early 1960s, Mr. Warhol's fame emanated, above all, from his innovative and influential pop art, his representation of commonplace commercial articles and circumstances as art iself. With his ever-present camera and tape recorder, he came, through his work, to be viewed as a recorder of society.

Established in 1962 by his celebrated *Campbell's Soup Cans*, Mr. Warhol's hallmark was his emotionless reproduction of the images around him. His underground films—*Eat, Haircut,* and *Sleep*—presented no more or less than unblinking views of mundane activities.

Later in his career, Mr. Warhol extended his activities into filmmaking and writing and became a fixture in the contemporary art world's social scene at such hotspots as Studio 54.

He continued to branch out as his career developed. In 1969 he created *Interview* magazine, a compendium of jet-set gossip.

In the 1970s he produced images of the glamorous and the famous that filled the entire fourth floor of the Whitney Museum of American Art in a 1979 show.

In recent months he produced a program for MTV called *Andy Warhol's Fifteen Minutes*—a reference to his widely quoted comment that in the future, everyone would be famous for 15 minutes.

Andy Warhol the celebrity maintained close ties to his family in Pittsburgh, especially with his mother, who became ill in the late 1960s and spent her last days at the old Wightman Manor nursing home in Squirrel Hill.

Still, Mr. Warhol seldom came to Pittsburgh. Instead, he would telephone his relatives regularly, said his brother, Paul. "After you get to New York, I guess Pittsburgh is a small town," Paul speculated.

Although he wouldn't visit Pittsburgh, brother John added, Mr. Warhol often expressed interest in his native town—the decline of steel, the changing economy, the rise of new skyscrapers.

SATURDAY, NOVEMBER 15, 1997

Stefan Lorant, 96
Author of Popular Pittsburgh History Book
By Torsten Ove, *Pittsburgh Post-Gazette*. Staff writer Bob Hoover contributed to this report.

He was known locally for his respected book chronicling the history of Pittsburgh, but the scope of Stefan Lorant's life was as sweeping as one of his presidential biographies.

Born in Hungary, imprisoned by Hitler, and later impassioned by American history, Mr. Lorant recognized the powerful connection between words and pictures. He became a pioneering editor in England and was often credited with the development of modern photojournalism.

He was the author of numerous books, among them *Pittsburgh: The Story of an American City*, and he counted many Pittsburghers among his friends.

But he also enjoyed relationships with some of the century's most famous figures, including Winston Churchill and German screen legend Marlene Dietrich, whom he once told to "go home, get married, and have babies" because she'd never make it as an actress.

When he fell ill a month ago, President Clinton called to wish him well.

Lorant, who lived in the Berkshires in Massachusetts, died yesterday morning at the Mayo Clinic in Rochester, Minnesota. He was 96.

"Two or three weeks before he was hospitalized, he visited us in Pittsburgh and we had dinner," said Dr. Thomas Detre, senior vice chancellor of health sciences at the University of Pittsburgh and a close friend of Mr. Lorant's. "He was in his element and sharp as a razor. He was very informed. There are not many people in this world who are as well-informed about local, national, and world politics as Stefan. He stayed on top of everything."

Mr. Lorant's reputation as an editor in Europe was cemented long before he came to Pittsburgh. He is often cited as one of the most important people of the century because of his work combining candid photographs with high-quality writing.

Edgar Kaufmann, a department store mogul and friend of Mr. Lorant, suggested in 1954 that Lorant write a book about the city. Mr. Lorant was incredulous at first. "A book on Pittsburgh?" he recounted telling Kaufmann in a 1988 interview. "You must be out of your mind."

After doing some research, however, Mr. Lorant came to see Pittsburgh as a "microcosm" of the country. His publisher, Harper & Row, wasn't as easily convinced. "I proposed this as the first serious book on an American city," he said, "and they said, 'Pittsburgh? Who will read it? It won't sell 5,000 copies.' I said, 'I don't care if it sells five copies. I must do it.'"

Mr. Lorant commissioned W. Eugene Smith to take the photographs. Doubleday published the book in 1964. The 50,000 volumes sold quickly. Mr. Lorant updated new editions four times, and sales have topped 120,000 volumes. He had nearly completed a fifth edition when he died.

William Block, publisher of the *Pittsburgh Post-Gazette*, met Mr. Lorant when he was first preparing the book and grew to know him over the years. "He would show up at the newspaper when he was planning another edition and wanted publicity," Block said.

To Block, Mr. Lorant was "an odd, eccentric man, but he was very clever and persistent. He wouldn't take no for an answer. He worked hard to get guarantees from a lot of Pittsburgh companies that they would buy so many copies of the book before he went ahead. But, when the book came out, it was a big success."

Despite that success, Lorant was known to be tight with a dollar. "I guess I'd call him pretty chintzy sometimes," Block said. "Really, in a lot of ways, Lorant was quite a rascal."

At least one Pittsburgh writer has complained about never being paid for his work for the book. Mr. Lorant also failed to return photos taken from the *Pittsburgh Press* and *Post-Gazette* files. In recounting the history of the book, which missed the original publication date more than once, one former *Press* editor wrote in 1984 that "just about everybody thought it was a boondoggle, or at least a bookdoggle."

If Mr. Lorant left some ill-will among contributing writers, he left a powerful impression on other Pittsburgh movers and shakers. Bruce Campbell, a Pittsburgh attorney who was executive secretary to former mayor Pete Flaherty, first met Mr. Lorant in 1974 when the author was preparing his second edition of the Pittsburgh book. "He made such an unbelievable and indelible mark," said Campbell. "He was very charming and charismatic. He was able to talk with anyone on any level. He would go to the Hilton, and he would be friendly with everyone from the person who picked up his bags at the door to the person who cleaned his room."

Even in his final years, Mr. Lorant remained the vibrant figure he'd been 20 years before.

"During his nineties he would pride himself on naming every president of the United States," Campbell said. "That's how he knew he was all right, because he could still do that. He was still unbelievably alert. He could remember almost every detail of his entire life. He could tell you about having lunch with Greta Garbo, and he could tell you what color the walls were."

Despite his local connections, the Pittsburgh chapter of Mr. Lorant's life is only one in a long biography. He was born in Budapest in 1901 and educated in Hungary. At age 19 he established himself as a leading cameraman in Europe with his first film in Vienna, *The Life of Mozart.* In Vienna and Berlin he created 14 films. He left filmmaking in 1925 and began writing for newspapers and magazines, and he soon became editor of a weekly magazine in Berlin, which he developed into the leading pictorial publication in Europe.

After Hitler came to power in 1933, the dictator's minions imprisoned Mr. Lorant because of his editorials criticizing the Nazi regime. Hungarian journalists managed to get him released and returned to Budapest, where he edited a Sunday magazine. In 1934 he moved to Britain and published his first book, *I Was Hitler's Prisoner.* It sold 1 million copies.

Roy McHugh, a retired columnist at the *Press* who knew Mr. Lorant, once asked him about Hitler. "He said he only met him once before he came to power, in a Munich beer hall where journalists got together to drink." Hitler was editor of a Nazi paper.

"Lorant said Hitler started making one of his political speeches, and he found it one of the most boring things he ever heard. He left. A day after Hitler came to power, Lorant was tossed in jail as an enemy of the Third Reich."

In England Mr. Lorant started *Weekly Illustrated* for Odhams Press. In 1937 he launched *Lilliput,* a pocket magazine. He sold it to Hulton Press and created *Picture Post* magazine, which reached a circulation of 1.75 million.

During Mr. Lorant's time at *Weekly Illustrated,* Winston Churchill asked him to travel to the United States to "take the pulse" of America for the British people. Lorant spent six months in the U.S. and wrote a series of articles in his newspaper. He was inspired by the freedoms in America and particularly impressed with Abraham Lincoln, whose biography he had read while in prison in Germany.

In 1940 Lorant emigrated and settled in the Berkshires. He became renowned for his pictorial biographies of Lincoln, Theodore Roosevelt, and Franklin Delano Roosevelt. He also wrote several books on the presidency itself and an illustrated history of Germany.

His book on Pittsburgh remains a fixture at local libraries. And although he never lived in Pittsburgh, he often professed his affection for the city.

"He loved Pittsburgh," said Campbell. "He said it was a wonderful place."

TUESDAY, JANUARY 15, 2002

Dahlen K. Ritchey, 91
Architect Designed Civic Arena, Three Rivers Stadium
By Patricia Lowry, *Pittsburgh Post-Gazette*

Dahlen Ritchey is the architect of Three Rivers Stadium. *Photo by Robin Rombach.*

In the mid-1930s, unable to find work as an architect during the Depression, Dahlen K. Ritchey spent a year designing window and furniture displays at Kaufmann's Downtown store.

It was a job that changed his life—and eventually the face of Pittsburgh.

Mr. Ritchey's early connection to store owner Edgar Kaufmann brought him several commissions, which in turn opened the doors to many more. Working with a series of partners over a career that spanned five decades, Mr. Ritchey designed Mellon Square, the Civic Arena, Allegheny Center, Three Rivers Stadium, and many school, university, and hospital buildings.

Mr. Ritchey, who was 91, died early Saturday morning of a heart attack at Allegheny General Hospital after suffering a seizure at his home in Bradford Woods.

He had been diagnosed with Parkinson's disease in 1982. Even so, "he had a wonderful drive and alertness to him," said University of Pittsburgh architectural historian Franklin Toker. "He was superbly well-educated and had a great sense of architecture and design and service to the public, and made an immense contribution to the betterment of Pittsburgh," Toker said.

Mr. Ritchey, who grew up in Oakland, Pennsylvania, became an architect at the urging of a Schenley High School teacher who recognized his drawing and math skills. After graduating from the Carnegie Institute of Technology in 1932, he won a scholarship to Harvard University, where he completed a master's degree. He then spent part of 1934 and 1935 traveling through Europe on a fellowship.

Back home in Pittsburgh, he took the job at Kaufmann's. Not long after, Edgar and Lilianne Kaufmann's good friends, Robert and Cecilia Frank, commissioned Walter Gropius and Marcel Breuer to design a house for them on Woodland Road in Shadyside. But Gropius wasn't licensed to practice architecture in Pennsylvania, and Kaufmann recommended Mr. Ritchey as the project's architect of record to handle all of the contracts.

By 1941 Mr. Ritchey and his partner, Carnegie Tech alum James Mitchell, were doing well enough to allow Mr. Ritchey and his wife, Katherine, to build a house in Bradford Woods. They dug the foundation in early December 1941, a day or two before the Japanese bombed Pearl Harbor. Mr. Ritchey went to war, and the house plans went on the shelf.

After serving in the navy aboard the USS *Saratoga*, he returned to Pittsburgh in 1946. The Ritcheys built their modern house high on a knoll and surrounded by rhododendrons and woods.

And the visionary Kaufmann soon had another project for him: In honor of the store's 75th anniversary in 1947, he commissioned the firm Mitchell and Ritchey to produce an exhibit that looked backward and forward in time, challenging the architects to imagine what Pittsburgh would look like in 75 years. The exhibit, mounted at Kaufmann's, was called *Pittsburgh in Progress*.

"They had plans for the Point, the Hill [District], the North Side," said landscape architect John Simonds, who worked with Mr. Ritchey on dozens of projects over the years. "Every single one of those dreams has been executed in one way or another."

In the late 1940s Kaufmann began pushing for a civic auditorium in the Lower Hill, putting up the early money for a theater to house the Civic Light Opera and Pittsburgh Hornets hockey team. It would have a dome that could open and close, Kaufmann decreed, and its architects would be Mitchell and Ritchey. When the building finally opened in 1962, Mitchell and Ritchey's arena was the world's largest dome— 415 feet in diameter—an engineering marvel that attracted international attention.

Late one Friday afternoon in 1949 Wallace Richards of the Allegheny Conference on Community Development told Mitchell and Ritchey about Richard K. Mellon and Paul Mellon's idea for a public square above a parking garage. The architects had Labor Day weekend to come up with a plan.

"The haste with which the drawings were demanded apparently bore upon the struggle then going on in the Aluminum Company of America over the location of its proposed skyscraper," wrote Fred Remington in a 1978 profile of Mr. Ritchey in *Pittsburgh* magazine. "Most of the Alcoa hierarchy favored a mid-Manhattan location. Richard K. Mellon didn't see it that way."

Mr. Ritchey's original plan for Three Rivers Stadium, an innovative, crescent-shaped building with an open end, was never built. "The idea came from Forbes Field," Mr. Ritchey told the *Pittsburgh Post-Gazette* last year. "You could sit in the stands and see Flagstaff Hill and Schenley Park. It was very nice. So the idea was to open it up and see the city." The design was changed, Mr.

Ritchey said, because it was thought the cutting-edge structure for the stadium's roof would cost too much.

After Mr. Ritchey's partnership with Mitchell ended in 1957, Ritchey formed D.K. Ritchey Associates (1957–1959), Deeter & Ritchey (1959–1965), and Deeter Ritchey Sippel Associates (1965–1979).

"Dahl was very much a hands-on architect, getting involved with details of the design and representing the firm at client meetings," said architect James Kling, who joined Deeter & Ritchey in 1964 and regarded Mr. Ritchey as a mentor.

Mr. Ritchey is survived by his wife, Beatrice. His first wife died of emphysema in 1973.

THURSDAY, SEPTEMBER 22, 2005

Molly Yard, 93
Dynamo Who Headed NOW
By Sally Kalson, *Pittsburgh Post-Gazette*

Molly Yard, a political activist for more than 50 years who became the eighth president of the National Organization for Women, died Tuesday night in her sleep. She was 93 and had been a resident of Fair Oaks of Pittsburgh, a retirement/nursing home in Dormont, for the past seven years.

Born in China to missionary parents, Ms. Yard played major roles in the movements for labor, civil rights, and women's equality. She worked for President Lyndon Johnson on the War

on Poverty; persuaded the YWCA of Pittsburgh to sign on as a sponsor of the historic 1963 March on Washington; wrested the Democratic nomination for a seat in the state legislature from entrenched party leaders; and, through NOW, forced the Democratic Party to ensure equal numbers of men and women delegates at its national conventions.

An ardent proponent of legalized abortion, affirmative action, and the Equal Rights Amendment, Ms. Yard was

Molly Yard, the president of the National Organization of Women (NOW), protests in support of Justice for Janitors in Washington, D.C. on April 1, 1988. *Photo by Melissa Farlow.*

known as a powerful leader who stood ramrod straight, blue eyes flashing from amusement to indignation. "She was a remarkable woman," said former National Republican Committeewoman Elsie Hillman, of Squirrel Hill. "We were on opposite sides of the political divide but together on so many things involving the community, especially improvements for women and the work force."

Eleanor Smeal, president of the Fund for the Feminist Majority and Ms. Yard's predecessor as NOW president, said: "Molly was indefatigable and brilliant in executing campaigns for social justice. When I met her in the 1970s, she had already beaten cancer, but she still left the rest of us in her dust.... You had to be there for the long haul.

"She gave the most stirring speeches," Smeal said, "and she was never afraid to ask for money. Once when I was speaking at a rally, she grabbed the mike and told me to be more forceful in my fund-raising pitch. The crowd loved it; I think we raised $90,000 that day."

Ms. Yard once described herself as a "born feminist" but declined to say when she was born. When she married labor arbitrator Sylvester Garrett in 1938, she told him she would not be taking his name because it indicated that a woman was the property of her husband. "I didn't see why I should obliterate the fact that I had existed," she said in a 1991 interview. "It's really a denial of what you were, like wiping out the beginning of your life."

The marriage lasted 58 years, until Garrett's death in 1996. They lived in Squirrel Hill and Point Breeze before taking up full-time residence at their 60-acre farm in Cook Township, Westmoreland County.

Ms. Yard's close friends knew her softer side. She was a great cook and gracious hostess who gave memorable dinner parties, said her friend Janet

Molly Yard. *Photo by Joyce Mendelsohn.*

Kreisman of Squirrel Hill, and at home, Yard would loosen her long white hair from its trademark bun.

"My mother was a competitor by nature, but she was a very accomplished homemaker as well," said her son, James Garrett of Mt. Lebanon, who as a child rode around in the back of sound trucks during political rallies. "She was from the old school that believed in family meals, a well-ordered house, and a childhood filled with adventure for her kids."

When it came to political work, Ms. Yard was all business. "Molly was hard-driving and vigorous," said Jeanne Clark, who was her press secretary at NOW in 1985 and was once arrested with Ms. Yard during a protest outside the Vatican embassy in Washington, D.C. "Most of the staff was much younger, but she was always the first one up and the last to bed. She never rode cabs when she could walk, and she was always calling out for us to walk up the escalator instead of ride."

Amy Isaacs, national director of Americans for Democratic Action, which Ms. Yard helped to found, said Ms. Yard was an enthusiastic but demanding mentor. "In 1975 I organized forums for Democratic presidential candidates," Isaacs said. "I had to face Molly's wrath because the women I had on the panel weren't feminist enough for her."

"The rest of us aged slowly over time," Isaacs said. "Molly stayed exactly the same until her stroke, and then she aged overnight."

Ms. Yard was elected president of NOW in 1987 and reelected in 1990. The following year, after leading a demonstration outside an airline ticket office over women's labor issues, she suffered a stroke in her Washington, D.C., office. She stepped down seven months later and was succeeded by her executive vice president, Patricia Ireland.

Born in Shanghai, China, the third of four daughters of Methodist missionaries, Ms. Yard started life with an international perspective on feminism. She once told the story of a Chinese friend who gave her father a brass bowl as a gift, his way of saying he was sorry she was not a boy. In those days in China, she said, the birth of a girl was a tragedy, and many were destined to live as prostitutes or servants. Sometimes, she said, "the girl babies were just thrown away."

She grew up in Chengdu, the capital of Szechuan province in West China, and came to the United States with her parents when she was 13. Her career as a social activist began while she was a student at Swarthmore College, where she received a bachelor of arts degree in 1933.

Through her positions as organization secretary and national chairwoman of the American Student Union, she developed a lasting friendship with Eleanor Roosevelt, whom she once described as "my second mother."

As a student, she led a successful drive to eliminate the sorority system at Swarthmore after a Jewish student was denied admission to the sorority to which Ms. Yard belonged, Kappa Alpha Theta.

She became active in Democratic Party politics, and in the late 1940s and early 1950s she worked with the Clark-Dilworth team to unseat the entrenched city machine in Philadelphia. Ms. Yard also worked for the Helen Gahaghan Douglas campaign for the U.S. Senate against Richard M. Nixon in California.

She moved to Pittsburgh in 1953 and worked in the gubernatorial campaign of Mayor David L. Lawrence in 1958, then headed the Western Pennsylvania presidential campaigns of John F. Kennedy in 1960 and George McGovern in 1972.

In 1970 she headed the unsuccessful campaign to get NAACP president Byrd Brown the Democratic nomination to congress; and in 1976 she was cochairman with Mayor Joseph M. Barr of the unsuccessful U.S. Senate campaign of Jeannette Reibman.

In 1964 Ms. Yard won the Democratic nomination for a seat in the state legislature. Kreisman recalled the *Pittsburgh Post-Gazette* headline: "Molly Yard Beats City Hall." She lost the general election, but the race gave rise to the 14th Ward Independent Democratic Club in Squirrel Hill, which remains a political force. She resigned as club president in 1977 due to acrimony over her support of Tom Foerster for mayor while other members had backed Richard Caliguiri in the 1976 election.

Ms. Yard became active in NOW while a resident of Squirrel Hill in 1974, and she joined the national staff in 1978 during the campaign to ratify the Equal Rights Amendment, serving as a lobbyist in Washington. She raised more than $1 million in six months.

A prime architect of NOW's political and legislative agenda, she was a senior staff member of the NOW Political Action Committee from 1978 to 1984. As NOW's political director from 1985 to 1987, she was instrumental in the successful 1986 campaign to defeat antiabortion referendums in Arkansas, Massachusetts, Rhode Island, and Oregon.

In April 1989 she and Elsie Hillman carried the banner for the March for Women's Equality/Women's Lives, which drew 600,000 marchers to Washington in support of abortion rights and the ERA.

Ms. Yard defeated Noreen Connell in the 1987 NOW election. Upon taking office she vowed to make the organization more visible and to work to defeat President Reagan's nomination of Judge Robert H. Bork to the U.S. Supreme Court. Bork ultimately was rejected by the U.S. Senate.

The membership of NOW grew by 110,000 during the years of her presidency, and its annual budget increased 70 percent to more than $10 million.

As NOW president she opposed U.S. involvement in the Persian Gulf War, saying Americans should not be fighting for "clan-run monarchies" in Kuwait and Saudi Arabia that denied women's rights.

Also in 1991 Ms. Yard was honored in Paris by the French Alliance of Women for Democratization for her work on reproductive rights; she had been a leader in the effort to get Paris-based manufacturer Roussel Uclaf to make the so-called "French abortion pill" available in the United States.

In addition to her son James, she is survived by another son, John Garrett of Rochester, New York, and five grandchildren.

FRIDAY, JANUARY 13, 2006

Reverend LeRoy Patrick, 90
"Bona-Fide Hero" of Civil Rights Movement
By Ervin Dyer, *Pittsburgh Post-Gazette*

The Reverend LeRoy Patrick was a steely figure at the center of the movement that confronted racism in Pittsburgh in the 1950s and 1960s.

While working to desegregate pools, restaurants, and public institutions, he was pelted with rocks, shoved into police vans, and threatened with death.

At the height of it, Mr. Patrick traveled with a tire iron in the front of his car in case of attack. He received reams of hate mail.

His civil rights activism began in 1951 with a campaign to integrate public swimming pools and spanned the ensuing decades as he championed equal opportunity in education, employment, and housing and served his community in myriad positions, including a stint as president of the Pittsburgh school board.

"A bona-fide hero of the civil rights movement," said the Reverend James Mead, pastor of the Pittsburgh Presbytery.

Mr. Patrick, one of the first black ministers to serve as moderator of the 226-church presbytery, died at his Oakland, Pennsylvania, apartment yesterday. He was 90 years old.

Politically and theologically progressive, he backed the presidential campaigns of Jesse Jackson and Shirley Chisholm and built Bethesda Center, now defunct, which he used to aggressively pursue social services for Homewood, Pennsylvania.

Some conservative black clergy thought he was too far afield of his ministry, but Mr. Patrick was not deterred from his Christian mission that faith without works is irrelevant and that action should be relevant to the common man. So he continued to march, pray, and sing freedom songs in Bethesda, the 94-year-old church considered a jewel of Pittsburgh's black presbyterianism. He presided over the church for 35 years.

His civil rights activism began with children. In the summer of 1951 Mr.

Patrick, a young minister from Eastern Pennsylvania, organized small groups of blacks and whites to swim in traditionally white-only pools. The children marched behind Mr. Patrick, a horn-rimmed pied piper, and jumped into the water when he jumped. The pools were not segregated by law, but black youth were routinely attacked with bricks and rocks for attempting to integrate them. Some people drained their pools rather than have blacks swim there.

Highland Park Pool was the first to integrate. Then came other city pools and eventually those around the county—a historic achievement led by a man who had never waded into water more than waist-deep.

In the late 1950s, his profile rising as a civil rights champion, he chaired the Allegheny County Council on Civil Rights and the Allegheny County Committee for Fair Housing Practices.

In the 1960s he sat at lunch counters and walked picket lines as he fought for equal opportunities in education, employment, and housing.

He led hundreds of demonstrations at the Pittsburgh school board, calling for racial integration, quality education, and racially balanced history and social studies lessons. He served seven years on the school board, which elected him president in 1976.

Mr. Patrick believed justice was advanced in a series of small steps and fought tirelessly for legal remedies. He was instrumental in bringing lawsuits against the University of Pittsburgh Medical Center and the Pittsburgh Police Bureau regarding hiring practices.

Tall and thin, Mr. Patrick was a stately figure in his black suits and white collar, which he unfailingly wore every Sunday while an active minister. He spoke in polished tones, his words clear and concise. Unlike those who stirred with the thunder of emotion, Mr. Patrick's métier was to lead with his intellect. "To call him meticulous is to underrate him," said Wendell Freeland, an attorney who met the minister in the 1950s during the pool protests. "He was more than eloquent. He was persuasive. An invaluable leader."

Every Saturday night the minister sat at his dining room table and wrote his sermon. Each was original. When he was 50, his sons gave him a pair of blue jeans. He never wore them. Until he retired, he'd never left home without shirt and tie.

Even in retirement, said Mr. Mead, "he could quiet the tension at the presbytery meetings when he stood to speak."

For more than 30 years Mr. Patrick led Bethesda Center, a social service mission supported by the church as an outreach to Homewood. Its inner-city ministry included recreation, employment, family development, and spiritual programming. Though it no longer exists, it was a model that other urban churches use today.

Away from church, Mr. Patrick served on the boards of the Pittsburgh NAACP and the Pennsylvania Historical and Museum Commission.

Mr. Patrick graduated from Lincoln University in 1939, uncertain about what to do with his life. He finally accepted that he was called to preach and repeatedly turned down offers to serve in church hierarchy.

He was born in Charleston, South Carolina, in 1915 to a lumber-mill worker and a homemaker who moved the family to Philadelphia in the 1920s.

He was the youngest of three sons. The oldest, Edgar, died of tuberculosis. His other brother was killed at age 16 by a white youth, and the case was never investigated—perhaps providing the spark for Mr. Patrick's commitment to civil rights.

Mr. Patrick served on the board of trustees at Lincoln University, where he once taught Greek, Latin, and religion. The school awarded him an honorary doctorate in 1964. He earned master's degrees in divinity and sacred theology from Union Theological Seminary in 1942 and 1946, respectively.

He is survived by sons Gregory of Sewickley and Stephen of Elizabethtown, Lancaster County, and six grandchildren.

SECTION
III

Business, Labor, and Industry

In legend and lore Pittsburgh made iron and steel, but in truth what Pittsburgh made was money—lots of money, gobs of it. Much of it helped the rich become even richer. Some of it allowed a few brilliant, hard-working, or just plain lucky members of the striving classes to become wealthy beyond the dreams of avarice. And some of it allowed working people to improve their lives and build hopeful futures for their children. H.J. Heinz and Andrew Carnegie built fortunes. Jock Yablonski and I.W. Abel were labor leaders. They and others were giants in their hometown and in the nation.

TUESDAY, MAY 15, 1919

H.J. Heinz, 75
Manufacturer of Food Products
By the *Pittsburgh Post-Gazette*

Henry J. Heinz, 75 years old, reputed to be the world's largest manufacturer of food products, noted internationally for his religious activities, and conspicuous figure in the business life of Pittsburgh for half a century, died at 3:00 yesterday at the family home, 7009 Penn Avenue. Death was from double pneumonia, which developed last Saturday morning.

Mr. Heinz had been unconscious since 10:00 yesterday morning, but the three physicians in attendance did not at any time abandon hope for his recovery. One son, Clifford Heinz, and his daughter, Mrs. John L. Given of New York, were at the bedside when the end came.

There are two other sons, Clarence now in Wisconsin for his health and Howard Heinz in Constantinople for the United States food administration.

Mr. Heinz had retained his active connection with the business since its beginning and was at his office last Friday afternoon engaged in looking after its affairs.

Started with Garden
Mr. Heinz was a native of Pittsburgh, the son of Henry and Anna M. Schmidt Heinz. He was born October 11, 1844. After receiving his education in the common schools and at business college, he turned to commercial pursuits.

After a lowly beginning through years of development, Heinz brought his business to the vast proportions which it now enjoys. His parents had intended to fit him for the ministry, but with the exception of a few years in his young manhood, his career has been concerned with the business side of the manufacture of pure food products.

During his boyhood days Mr. Heinz assisted his father, who was a manufacturer of brick on a small scale. His father's family having moved to Sharpsburg, then only a small village, where a garden of about three acres surrounded the house, he became interested in gardening, and three-quarters of an acre was set aside for his use. As the garden yielded more than the family required, the surplus was disposed of among the villagers. The success which he met in handling garden products suggested to him the idea of engaging in the business and packaging pure food products, which was commenced in a modest way in 1869. His first factory consisted of the basement and one room of the dwelling in which is father's family lived prior to moving to a new home just before the business was commenced. The first product was horseradish, packed in bottles. Soon the packing of pickles, sauces, and other foods was added.

Insisted on Cleanliness

From the beginning Mr. Heinz insisted on the cleanliness of the surroundings, and purity of the products and quality was ever his aim. This policy resulted in the rapid growth of the business so that by 1872, greater facilities were needed, and the business was moved to Pittsburgh. It grew steadily until now the main establishment in Pittsburgh occupies a floor space of more than 30 acres, which is increased to more than 70 acres by including the branch houses.

The company was incorporated in 1905, with Mr. Heinz as president. It operates, in addition to the main plant, 10 branch factories—three of these being in England, Canada, and Spain, and 30 agencies in all parts of the world, which constitute the machinery of distribution.

Mr. Heinz's interest in higher education is indicated by the fact that he was largely instrumental in founding, and was one of the chief supporters of, the Kansas City University, also having been president of the board of trustees of that institution from the beginning.

Sunday Social Worker

When he was a young man he joined the Episcopal Methodist Church of Sharpsburg and became a teacher and later superintendent of the Sunday school. In 1877 he became a member of the Grace Methodist Protestant Church in Sharpsburg, was superintendent of the Sunday school for several years, and, a number of years ago, was elected honorary superintendent of the school for life.

It had been his habit for a number of years to visit one or more Sunday schools each week, wherever he might happen to be. On Sunday, May 4, the last Sunday he was able to get out of his house, he made a visit to his old school at Grace church. After he removed to the Homewood district he became connected with the East Liberty Presbyterian Church and retained that membership.

In Sunday school work Mr. Heinz was an international figure. He was chairman of the executive committee of the World's Sunday School Association, for many consecutive years president of the Pennsylvania Sabbath School Association, and in 1916 was elected a vice president of the Sunday School Union of London. This is considered a great honor of the Sunday school world and is one which has been accorded to only two other Americans: Bishop John H. Vincent and John Wanamaker. The Sunday School Union is the oldest national sunday school organization in the world. The chairman of the national council is Sir George Cloydon Marks M.P., and among the associates of Mr. Heinz as vice presidents were the Earl of Aberdeen, Lord Kinnaird; the Bishop of Hereford, Lord Hullendon of Leigh Principal daivie; and Reverend F.H. Meyer.

During all of his career Mr. Heinz took an advanced position on the social problem of the proper relationship between employer and employee. In outlining pivotal projects and in carrying them forward to a successful conclusion, he always showed genius of a high order.

Mr. Heinz always took a great interest in civic affairs, and as a member of the Pittsburgh flood commission, his keen ideas stoked the attention of some of the country's shrewdest engineers. His suggestions as to city improvements were always welcomed. For many years he was a director of the chamber of commerce.

Had Many Interests

Besides his connection with the Heinz Company, Mr. Heinz was a director of the Union National Bank, the Western Insurance Company of Pittsburgh, and the Winons Interurban Railway Company of Indiana; former president of the flood commission of Pittsburgh, vice president of the civic commission of Pittsburgh, vice president of the Western Pennsylvania Exposition Society, president of the Pennsylvania State Sunday School Association, and chairman of the executive committee of the World Sunday School Association.

Mr. Heinz was an extensive traveler and was the possessor of a large collection of art objects and antiquities, his collection of ivory carvings and antique watches being one of the largest private collections in the world. Mr. Heinz's collection of curios, which represented many foreign lands and distant areas, was placed on exhibition in 1914 in a museum in the rear of the Heinz home. The museum is open to the public.

Mr. Heinz was an extensive traveler, and it was his custom to visit Europe annually up to 1914. It was on these trips that he indulged in his fondness for collecting souvenirs and antiques of his travels. His collection is a notable one. Because of his interest in art and antiques he was made an honorary curator of ivories, timepieces, and textiles of the Carnegie Museum a few years ago.

Mr. Heinz was a great lover of children, and no organization having for its object the health and happiness of children ever appealed to him in vain. It was this interest that led him to erect and equip the community house known as the Sarah Heinz House at East Ohio and Heinz Streets on the north side, which was designated for the use of boys and girls of that community and which received its name by reason of the fact that it was a memorial to his wife.

His son, Howard Heinz, had become interested in boys' club work while attending Yale University, and when he returned home he desired to establish a work for boys and girls. In this work Mr. Heinz always took a great interest and gave his son encouragement and support, and when the father saw the fruits of the work, he decided to erect a special building with modern equipment to be used in carrying on the work.

Mr. Heinz leaves three sons, Clarence N., now at Lake Geneva, Wisconsin, and Howard and Clifford Heinz of this city; one daughter, Mrs. John L. Given of New York; two brothers, John H. of Atlanta and P.J. Heinz of Lake Geneva; and three sisters, Mrs. Sebastian Mueller, Miss Mary A., and Miss Henrietta D. Heinz, all of Pittsburgh.

TUESDAY, AUGUST 13, 1919

Andrew Carnegie, 84
Steel King
By the *Pittsburgh Post-Gazette*

Although Mr. Carnegie, who was in his 84th year, had been an invalid since 1917, when he suffered an attack of grip, the news of his death was a shock to old friends and former business associates here. Since his previous serious illness he had been under the care of two nurses.

Identified so long with the international peace movement, Mr. Carnegie was said to have been more severely affected by the world war than most men. It came as a hard blow to him and the cause which he had so close at heart.

Owing to his ill health, Mr. Carnegie for some time had led a secluded life, and his withdrawal from all public activities gave rise to frequent statements concerning his health. After his retirement he was compelled to limit the number of his daily visitors, and until his last illness he met and spoke with only a few of his oldest and closest friends.

Mr. Carnegie's physicians decided he frequently overtaxed his strength by seeing all callers at his Fifth Avenue home here.

Shadow Brook Refuge

Two years ago Mr. Carnegie found a refuge at Shadow Brook, his new summer home at Lenox, which he purchased from the estate of Anson Phelps Stokes. It was the first country place owned here by the former steel master.

Previously Carnegie had spent his vacations at Skibo Castle in Dunfermline, Scotland. When he purchased the Lenox property it was announced that neither he nor any member of his family would probably ever again visit Skibo because of changes—physical and sentimental—caused by the war.

The marriage of Mr. Carnegie's only daughter, Margaret, on April 23, to Ensign Roswell Miller of the U.S. Navy was the last social affair the aged philanthropist and peace advocate attended here. The ceremony was performed at Mr. Carnegie's townhouse in the presence of 106 guests, with the bride standing in the floral bower with Scotch bagpipes playing in accordance with her father's wish.

The bridegroom—son of the former president of the Chicago, Milwaukee, & St. Paul Railroad, who died in 1913—had not completed his college course when war was declared. In 1916 he left Stevens Institute in Hoboken, New Jersey, where he was taking a course in civil engineering, to drive an ambulance in France. When the United States became involved, Miller entered the navy as an ensign.

It was said at the time of the wedding that after the honeymoon, Mr. Miller and his bride would go to Princeton, New Jersey, where he would complete his studies before entering upon a professional career. The former Miss Carnegie, heiress of her father's millions, is 22 years old. Her husband is two years her senior.

Was Highly Honored

Mr. Carnegie, at the time of his death, was the holder of numerous honors and decorations bestowed upon him by rulers and peoples over all the world. He received as a result of his benefactions abroad the freedom of 54 cities in Great Britain and Ireland. Altogether he endowed 2,000 municipal libraries in the United States in addition to his numerous other philanthropic enterprises.

He was lord rector of St. Andrew's University from 1901 to 1907 and of Aberdeen University from 1912 to 1914, and he held the honorary degree of doctor of laws from the Universities of Glasgow, Edinburgh, Birmingham, Manchester, McGill, Brown, Pennsylvania, Cornell, and other American colleges.

Mr. Carnegie was a member of numerous philosophical, civic, and scientific bodies, among them the American Institute of Architects, the American Society of Mechanical Engineers, the American Institute of Mining Engineers, the National Civic Federation, the American Philosophic Society, and the New York Chamber of Commerce. He was a commander of the Legion of Honor of France and had also received the grand crosses: Order of Orange, Nassau, and the Order of Danebrog. He was a member of the Union League Club, New York Yacht Club, Authors Club, Lotos Club, St. Andrew's Club, and the Indian Harbor Yacht Club.

SATURDAY, JANUARY 10, 1970

Joseph A. "Jock" Yablonski, 59
United Mine Workers Official

By Alvin Rosensweet, *Pittsburgh Post-Gazette*

Joseph A. "Jock" Yablonski, the murdered official of the United Mine Workers Union, his wife, Margaret, and their daughter, Charlotte Joan, were buried here today on a snow-covered knoll swept by blasts of subzero air.

Huddled with several hundred mourners beneath a canopy, Monsignor Charles Owen Rice intoned the prayers at the graveside.

"I am the resurrection and the life. He who believes in me shall never die."

Then after the mourners—fingers and faces numbed by cold—had recited the Lord's Prayer, Monsignor Rice, who had married the Yablonskis, prayed: "May they rest in peace. Grant this mercy to your dead servant. Eternal rest grant unto them."

Sons Kiss Coffins

Before the three caskets were lowered into the frozen earth, Yablonski's sons, Kenneth and Joseph, knelt and kissed

United Mine Workers official Joseph "Jock" Yablonski on January 4, 1966. *Photo by Al Hermann.*

the coffins. Then they laid a red rose on each, as Yablonski's 89-year-old mother wept uncontrollably.

The graveside service in Washington Cemetery was preceded by a solemn requiem mass at the Church of the Immaculate Conception in Washington, Pennsylvania, where Monsignor Rice, in his homily, marked the difference between the Yablonski murders and the assassinations of the Kennedys and Dr. Martin Luther King Jr. For the Yablonskis, he said, "There was the element of cold-blooded preparation…the chilling and premeditated murder of two women, and, if there were an insanity here, it is the sort to curdle the blood."

About 850 mourners almost filled the Gothic-style church as three priests, wearing the white vestments of the Mass of the Resurrection, conducted the service. The caskets had been brought from Millsboro, Pennsylvania, about 15 miles outside Washington.

One group of mourners was made up of women employees of Centerville Clinic, founded by the slain UMW leader. Joseph Rauh of Washington, D.C., who was Yablonski's attorney, and Representative Ken Hechler, whose West Virginia congressional district includes soft coal fields, attended the mass. It was presided over by Monsignor Rice, former pastor of Immaculate Conception, the Reverend Joseph Koloszczyk of the Yablonski's Clarksville, Pennsylvania, church—St. Thomas, and the Reverend Armand Jean Baldwin, OSD, of St. Vincent Seminary in Latrobe, Pennsylvania.

Miners Are Pallbearers

As the organ prelude, a selection from Gabriel Faure's Requiem Mass, pealed forth, 19 pallbearers carried the white-covered caskets to the altar rail at the sanctuary. Eighteen were coal miners; the 19th was Kenneth Yablonski, a son, who helped carry his mother's casket.

Now the mourners stood for the Responsory: "Come to their aid, O saints of God," then joined in the Introit: "'I

am the salvation of the people' says the Lord." A choir of children, directed by a nun, sang from the choir loft before the recitation of the Epistle: "Allelula, allelula, allelula."

"Let the sympathy of the priests and the community be known to the sons of Joe and Margaret Yablonski and their daughter, Charlotte," Monsignor Rice said before giving the homily.

Work Unfinished

Monsignor Rice called Joseph Yablonski a strong, buoyant, and charismatic man who was taken from this life with his work unfinished. "It was necessary for him to tramp on toes. He made friends and enemies," Pittsburgh's "labor priest" said.

Monsignor Rice said "the killers took his charming wife, poised and intellectual, companion as well as homemaker, and the lovely daughter, Charlotte, a person of idealism and compassion… this was a new and frightening dimension."

"As we contemplate these three caskets, we ask why and who and want to find the answer if only so that suspicion will be taken from the innocent and that fear of the unknown may be dissipated."

Honorary Pallbearers

Waving incense, Monsignor Rice passed among the caskets invoking the final blessing. And then, almost startling in its suddenness, Kenneth Yablonski arose and faced the mourners. His voice quivering only slightly, he said in a loud and resonant voice: "My father worked long and hard to reach his goal. He truly loved and believed in the miners. He said the heart of the miner is in the chests of the men. We entrust our father to the coal miners he loved so much."

He named members of the honor guard and pallbearers, then concluded:

"We ask all coal miners of North America to serve as honorary pallbearers for our father, mother, and sister."

TUESDAY, OCTOBER 17, 1978

Willard F. Rockwell, 90
Rockwell Manufacturing Chairman
By Alvin Rosensweet, *Pittsburgh Post-Gazette*

Colonel Willard F. Rockwell, who built three major industrial firms and was a leading spokesman for the free enterprise system, died yesterday in a Westmoreland County convalescent home.

Colonel Rockwell, 90, had been chairman of the board of the former Rockwell Manufacturing Co. and the former Rockwell-Standard Corp., with headquarters in Pittsburgh. He became honorary chairman of the giant Rockwell International Corp., which the two companies formed.

In July 1973 the colonel entered the Murray Manor Convalescent Home in Murrysville, Pennsylvania, after suffering an overdose of oxygen during a home inhalation treatment. At that time, his doctors said his condition was similar to a minor stroke, but he was reported to be in excellent physical condition.

Although everyone called him "Colonel" (he was never known simply as "Mr. Rockwell"), he served as a civilian in World War I. He did become a lieutenant colonel in 1930 in the Army Quartermaster Corps. He was a man of distinguished military bearing, wore a well-cropped moustache, and, in his later years, grew a small, gray chin beard.

Colonel Rockwell's principal work was as an inventor and industrialist. Before Rockwell-Standard Corp. merged in September 1967 with North American Aviation Inc., it had attained sales of $636 million in 1966. Rockwell Manufacturing Co., which he built from a meter-manufacturing company, rang up $202 million in sales in 1967.

But it was as an outspoken conservative that Colonel Rockwell most often entered the public eye and won the sobriquet of "the rebellious colonel." He once told an audience of businessmen that "the most obvious difference between me and most of you is that I am a relic of the 19th century." He said he considered it to be a compliment when he was referred to as a "pre-McKinley industrialist."

He placed the blame for many of this country's problems on two developments in 1913. Marked changes in our freedom, he contended, were brought about by amendments passed in that year providing for a federal income tax and election of U.S. Senators by direct popular vote. The latter legislation, he said, "made it possible for the most despicable demagogues to become senators."

Colonel Rockwell pushed reductions in foreign aid "if American business is to survive." He warned in 1960 that this country had embarked on a program of "international socialism" embodied in both the Democratic and Republican platforms of that year.

He said the income tax implemented socialistic theory and that "our government practices socialism here more than in some nations where socialism is openly avowed."

"Turn back to the principles of free enterprise that guided America until 30 years ago," he urged. Speaking at the national convention of the Sons of the American Revolution in Detroit in 1964, when he was given SAR's highest award, Colonel Rockwell criticized government spending and federal deficits. He said the United States has "both socialism and a dictatorship."

He criticized "bureaucratic despots in Washington," accused the Interstate Commerce Commission of "50 years of bungling," and attacked antitrust and "antibusiness laws and destructive taxes," which, he said, harassed business.

He favored public works by local communities instead of by the federal government, opposed removal of tariff barriers, and once suggested that a small recession might have a beneficial effect by checking inflation.

In 1951 Colonel Rockwell said communism was declining. In 1955 he predicted that lowering tariff barriers

iers would throw millions of Americans out of work. In 1956, after Israel won a war, he predicted that President Nasser of Egypt would soon be out of office.

He said high state taxes drove industry out of Pennsylvania and continually asked for tax relief for Pennsylvania industries to stimulate industrial growth. In 1964 Colonel Rockwell was finance chairman of Western Pennsylvanians for Goldwater.

He was born on March 31, 1888, in Dorchester, Massachusetts, a suburb of Boston. He graduated from Massachusetts Institute of Technology in 1908 and became chief engineer of a chemical plant, where he earned $10 a week.

An owner of Torbensen Axle Co. was attracted to Rockwell in 1915, and Rockwell joined that firm in Cleveland as a factory manager, later becoming vice president. During World War I he served as a civilian specialist in the Motor Transport Division of the Quartermaster Corps and advocated the use of heavy-duty trucks for the armed forces.

Colonel Rockwell developed several product innovations at the axle company but resigned in 1919 because he believed his employees would not accept his new concepts. He reorganized a small axle company in Oshkosh, Wisconsin—the Wisconsin Parts Co.—of which he became president, pinning his hopes on the double-reduction axle that he had invented and patented.

But the 1920 depression and the government's decision to sell its World War I army trucks for less than a truck axle cost hurt the firm. But Col. Rockwell got a truck manufacturing company to use his axle rather than the worm drive then in general use.

In 1925 the Mellon family of Pittsburgh got Rockwell to take over the Equitable Meter Co. He continued to head the Wisconsin company while expanding the Pittsburgh firm by several acquisitions. This was the genesis of Rockwell Manufacturing Co.

In 1933 Timken-Detroit, then the largest producer of heavy-duty axles, took over Wisconsin Parts Co. and elected Rockwell president to pull it out of its Depression doldrums. Three years later, the Mellons asked Rockwell to take over Standard Steel Spring Co., auto spring makers, of Coraopolis, Pennsylvania. At that point, he was president of Timken-Detroit, chairman of Standard Steel Spring, and chairman and president of what was then Pittsburgh Equitable Meter Co.

Standard Steel Spring was merged in 1953 with Timken-Detroit, forming Rockwell Spring & Axle Co., with Rockwell as chairman. Five years later, while diversifying into other product lines, the name was changed to Rockwell-Standard Corp., now merged into North American Rockwell.

In the meantime, Rockwell had purchased additional stock in the meter company here and took a controlling interest. Water meters, valves, taxi meters, parking meters, power tools, industrial meters and controls, locomotive parts, and large castings were added to the product lines of Rockwell Manufacturing Co. A major factor in the growth of Rockwell Manufacturing had been the acquisition of Merco-Nordstrom Valve Co. of Oakland, California, in 1933.

During the 1920s and 1930s, Rockwell, an expert in military mechanization, worked with the armed services in the development of trucks and tanks. In World War II, he was director of the Production Division of the U.S. Maritime Commission but kept his hand in business. Timken-Detroit produced approximately 80 percent of the axles for tactical and transport vehicles, and Rockwell companies made other war material.

After World War II Colonel Rockwell's only son, Willard Jr., joined Rockwell Manufacturing as general manager, and the firm expanded to 12 plants with 6,000 employees.

In the postwar period, Colonel Rockwell wrote an ad titled, "How Long, Oh Lord, How Long?", protesting strikes, and he increasingly spoke out against government waste and in defense of the free enterprise system. He sued a union for $15 million because of work slowdowns and effected employee benefits. But his sense of humor compelled him to hang a sign around his neck and join pickets at the Homewood, Pennsylvania, plant in 1918.

In 1965 Colonel Rockwell sponsored the Rockwell Polar Flight, a 26,203-mile journey circling the world by crossing both the North and South Poles in 51 hours, 27 minutes. Colonel Rockwell, then 77 years old, served as senior flight observer.

Colonel Rockwell lived in a 16-room home on a five-acre estate on West Hutchinson Avenue in Edgewood. There, he and his family enjoyed a swimming pool and tennis court, and the colonel frequently indulged in a game of pool after dinner. He enjoyed his prize chrysanthemums, roses, and a large vegetable garden; cleared a field for his family to play baseball and football; and got the cobwebs out through his hobby of building walls.

His first wife, the former Clara Whitcomb Thayer, died in 1965. His second wife, the former Dorothy Morgan, died in 1974.

He is survived by his son, Willard Jr., chairman of the board of Rockwell International; three daughters, Mrs. H. Campbell Stuckeman of Pittsburgh, Mrs. Orin M. Raphael of Oakmont, and Mrs. William S. Potter of Coral Gables, Fla; 19 grandchildren; and 37 great-grandchildren. Another daughter, Mrs. Charles S. Bygate, died in 1973.

TUESDAY, AUGUST 11, 1987

I.W. Abel, 78
Former United Steelworkers Leader
By Jim McKay, *Pittsburgh Post-Gazette*

I. W. Abel, who presided over 12 years of labor peace and made the United Steelworkers the best-paid industrial workers in America, died of cancer yesterday at his home in Malvern, Ohio. Born August 11, 1908, he would have been 79 today.

Iorwith Wilbur Abel—"Abe" to those who knew him well—began his labor career as a volunteer member of the Steelworkers Organizing Committee, the forerunner of the 50-year-old union, and later served three terms as the third president of the USW from 1965 to 1977, when he retired.

When he retired as union president membership was at its peak. Strikes were a negotiated thing of the past and well-paid mill jobs appeared to be secure.

"Abe was a determined, innovative bargainer whose efforts at the negotiating table brought working people more leisure time so they could enjoy the fruits of their labor," said Lynn R. Williams, the union's incumbent president.

Despite many accomplishments at the bargaining table, in the legislative field, and in the political arena, Abel perhaps will be best remembered for the Experimental Negotiation Agreement signed with the steel industry in 1973. The ENA, discontinued by the steelmakers as too expensive in 1980, banned industry-wide steel strikes while guaranteeing workers a 3 percent annual wage increase and unlimited cost-of-living protection.

The son of an Ohio blacksmith of German ancestry, Abel joined the labor movement in 1936 following a Depression job firing kilns in a brickyard. That job, he would say later, helped develop his social thinking. "I worked for 16¢ an hour, 12 hours a night, seven days a week—half my life—and I drew 29 bucks on payday," Abel recalled

I.W. Abel. *Photo courtesy of the* Pittsburgh Post-Gazette.

in an interview at the union's 1986 convention in Las Vegas.

Born in Magnolia, Ohio, Abel attended Magnolia High School and a business college in Canton, Ohio. In 1925 he went to work for the American Sheet and Tin Mill plant in Canton and learned the molding trade. Later he worked for the Canton Malleable Iron Co. and the Timken Roller Bearing Co.

In 1930 he married Bernice N. Joseph of East Sparta, Ohio. Six months later, a victim of the Depression, he lost his job at Timken. He then found the brickyard job.

Abel became a volunteer for the Steel Workers Organizing Committee (SWOC) in 1936 and helped to organize Local 1123 at the Timken Roller Bearing Co. He served as the local's financial secretary, vice president, and, eventually, president. He was a dues-paying member of Local 1123 at his death.

The late Philip Murray, founding president of SWOC, chose Abel in 1942 as provisional head of the union's newly created District 27 headquartered in Canton. He later was elected a director by the district's members. In 1952 Abel was the unanimous choice for the office of international secretary-treasurer. He was first elected international president in 1965 and was reelected in 1969 and 1973.

"Abe was not only a lifelong and dedicated trade unionist who helped forge landmark improvements in the lot of working people, he was also a compassionate human being who strove to improve the total society in which we live," Williams said.

As USW president, Abel fought for the Occupational Safety and Health Act—health and safety legislation covering workers in mines and industry.

A familiar figure on Capitol Hill and in the White House during the Johnson presidency, he also was instrumental in passage of the Employment Retirement Income Security Act, under which the government polices and guarantees certain company pension plans. "It's no good to just have a company say, 'Okay, we'll agree to a pension, and we'll agree to fund it,' and then do nothing about it," Abel said in the convention interview.

Under the Abel administration, the union helped to change the shape of the civil rights landscape in the United States. He was an outspoken champion of equal opportunity. "The landmark basic steel consent decree of 1974 opened doors to advancement previously denied to minorities by creating an affirmative action program and laid the groundwork for the first training program in a labor agreement," Williams said.

The Experimental Negotiating Agreement which Abel pioneered was an attempt to eliminate the costs of cyclical stockpiling before contract negotiation. It also worked to dampen demand for steel imports and to set the ground rules for contract negotiations.

Labor relations with the steel industry were stable during Abel's tenure.

Membership grew from about 800,000 to 1.4 million, with nearly 250,000 of that coming through mergers with other unions. The USW's dues-paying membership now stands at about 650,000.

The union made impressive gains in wages and benefits through the now-defunct coordinated bargaining system, under which the USW negotiated contracts with the industry as a group.

Abel, who made his home until recently in Sun City, Arizona, is survived by his second wife, the former Martha L. Turvey. His first wife, Bernice, died in 1982. He is also survived by two daughters, Karen Jones of Fort Washington in Montgomery County and Linda Goldberg of Fairfax Station, Virginia, and five grandchildren.

SECTION

IV

Characters in Character

What would any city be without its characters? A colorless urban center full of careerists. A set of buildings jammed full with anonymous toilers. A place with, well, no character. Pittsburgh is many things, but none can deny that it is a city of character. And, as you will see, a city with its share of characters.

TUESDAY, JULY 8, 1952

William A "Gus" Greenlee, 56
Sports Promoter
By the *Pittsburgh Post-Gazette*

William A. "Gus" Greenlee, 56, one of the two men credited with introducing the numbers racket in Pittsburgh back in 1926, died yesterday at his suburban home, 10900 Frankstown Road, Penn Township.

One of the Hill District's most colorful figures, Greenlee quit the racket years ago and branched out into sports promotion and the restaurant and hotel business. He opened the original Crawford Grill on Wylie Avenue; operated the Pittsburgh Crawfords, a Negro baseball team; helped establish Greenlee Field, now the site of a housing project; and at one time managed John Henry Lewis, former light heavyweight boxing champion.

Greenlee, a native of North Carolina, spent most of his life in Pittsburgh. Like his one-time reputation of never failing to pay "Woogie" Harris, he was well known for his readiness to answer any charitable call. While they were in the lottery business together they built a reputation of never failing to pay off—no matter how hard their numbers pool was hit.

A veteran of World War I, Greenlee had been a patient at the Veterans Hospital in Aspinwall, Pennsylvania, for several months but recently was removed to his home. He leaves his wife, two brothers, and two sisters.

FRIDAY, JUNE 11, 1999

Robert R. Lansberry, 69
Couldn't Get His Mail
By Timothy McNulty, *Pittsburgh Post-Gazette*

Imagine what was going on in Robert R. Lansberry's mind.

He had been carrying his black-and-white sandwich boards around his neck for years—since he first felt the silent mind-controlling radio waves sent by the CIA in the 1970s. In the beginning he protested by sending the government letters, but when he started to suspect that the Feds—through their agents at the U.S. Postal Service—were censoring his mail, he took his protest to the streets.

Though his signs—which Mr. Lansberry wore Downtown and at most big public events citywide—said lots of things over the years. A usual target was U.S. Representative Bill

Robert Lansberry may not get any mail, but he did get 14,000 votes for Congress. *Photo by Bill Levis.*

Coyne, a Democrat of Oakland, Pennsylvania. Coyne was a federal official, after all, and he hadn't cracked the mail censorship case, let alone the greater CIA conspiracy underneath it.

Then came the parade.

Mr. Lansberry was there as usual with his signs, getting the message out, and who should come walking down the street but Coyne himself, at the head of a large group of marchers. As the group got closer to Mr. Lansberry, he saw they were federal employees—and letter carriers at that.

Imagine.

"Get me my mail!" Mr. Lansberry yelled.

After a quarter of a century as a grizzled fixture of city life, Mr. Lansberry of Stowe, Pennsylvania, died yesterday morning of pneumonia after a long battle with cancer, said a spokeswoman for the VA Medical Center in Oakland. Lansberry was 69.

Mr. Lansberry, a former sailor and grocery store owner, wore his first "Why Can't Lansberry Get Mail" sandwich board during the 1978 Three Rivers Arts Festival. He had been writing protest letters to the government for years, questioning everything from CIA mind-control studies to the price of milk, but he switched to the placards after sensing the mail censorship. The tip-off, he said to anybody who'd listen, came when his sympathizers said they had been sending him money through the mail, but it didn't arrive.

So he took his message to the streets, marching along Grant Street and other crowded places with the two white placards strapped around his shoulders for 12 to 14 hours a day. Afterward he'd stop by a Smithfield Street tavern for his customary six bottles of Rolling Rock.

The routine didn't change, but the messages did. They ranged from the lengthy—"Stop Thornburgh Mail Thief" and "Ask Mayor Caliguiri about Biofeed Slaves, Tortures, Guinea Pigs, Postal Theft"—to the shorter and more declarative, such as the "Murphy Is a Rat" and "Coyne Sucks" placards he wore the last few years.

In 1990 Pittsburgh police arrested Mr. Lansberry for obscenity for wearing a sign saying Coyne "suks, socks, scuks." Though he had deliberately misspelled the word to stay out of trouble, a city magistrate agreed the message was obscene and sentenced him to 25 days in the county jail. (He spelled it correctly in the last few years, and no one seemed to mind.)

Coyne so rankled Mr. Lansberry that he spent his entire life savings ($610) to run against the incumbent congressman in the 1992 Democratic primary and got 13,871 votes to Coyne's 44,616. The day after the election, he explained his loss with a new sign: "Election Was Fixed."

The anger at Coyne started after the former Pittsburgh city councilman entered congress in 1980. Mr. Lansberry told Coyne's staff he wasn't getting mail. They checked with the U.S. Postal Service, found nothing amiss, and told him so. Thereafter, Mr. Lansberry's growing anger at the federal government became associated with one man: Coyne. The congressman knew Mr. Lansberry was troubled and brushed the placard campaign off.

"It's very bad to hear he passed," Coyne said yesterday from Washington, D.C. "Obviously it was not the easiest life to have to live."

In 1983, a year after the loss to Coyne, Mr. Lansberry ran in the Democratic primary for Allegheny County Clerk of Courts. It was another losing effort, but he got 33,880 votes in the countywide race.

Mr. Lansberry advised his fellow Downtown habitues to adopt his tactics. At the corner of Smithfield and Fifth Avenue—a Lansberry stomping ground and the big leagues of Downtown eccentricity—he insisted to Ron Sicilia, the bellowing lunchtime street minister, that sandwich boards were the way to go. "He told me many times to carry a sign, but it wasn't my style," said Sicilia, who's stood at the corner, yelling, for 18 years.

Nearby, Mr. Lansberry made one of his best friends, Jim Selelyo, who first met him 30 years ago at his Four Seasons Floral stand. Lansberry'd talk about the silent radios that control the mind, politics, how he loved traveling— he'd been to Hawaii, Germany, Cancun, and spent several summers protesting in Washington, D.C.—and how he missed his three kids.

Mr. Lansberry honestly believed his messages, Selelyo said. "He was a very,

very educated individual and claimed the post office stole his mail because they didn't want him to pursue his cause," he said. "If everyone was as honest as Lansberry, you'd never need police."

Mr. Lansberry grew up in Morningside, Pennsylvania, and graduated from Peabody High School in 1948. He graduated from Penn State with a business degree in 1952, joined the navy for four years, then came back to the area for jobs with IBM and Westinghouse. In 1956, back from Korea, he changed his party affiliation from Democrat to Independent, county elections department records show.

He lived in Plum, Pennsylvania, in the 1960s, opened up two grocery stores—Lansberry's General Store and the Manor Village Market—and owned properties in Highland Park and Penn Hills.

In 1971 Mr. Lansberry started writing his letters. In 1974 his wife tried to confine him to a mental institution, he told *Pittsburgh Post-Gazette* reporter Tom Hritz. Soon after, Lansberry left his wife and the children and moved Downtown, sometimes sleeping outside and sometimes paying rent with his Social Security and pension checks. In 1977 he started living Downtown in the Edison Hotel, then, over the years, moved on to McKees Rocks, the South Side, Lawrenceville, and finally Stowe.

In 1978, at the beginning of his crusade, he registered again as a Democrat. He rarely missed an election, and he cast his last vote in November, when esophageal cancer forced him to stop marching.

THURSDAY, JANUARY 9, 2003

Dante "Tex" Gill, 72
Massage-Parlor Owner
By Torsten Ove, *Pittsburgh Post-Gazette*

In all the old newspaper stories about Dante "Tex" Gill, she was always "the woman who prefers to be known as a man" or some variation of that description, and she sure looked and acted the part. Short and dumpy, she wore men's suits and short hair, she talked tough, and she may even have undergone the initial stages of a sex change that made her appear masculine.

During the 1970s and 1980s she was a bizarre fixture in the red-light world of Pittsburgh's massage-parlor district along Liberty Avenue. For years, according to police, Ms. Gill ran a string of parlors as fronts for prostitution, all the while insisting that she was a man and telling everyone she wanted to be known as "Mr. Gill."

In 1984 she went on trial in U.S. District Court for tax evasion and ended up in federal prison for seven years.

Ms. Gill of Brentwood died yesterday in UPMC McKeesport. She was 72

Dante "Tex" Gill was named Dubious Man of the Year in 1984. *Photo courtesy of the* Pittsburgh Post-Gazette.

and had been undergoing dialysis for some time.

Born Lois Jean Gill in the city, Ms. Gill was a savvy businesswoman who became one of the most notorious of the city's massage-parlor operators. State and local authorities had long believed her parlors, including the Japanese Meditation Temple, were little more than brothels, but she seemed beyond the reach of the law for years until the Internal Revenue Service stepped in.

IRS agents caught her for tax evasion—not prostitution—by comparing the money she spent with the income she reported. In 1984 she was convicted of conspiracy and evading income taxes from 1975 to 1983.

Those who knew Ms. Gill said she was every bit as colorful as the news stories about her suggest. An unabashed lesbian in a less sexually liberated age, she married a woman in Hawaii and lived with her in Pittsburgh for a time before they eventually split.

"She was just a hell of a lot of fun," said lawyer Carl Max Janavitz, who met her in the 1970s and sometimes represented her. "She was just laughing at the world. And naturally, the authorities don't like that. She was a very good businesswoman, but she just had a different lifestyle."

Before her entry into the massage parlor industry, Ms. Gill was involved in several other ventures. In the late 1950s she worked as a blacksmith at the old horse stables in Schenley Park, where children and adults would come to learn to ride. She went by the name Lois back then, but she wore her hair short and covered with a cowboy hat, and she was known as gruff and no-nonsense. If a horse acted up while she was shoeing it or cleaning its hooves, she smacked it on the rump. She was apparently an accomplished horsewoman in her youth.

Barry Paris, a *Post-Gazette* film critic and Ms. Gill's cousin, said she was an anomaly for her day, someone who had to hide her sexuality as a single woman in the transgender community, which at the time was so underground it had yet to acquire that label.

"She scared the hell out of us when my cousins and I took riding lessons from her as kids at Schenley stables, and she got involved early on with the proverbial 'wrong crowd,'" he said. "But she was personally gentle and nonviolent, and she made a nice corrupt life for herself in a nice corrupt American society."

In her later years, before she went to prison, Janavitz said Gill ran various businesses in town, including a baby furniture store and a frozen foods store. She got involved in the massage parlors through business contacts, Janavitz said, and did it because she needed money to care for her ailing mother, Agnes, who eventually died of cancer in 1973.

Janavitz, who had a falling-out with Ms. Gill and hadn't talked with her for the last 10 years, characterized her as a true free spirit who did things her own way. "You're talking about a person who was very complex," he said. "She was very tough. A lot of fun. She drank a lot. She partied a lot. She could recite poetry endlessly. Irish poetry."

SECTION

V

Classic Pittsburgh

You hear the phrase "classic Pittsburgh" everywhere—in political centers, in the cultural district, in the malls, in the crowded restaurants of Downtown at the noon hour. No one can define the term properly. No one can deny the richness of the phrase. Perhaps the best explanation becomes clearer after considering the people who comprise this section. Classic Pittsburgh, indeed.

SATURDAY, OCTOBER 9, 1954

John Minadeo, 15
School Safety Guard
By the *Pittsburgh Post-Gazette*

In the four years since he came here from Italy, young John Minadeo had made the most of his opportunities as an American. As a member of the ninth grade at Hazelwood's Gladstone Junior High School, his reputation for dependability and good behavior led to his election two weeks ago as captain of the safety patrol. After school hours he worked as a stock boy in a fruit market. That was to help his father, who labors in a cemetery.

When school let out on Thursday afternoon, there was hardly a prouder or more impressive looking lad in all of Hazelwood than 15-year-old John Minadeo. Resplendent in a white Sam Browne belt, symbol of his leadership and responsibility, he stood in the bright October sunshine directing schoolmates across a busy street intersection.

Suddenly there was a commotion up Hazelwood Avenue. Down the hill toward the intersection an automobile sped crazily out of control, its driver shouting that the brakes had failed. Captain Minadeo reacted promptly, pushing the child nearest him to safety. But the car plunged onto a group of children.

When this brief nightmare had ended, Captain Minadeo lay dying of a skull fracture. He had responded heroically to the last opportunity afforded by his adopted land.

The short life and tragic death of John Minadeo are at once a challenge and a rebuke: a challenge to all who believe that in every human soul there is an infinite potential for good, a rebuke to all who for reasons of color, creed, or national origin discriminate against any American school child.

FRIDAY, APRIL 12, 1996

Ivo Fatigati, 73
His Steaks Almost as Big as His Heart
By Matthew P. Smith, *Pittsburgh Post-Gazette*

There is a wonderful little love story about Ivo Fatigati that is almost as delicious as the enormous steaks he used to serve up to his customers at his out-of-the-way restaurant in Pennsylvania's South Fayette Township.

Mr. Fatigati, who was chef and co-owner of Fatigati's Restaurant, a favorite of Steelers players and others with big appetites, died Tuesday in St. Clair Memorial Hospital of pancreatic cancer. He was 73.

More about the restaurant will follow, but back to the story, which is best told by Mr. Fatigati's wife Ellenore.

Mr. Fatigati, who was an aircraft mechanic with the Army Air Corps during World War II, returned to the United States after the war and finished a degree in business administration and commerce at the University of Notre Dame.

After graduation he joined the State Department and began working overseas at several embassies as a code clerk, a job that required him to have a special clearance to handle sensitive and often top-secret documents. The job took him around the world and included stops in Kuala Lumpur in Malaysia, Singapore, and Korea.

He almost didn't survive his posting in Korea in the early 1950s. He was among the last Americans to flee the country as war broke out, and occasionally he talked about the time he and other embassy staffers had to jump out of the Jeep they were driving to avoid being strafed by a North Korean fighter plane. It earned him a special citation from Dean Acheson, the secretary of state under President Truman.

It was while he was in Singapore that another State Department employee told him about Ellenore Meller, who was a secretary at the U.S. Embassy in Athens, Greece. "You'd like her," the friend said. "She's a nice Catholic girl."

They started corresponding, but circumstances prevented them from meeting until they both returned to the

United States. They finally got their chance in the summer of 1953. Ellenore, who lived in Milwaukee, and a sister drove to New York to visit some friends. On their return trip, she arranged to meet Mr. Fatigati face to face.

They decided they wanted to meet somewhere that they would easily find each other. They agreed to meet on the steps of the state capitol in Harrisburg.

And?

"It was love at first sight," she said. "It was like it was something that was meant to be."

They were married in 1956 in the Log Chapel at Notre Dame and settled in Pittsburgh. At the urgings of his father, Mr. Fatigati left the State Department and went to work at the family's restaurant on Route 50 in the Cuddy section of South Fayette.

Mr. Fatigati, already an accomplished cook, changed its name from the White Front Bar & Grill to Fatigati's and had the place renovated.

It also developed a reputation. Some restaurants are known for their fine food, some for big portions. But very few were anything like Fatigati's, where the steaks never fit on the platter.

In a competitive business, where the biggest steak at a restaurant might be 20 ounces, Mr. Fatigati was known to serve his customers T-bones and New York strips that weighed three or four pounds. "My father never wanted people to go away hungry," said Fatigati's son, Gregory, who is the executive chef of Chestnut Ridge Inn on the Green in Blairsville, Indiana County.

The oversized portions made the restaurant popular with many former

Steelers, among them were L.C. Greenwood, Jack Ham, Andy Russell, and Terry Bradshaw. "I remember watching L.C. Greenwood finish off one of those big steaks and a big platter of homemade pasta. There weren't many who could do that," Gregory Fatigati said.

But it wasn't just the portions that made it popular. Fatigati's was known for its homemade pasta, sauces, and salad dressings.

Fatigati's was also something of a training ground for budding chefs. Sixteen people who worked in the restaurant's kitchen went on to the prestigious Culinary Institute of America in Hyde Park, New York, including Gregory Fatigati.

Carl Apone, retired music critic for the *Pittsburgh Press* and a longtime friend of Mr. Fatigati's, said they met while they were students at Notre Dame in the 1940s. "He was a sweet man," said Apone. "He was loved by just about everybody who knew him."

Apone said the only problem he had with Mr. Fatigati was trying to pay his dinner bill. "Ivo was very big-hearted," he said.

Gregory Fatigati said his family was struck by the fact that two of Mr. Fatigati's closest friends in the restaurant business also died recently. Louis Tambellini of Tambellini's Restaurant on Route 51 died on April 1, and Frank Sgro, who operated Sgro's Restaurant off the Parkway West in Robinson, Pennsylvania, died last Friday. "(My father) and Frank were probably the closest, but there was a lot of mutual respect among all three of them. Frank always said my father made the best lamb chops of anyone," Gregory Fatigati said.

Mr. Fatigati also is survived by a son, Francis of Seattle; three daughters, Ellen Fatigati and Mary Birnie, both of Washington, D.C., and Ann Casiere of Mt. Lebanon; two brothers, Mario and William, both of Cecil; and five grandchildren.

THURSDAY, JANUARY 30, 1997

Joey Diven, 66
Fabled Street Fighter
By James O'Toole, *Pittsburgh Post-Gazette*

Joey Diven, a man who seized life in the massive fists that made his reputation, died yesterday morning. He was 66. He leaves behind a wife, two sons, and a million stories—many of them true.

Hours after his fatal heart attack in Montefiore University Hospital, friends and relatives crowded into the neat Brookline, Pennsylvania, home he shared with his wife, Barbara. Their embraces and condolences were punctuated with laughter as they exchanged tales of the legendary street fighter, sometime politician, and perennial soft touch.

"Remember the time he stole the fire truck?" ventured one cousin.

"Nah, that was Billy Neumont who stole the fire truck. Joey stole a trolley—no, it was a bus," his wife said quickly, to set the record straight.

As the tale goes, an unsuspecting bus driver stopped for a cup of coffee at the old Gammon's restaurant on Forbes Avenue in Oakland. Mr. Diven and a friend knew an opportunity when they saw it. They commandeered the bus and drove off, patrolling the streets of his beloved Oakland for hours, picking up old ladies at bus stops and dropping them off at their doors.

Then there was the time Mr. Diven somehow ended up with a pony from a circus that had closed its run at Forbes Field, and he decided to take it home to his nephews. On the way, he and the pony startled patrons at the old Cardinal Lounge on Forbes Avenue as, together, they interrupted their journey for a cool drink.

"He thought he could get it home by tying it to the bumper and driving real slow, but he couldn't get it through the tubes—thank God," Barbara Diven said.

But perhaps the quintessential Joey Diven story involves the time he took on and bested a significant portion of the Pitt football team in the autumn of 1954.

As recounted by Roy McHugh, the former *Pittsburgh Press* columnist and sports writer, Mr. Diven and a variety of burly undergraduates engaged in a battle that moved along Forbes Avenue from Atwood Street to an alley behind the old Strand Theater. In the wake of this vigorous conversation, Mr. Diven was mildly bruised, several Pitt athletes were badly battered, and countless innocent bookies burned as Pitt unexpectedly failed to cover the spread for the next afternoon's game.

But Mr. Diven held no grudge against Pitt. Among the mementoes in his basement game room is a Dan Marino jersey from the years Marino quarterbacked the Panthers. It's a few feet from one of Terry Bradshaw's helmets, one of Roberto Clemente's bats, and myriad autographs and artifacts from the Major Leaguers and umpires with whom Mr. Diven loafed. The bats decorate a corner of a bar salvaged from the Oakland Café, one of his neighborhood haunts.

In his prime Mr. Diven was a battleship of a man, 6'3", 285 pounds, with hulking shoulders supporting a 19-inch neck. His father's family followed an archetypical Irish immigrant pattern, having fled the potato famine in the 1840s. The father was a policeman, as were Mr. Diven's five brothers.

He was born on Dawson Street in Oakland, later moved to the Sheraden area, then back to Oakland, where he lived until 1964, when he moved to Brookline.

Mr. Diven's varied career also touched on law enforcement. At different times, he was an elected constable in Oakland and served as a county detective. He was also a salesman for the old Duquesne Brewery and later held several positions in county politics.

Working for the prothonotary's office and later as an assistant to county commissioner Tom Foerster, Diven frequently managed his vaguely defined duties from "his office"—a corner barstool down the street at Mitchell's, the venerable courthouse hangout.

His son, Michael, of Brookline, said that in their youth, his father and uncles honed their toughness with a friendly game called one-punch. The name suggests the elegant simplicity of its rules. A brother would stand still while another hauled off and punched him as hard as he could. If the sibling on the receiving end felt up to it, he returned the salute.

Michael and Mr. Diven's other son, Joseph R. Jr. of Beechview, recalls family combat that was slightly less rigorous. Their father regularly supervised fraternal boxing matches in which they faced one another wearing boxing gloves that had belonged to Billy Conn, the boxing champion who was Diven's lifelong friend.

Mr. Diven's toughness was at the core of his legend, but friends said yesterday that it was only a portion of his character. "The most important thing to Joey was to help people, no matter who they were," Foerster said. "I was having dinner with Joey down in Mitchell's one night, and there was somebody who needed money. [Mr. Diven] pulled out what I knew to be his last $5. He would never turn anyone down."

McHugh called Diven the king of the barroom brawlers. The writer Frank Deford, in a memorable *Sports Illustrated* profile of Billy Conn, called Mr. Diven the greatest street fighter who ever lived. But, McHugh said, "The street fighting thing wasn't the essence of Joey Diven. He had an ingratiating personality. He was really a genial companion."

"You could always tell the difference between people who knew my father and people who knew of him. The people who would tell you he was the toughest son of a bitch in the world knew of him," Joey Jr. said. "The people who said he had a big heart knew him."

Mr. Diven prided himself on never throwing the first punch in a fight. But no one was immune to his quick needle.

Name a memorable moment in modern Pittsburgh history, and Mr. Diven was there. When Bill Mazeroski hit his home run to win the 1960 World Series, Mr. Diven was working the door of the Pirates locker room at Forbes Field. When John F. Kennedy came to Pittsburgh the same year, there was Mr. Diven with him on stage at Syria Mosque. When the Steelers traveled to New Orleans for their first Super Bowl, the late Art Rooney assigned Diven to handle security for the players.

Like Woody Allen's character Zelig, Mr. Diven seemed to show up everywhere. But unlike the chameleon-like character who constantly changed to fit new circumstances, Mr. Diven was the same with everyone.

On travels to New York City, often with Billy Conn, Mr. Diven could be found at the legendary bar, Toots Shor's.

One evening in 1958, Mr. Diven's sister, Virginia, was in her kitchen in Terrace Village when the phone rang. Frank Sinatra was on the other end of the line. Mr. Diven thought she'd like to say hello.

Mr. Diven's health had begun to ebb in recent years. He was diagnosed with diabetes in 1970, and in 1991 one leg was amputated because of the disease.

THURSDAY, MAY 7, 1998

James Blandi Sr., 72
The Man Behind LeMont

By Gene Collier, *Pittsburgh Post-Gazette*

James "Jim" Blandi, owner and founder of the LeMont, holding rare brands of wine. *Photo by Dale Gleason.*

They called him "the Chief" in the elegant landmark panorama that is LeMont.

The restaurant he founded on Mount Washington in 1960, the one that still flourishes for a new generation of Pittsburghers, reflected both Jim Blandi's personal warmth and his professional aptitude—a combination that made him a giant of local business. "A wonderful restaurateur and a wonderful human being, an absolute heart of gold," Robi Ehrhardt was saying in the restaurant as the dinner shift filtered in. She's LeMont's controller. "Mr. Blandi used to live here. He was here day and night up until 10 years ago, when he kind of semiretired. Eight years ago, that's when Jim Jr. stepped in."

James Blandi Sr. died yesterday at age 72 in Mercy Hospital of renal failure, a complication from an aneurism he had suffered in 1989, but remembrances of his generosity were still vivid.

He started the Gourmet Dinners for Children's Hospital through the *Pittsburgh Press* Old Newsboys Fund just two years after LeMont opened. Those dinners raised $600,000 for the Free Care Fund before they were discontinued in 1993. These were lavish, seven-course dinners that guests paid up to $200 to attend. Mr. Blandi and his uncle, Frank Blandi, the former owner of the old Park Schenley Restaurant in Oakland, took care of the expenses.

Children's Hospital chairman and CEO Robin Violi issued a statement yesterday from California: "The hospital deeply regrets the passing of Mr. Blandi. He's been a friend and a major contributor for many years through his annual gourmet dinners. He'll be sorely missed. Our sympathies to his family."

"Nothing has given me more satisfaction," Mr. Blandi once said, "than raising that kind of money for kids whose parents can't afford their medical care."

A good part of Pittsburgh's societal history is linked to Mr. Blandi's vision for LeMont and to a kind of golden age of Mount Washington dining that included contemporaries such as Tambellini's and Christopher's. "There was a period

in the 1960s and 1970s where that's all there was, was Mount Washington dining," John Tambellini said yesterday. "Mount Washington was everything, and LeMont was one of the most beautiful restaurants ever built in Pittsburgh. We were not competitors. We were very good friends. He was a great man. It's a very sad loss."

The grandson of Italian immigrants, Mr. Blandi was part of a large family business that owned wineries in Dunkirk, New York, as well as Pittsburgh restaurants.

An only child born in Buffalo, New York, Mr. Blandi took his first job at age three during Prohibition, licking labels for the bottles of liquor sold at his grandfather's restaurant, said his son, James A. Blandi Jr.

The family moved to Pittsburgh, and Mr. Blandi was raised in East Liberty.

As a young man, he owned the former Fox Head Grill in Dormont in the 1950s. Later he was a partner with his uncle at the Park Schenley.

Mr. Blandi later lived in Fox Chapel and Oakmont, and he remained in the restaurant business.

"LeMont was Jim Blandi's personality, from the ambience to the whole class of the place," said Alex Colaizzi, the LeMont maitre d', who worked for Mr. Blandi for 37 years. "In 1960, when this place opened, you couldn't make a reservation for three months. The day it opened, he contracted for an addition that would make room for 32 new tables. It was a whole different era. Its magnificence had not been seen before."

Jim Blandi Jr. said his father never steered him to the business. "My father was a very loving, nurturing man who always wanted me to go in my own direction and never asked me or told me to come into the business," he said. "It was my own choice, and I made it when I was 13. Now I'm 32. My father

was my life. It's a very difficult loss."

In addition to his uncle and son, Mr. Blandi is survived by a daughter, Christina Marie James, and three grandchildren.

SATURDAY, DECEMBER 27, 2003

George Zambelli Sr., 79
Headed One of Oldest Fireworks Companies
By Michelle K. Massie, *Pittsburgh Post-Gazette*

George Zambelli Sr., head of the famed Zambelli Fireworks Internationale, who, with his business acumen expanded his company far beyond its Western Pennsylvania borders while keeping it firmly rooted in the region, died Thursday. He was 79. Mr. Zambelli died of complications from the flu. His 10-year battle against cancer also weakened his immune system.

In 1946, upon graduating from Duquesne University, Mr. Zambelli sat down with his father and brothers and asked if he could take the helm of the family business, which was founded in 1893. His family agreed and allowed him to lead the way. Since then, as president and owner of the company, Mr. Zambelli became an innovator in the fireworks industry, becoming the first to introduce choreographed fireworks displays to the country.

He also pushed the industry forward with how it staged such pyrotechnic displays. He saw the usefulness of displays beyond the major holiday celebrations. Mr. Zambelli incorporated

George Zambelli of the New Castle–based Zambelli International Fireworks Co. *Photo by V.W.H. Campbell Jr.*

fireworks into more intimate settings, such as weddings and cultural and religious festivals.

Ida D'Errico, of Mt. Lebanon, Pennsylvania, a consultant and former producer of such Pittsburgh events as the Three Rivers Regatta, knew Mr. Zambelli for more than 20 years, both as a friend and as a professional colleague. "What he loved more than anything was seeing people of all ages smile. And his fireworks brought happiness around the world. He reminded me so much of Santa Claus, so it's ironic that he would die at Christmas," D'Errico said.

"When George walked in the room, he lit it up more than he did with the fireworks," said Wayne Hettinger, a producer of Thunder Over Louisville who worked with Mr. Zambelli for the past 15 years on displays. "When we were searching for fireworks vendors, and we looked at a lot of them, George was very interesting. He did what he did best. He introduced himself and became a friend," Hettinger said. "And on the business end, he backed up everything he said he was going to do."

Because of his business savvy, stringent work ethic, and devotion to fireworks, Mr. Zambelli successfully ran the nation's largest fireworks manufacturer from its corporate headquarters in New Castle, Lawrence County, and earned several nicknames over the years including, "Boom Boom," "the Great Zambelli," and "Mr. Fireworks."

"In the 1950s and 1960s we were doing displays in Central America and later on in Kuwait, Switzerland, and other places around the world," said George Zambelli Jr., 55, of Marshall. "But the company started here. My dad never forgot his original customers— his loyalty and wanting to give back to the community who supported the company."

George Jr., an ophthalmologist, said that he started hanging around his father's office when he was five years old, and by the time he was six, he was answering telephones as an operator at the company.

Each year, Zambelli Internationale produces more than 3,500 fireworks shows throughout the world. From weddings to community festivals to company picnics and ball games to displays before U.S. presidents (the company has done displays for every president since and including John F. Kennedy) and visiting dignitaries to the most popular of all— annual Fourth of July celebrations, Mr. Zambelli; his wife of 59 years, Constance; his five children; and throngs of grandchildren have all been a part of the family business. Mr. Zambelli expected the family to be with him at the fireworks displays, George Jr. said.

Mr. Zambelli's father, Antonio Zambelli, a laborer and fireworks maker, emigrated from Cassarta, Italy, to New Castle and brought with him a knowledge and artistry of pyrotechnics which blossomed into Zambelli Fireworks Manufacturing Co.

"[George Zambelli Sr.] was a good friend of mine and a remarkable man," said Allegheny County chief executive Jim Roddey. "When I came to Pittsburgh 25 years ago, I was amazed that Pittsburgh had so many parades and fireworks.... The Zambellis were a big part of that. They're a unique family. They're the first family of fireworks, and I think they're a lot more famous worldwide than they are locally. George has created a legacy, and the family should have no problem carrying it on."

Despite the success of the company, Mr. Zambelli played down much of his fame. "George was the most genuine human being," D'Errico said. "George wasn't like other famous people. He did what he did to bring joy to people."

D'Errico worked with Mr. Zambelli and his company to produce Millennium Pittsburgh on January 1, 2000, which was the largest live New Year's Day fireworks display in the country.

The Zambellis were known for pleasing their audiences and doing all they could to accommodate a crowd— no matter how large or how small the budget for the event. "He always thought fireworks were magic," said George Jr. "He was like a painter who painted the sky."

Mr. Zambelli, his family, and the company have been highlighted in television specials and in a recent biography titled *Zambelli: The First Family of Fireworks.*

"His life was the fireworks business," said Marcy Zambelli Fumagali, of Boca Raton, Florida, one of Mr. Zambelli's daughters. "He'd be up at 5:00 AM and work until 10:00, 11:00 at night. Fireworks consumed most of his time, but he loved to be around the crowd. It was a labor of love."

Mr. Zambelli often contributed to a number of charitable organizations, including Children's Hospital of Pittsburgh.

Besides his wife, son, and daughter, Mr. Zambelli is survived by three other daughters; Donnalou Zambelli McVay and Annlyn Zambelli Richards, both of New Castle, and Danabeth Zambelli Trasatti, of Boca Raton, Florida; a brother, Louis Zambelli of New Castle; and 10 grandchildren.

TUESDAY, JUNE 21, 2005

William Block, 89
Longtime Publisher of the *Post-Gazette*
By Michael McGough and James O'Toole, *Pittsburgh Post-Gazette*

William Block, whose self-effacing and socially conscious leadership shaped the *Pittsburgh Post-Gazette* for nearly 60 years and infused it with his wide-ranging interests in art, music, and altruism, died yesterday at UPMC Shadyside of pneumonia. He was 89 and lived in Oakland, Pennsylvania.

A member of a now four-generation newspaper family, Mr. Block began his career as copublisher of the *Post-Gazette* in smoky post-World War II Pittsburgh at a time of intense competition among three daily metropolitan newspapers. He ended his formal involvement with the paper in 2001, when he stepped down as chairman of Block Communications Inc., the company that runs what had become—and remains—the region's dominant news organization.

In the Hilton Ballroom on January 18, 1993, William Block Sr. holds aloft the first edition after an eight-month strike that saw the *Pittsburgh Post-Gazette* emerge as the region's leading paper. *Photo courtesy of the* Pittsburgh Post-Gazette.

A patron of the arts and art education, Mr. Block was a member of the boards of the Pittsburgh Symphony and the Pittsburgh Glass Center. His civic contributions included efforts to promote literacy, coordinate the work of the region's charities and foundations, and spotlight the human impact of urban development and renewal.

His dedication to excellence and to making sure that the newspaper he loved remained a strong presence in a changing marketplace made it possible for the *Post-Gazette* to buy the bigger *Pittsburgh Press* in 1992 after a traumatic newspaper strike that threatened the survival of both papers. "If the *Post-Gazette* had not been a quality editorial product for so many years, we could not have purchased the *Press*," recalled Raymond Burnett, who served as business manager for the *Post-Gazette* before it acquired the *Press* after 31 years in which the newspapers were linked in a joint operating agreement.

As chairman, publisher, and, before that, copublisher with his brother Paul Block Jr., Mr. Block set high standards for the *Post-Gazette* even as he entrusted day-to-day operations to a series of strong-willed editors, including Frank N. Hawkins in the 1960s and 1970s and John G. Craig Jr. in the 1980s and 1990s. "Some people are in the right place at the right time, and Bill was such," said Craig, who retired in 2003. "For more than half a century Pittsburgh was served by a newspaper and newspaperman whose values and aspirations were synonymous with the best of his hometown's...because he knew of—and was of—Pittsburgh.

"When I met him in 1976, resident journalistic involvement of this sort and a willingness to spend the money to support it was in rapid decline; today it is all but gone in the nation's major cities."

Somewhat paradoxically, Mr. Block was both a publisher who deferred to his editors and a constant—and accessible—presence at the newspaper. "I can say that in all the time that I worked for him—and that was a hell of a lot of years—he never approached me in one of my spots to say, 'I think we should do this' or 'I think we should do that,'" said James E. Alexander, a former *Post-Gazette* city editor and managing editor who worked with Mr. Block for decades. "I can't believe that's a possibility for some publishers."

Mr. Block preferred to be addressed as "Bill" in the relaxed conversations he would strike up with reporters at the newspaper's Downtown offices. His unassuming manner belied the reality that he had been chairman of a publishing and broadcast enterprise that at various times included several newspapers and television stations (including, for some time, Pittsburgh's Channel 11), WWSW Radio, three cable systems, and an advertising distribution firm.

"He was such a gentleman and so easy to work for," Burnett recalled. "It's hard to convey how nice he was without sounding maudlin."

"My memories of Bill Block are like those of all the old-time *Post-Gazette* people," said William E. Deibler, a former managing editor who is now retired. "He was not only a kind and generous employer; he was a friend. Everybody thought of him that way, from copy boys to the top editorial people."

Deibler first joined the *Post-Gazette* as a correspondent in Harrisburg, where he had previously worked for the Associated Press. When he flew into Pittsburgh for an orientation session, he discovered that the city's hotels were on strike. "I came back to the office and said, 'I really don't know what I'm going to do,' and Bill Block said, 'Don't worry, you're going to stay with me.' And so we went out to his home."

In November 1974, Tim Menees, then a reporter in Seattle, had decided he wanted to be an editorial cartoonist and sent applications around the country. His work caught Mr. Block's eye, and he flew Menees in for an interview. Mr. Block was interested, but he wasn't ready to make a commitment. "Cy Hungerford has been here in Pittsburgh for years," he told the aspiring cartoonist. "I'm not going to force him to retire. This is his life and it would kill him."

Menees was impressed, he later told longtime associate editor Clarke M. Thomas in an interview for *Front-Page Pittsburgh*, a recently published history of the *Post-Gazette*. "As much as I wanted the job, I thought, 'Wow! If this is the attitude of the owner of the paper, it must permeate the place,'" Menees told Thomas. "'He must care about people so much that he's not going to farm out an elderly employee just to get new blood.'"

Hungerford was in his late eighties. A year and a half later, Hungerford, who died in 1983, decided to cut his workload, and Menees was hired. He's been at the *Post-Gazette* ever since.

A Great Civic Leader

Mr. Block's influence as publisher was perhaps most evident on the editorial page. "I've always been that horrible term—*liberal*—more so than my editors," Mr. Block said in an interview for *Front-Page Pittsburgh*.

"When I got back [from military service] in 1946, I veered the editorial policy more to the center," he said. It was a new line for a newspaper that, in his father's day, had been a critic of Franklin D. Roosevelt's New Deal. "We've been liberal in connection with civil rights, conservative on economics. That is my personal feeling and the road that we followed," Block said.

Under Mr. Block's leadership, the *Post-Gazette* backed President Harry S. Truman when he fired General Douglas MacArthur for exceeding his authority during the Korean conflict and stood behind Roy Harris, a composer-in-residence at Chatham College who had been condemned, unjustly, in the paper's view, as a communist sympathizer. Over the years, the paper endorsed both Democrats and Republicans for national and statewide offices.

The newspaper was especially supportive of the postwar smoke-control efforts of Richard King Mellon and Mayor (and future governor) David L. Lawrence, a duo he once described as an unlikely couple—"Lawrence the poor Irishman, Mellon the blue-chip aristocrat"—who were nevertheless able to work together. Mr. Block got to know Lawrence, and the two men would get together at Golden Gloves boxing matches sponsored by the Dapper Dan Club, a *Post-Gazette* charity.

Although Mr. Block encouraged the newspaper's editorial writers to engage in give-and-take on controversial subjects—and sometimes acceded to a consensus even when he disagreed with it—at other times he insisted on exercising the publisher's prerogative, especially when it came to election endorsements. "He'd say, 'Let's take a vote on this,' but in the end he would make the final decision," recalled Thomas.

Sometimes Mr. Block wrote signed columns for the *Post-Gazette*, usually after returning from one of his many trips abroad, some in connection with his involvement with the International Press Institute. He served as chairman of the IPI's American Committee from 1973 to 1977.

During a three-week trip to mainland China in 1978, Mr. Block wrote a letter to the editor of the *People's Daily* complaining about the incessant horn-blowing of motorists and truck drivers. The editor wrote that he agreed with his position; his letter also was aired over the official state radio. But the din of Beijing remains—attesting to the limits of the power of the press in that nation as in this one.

Arriving in his adopted city after World War II, Mr. Block found a newspaper staff that was all white, like those of the other mainstream papers in the city and most of their counterparts across the country. In 1955, at the insistence of Mr. Block, according to Thomas' history of the paper, the *Post-Gazette* became the first mainstream Pittsburgh newspaper to hire an African American reporter, Regis Bobonis, who later left the paper to become editor of the *Pittsburgh Courier*, the city's nationally known African American paper.

Although Mr. Block's primary influence on Pittsburgh was through his newspaper, he was active as an individual in civic, charitable, and cultural activities. He was a former chairman of the Health and Welfare Planning Association, an advisory panel that helped evaluate and coordinate the work of the various charities and foundations in the region. In the mid-1960s he chaired the newly created Social Planning Committee of the city of Pittsburgh's Planning Department. That panel was charged with examining the human impact of urban renewal projects.

"He was a great civic leader, especially in the areas of human services and social policy," said Morton Coleman, director emeritus of the Institute of Politics at the University of Pittsburgh. "He was concerned a lot about the impact of development on people, on how it affected how people actually lived their lives."

Mr. Block also was a longtime supporter of NEED—the Negro Educational Emergency Drive—a local program established in 1963 that raised funds to help African American students attend college.

Mr. Block was willing to put himself on the line when the interests of the newspaper and its readers were at stake. In 1954 the *Post-Gazette* joined with the *Greensburg Daily Tribune* and *Morning Review* and other news organizations in challenging a judge's order forbidding the taking of photographs inside the Westmoreland County courthouse.

While sheriff's deputies were focused on one *Post-Gazette* photographer carrying a large, conventional camera, another used a concealed infrared camera strapped to his waist to take a picture of convicted murderer J. Wesley Wable, known as the Turnpike Killer, as he was being escorted to a courtroom.

The photographers, a *Post-Gazette* reporter, its editor, and Mr. Block were found to be in contempt of court after a hearing in which Mr. Block defended the photographing of Wable, saying his trial was of national importance and "that made it seem to us a part of our responsibility to the public to cover it reportorially and with picture coverage."

In 1956 the Pennsylvania Supreme Court upheld the contempt judgment but threw out five-day jail sentences for Mr. Block and his employees because the photographs were part of a "test case" of an order that several Pennsylvania newspapers considered a violation of the First Amendment. The legendary Justice Michael A. Musmanno dissented from the decision upholding the contempt sanction. He wrote: "Freedom of the press means freedom to gather news, write it, publish it, and circulate it. When any of these integral operations is interdicted, freedom of the press becomes a river without water."

In an era of chain ownership and cost cutting to maximize profits, Mr. Block ran counter to the trend in several ways. He surprised fellow publishers in 1962 when he announced that, while there were fewer newspapers around, the survivors were better and that part of the credit went to the Newspaper Guild, the union that represented his newsroom staff.

Mr. Block's views about unions proved to be an asset for the newspaper during its purchase of the strikebound *Pittsburgh Press* in 1992, a transaction that boosted the *Post-Gazette*'s circulation and bucked a national trend toward chain ownership of big-city dailies. The sale was conditioned on the *Post-Gazette*'s reaching agreements with the labor unions that had failed to settle with Scripps Howard, the chain that owned the *Press*.

"Across the years Bill Block built a feeling of fairness and trust that helped in the labor dispute," recalled Thomas. "The labor guys were willing to settle for him rather than Richard Mellon Scaife [publisher of the *Greensburg Tribune Review*, who also was interested in buying the *Press*]. Bill was a trusted person."

Of the *Post-Gazette*'s purchase of the *Press*, Mr. Block himself said, "It was like Jonah swallowing the whale. I was gradually gliding into a sedentary retirement until the strike and the decision by Scripps [Howard] to sell brought me back into nonstop exertion."

At his 80th birthday party in 1995, a family and corporate celebration on a sunny afternoon at the Pittsburgh Zoo, an employee thanked him for saving the *Post-Gazette* and, with it, his job.

Mr. Block, typically, demurred. "Oh, I should be thanking you," he said. "I wouldn't have a job if all of you weren't there."

A Life in Full

William Block was born in New York City on September 20, 1915, the son of

Paul Block Sr. and Dina Wallach Block. The family had entered the publishing business in 1897 when his father founded Paul Block Associates. At one time or another, the family company owned the *Brooklyn Standard-Union*; the *Duluth Herald*; the *Lancaster* (Pennsylvania) *New Era*; the *Milwaukee Sentinel*; the *Memphis News-Scimitar*; and the *Newark Star Eagle*. Paul Block acquired the *Post-Gazette* in 1927.

Mr. Block attended two private schools in New York before enrolling in the Hotchkiss School in Lakeville, Connecticut. After graduation from Hotchkiss, which honored him with its Alumni Award in 1982, he entered Yale University, graduating with a bachelor of arts degree in 1936.

After Yale, Mr. Block worked briefly at the *Post-Gazette*, helping to oversee construction of a new newspaper plant on Grant Street. His education in the family business continued at the *Blade*, the family's newspaper in Toledo, Ohio, where he started on the ground floor in several departments. Among the tall, skinny heir's duties in that preautomation age were shifts carrying heavy bundles of papers from the presses to the mailroom tables. "The pressmen loved the idea of putting me on the fly...to carry all those papers," he recalled in his privately printed memoirs. "I wouldn't let on that it was practically breaking my back."

Drafted several months before the attack on Pearl Harbor, Mr. Block was an enlisted man for 15 months; in June 1942 he was commissioned a second lieutenant in the Coast Artillery Anti-Aircraft and was assigned to Fort Stewart, Georgia.

Racial segregation was omnipresent in the South of that era as well as in the army. The newly minted lieutenant found himself assigned to a unit consisting entirely of black enlisted men, commanded, with few exceptions, by white officers. One day, he recalled in his memoirs, he was having lunch at a table with two chaplains, who were black, and one of the unit's few black officers.

The regimental battery commander, a Mississippi native, entered and ordered the three blacks to leave the table. Mr. Block recounted that, while uncomfortable at this slight, he at first did nothing. But the next day, when the scene was repeated, Block said, "Captain, don't you think we ought to fight one war at a time?"

With that, he left the table along with the three black officers. Young Lieutenant Block was transferred out of the unit the next day. He later was sent to Camp Haan, California.

Mr. Block had happier memories of that assignment. On his first night in California, at the Mission Inn in Riverside, he spotted a woman whose name, he would soon learn, was Maxine Horton. "There was a very beautiful girl playing the saxophone in an all-girl band," he recalled. "That was the evening I met the young lady who was later to be my wife. It was September 13, 1943."

Mr. Block juggled the wartime romance with military duties, and before long the couple was determined to get married. "Finally the colonel said I could have a long weekend," he recalled. "We rushed to a jewelry store in Riverside and got a ring...we drove to

Las Vegas and were married by a justice of the peace; I think his name was O'Malley. His wife and a policeman were witnesses."

Five months later Mr. Block applied for assignment to a planned postwar Far Eastern Military Government and was sent to Charlottesville, Virginia, and Yale to study Japanese. He shipped out to Yokohama after V-J Day, where his ship rode at anchor for days. Then, with a logic known only to the military, it was decided that Mr. Block's unit, after its months of training in Japanese language and culture, should be sent to Korea, a nation whose language was totally unknown to him and most of his compatriots.

Mr. Block served in the military administration that helped Korea make the transition from Japanese occupation until he left the service in 1946. By then his father, Paul Block Sr., had died and Paul Jr., Mr. Block's older brother, was in command in Toledo. Mr. Block, along with Maxine and their infant son, William Jr., returned to take over the family's operations in Pittsburgh.

Newspaper Wars

Mr. and Mrs. Block made their first temporary home here in a suite at the old Schenley Hotel, now the University of Pittsburgh's student union. This was still the Pittsburgh of soot-belching steel mills and a population that shrugged off grimy skies as a cost of prosperity.

Block said: "Our train arrived from Chicago about 7:00 AM, and we went to the hotel. It was a very warm August day. I opened all the windows (there

was no air conditioning) and ordered breakfast for Bill Jr.…. There was a glass of milk for Bill, and by the time Maxine had him all cleaned up and ready for breakfast, a film of soot had settled on the glass of milk. I remember Maxine looking at it and shuddering. She said, 'My God, do we have to live here?' I answered, 'This is where the job is.'"

"The job" proved satisfying but also frustrating as the Block family encountered resistance to various expansion plans. In 1949 the Blocks launched a Sunday edition with a lavish event that filled the 17th floor of the William Penn Hotel. But, as Mr. Block later recalled, "Hearst [then the owner of the *Pittsburgh Sun-Telegraph*] and Scripps Howard really ganged up on us…a lot of dealers refused to handle the *Sunday Post-Gazette*." The result was a Sunday edition that lost money and closed in less than a year.

But the ambitions of Mr. Block and his brother for the potentially lucrative Sunday market remained. An opportunity more than a decade later to buy and absorb the rival *Sun-Telegraph* seemed the gateway to realizing it. The effort produced another failure, however—one that Mr. Block would remember as the low point of his career in journalism.

The Hearst paper was by then much weaker than the publication that had helped doom the *Post-Gazette* Sunday edition in 1949. The *Sun-Telegraph* had been a six-day afternoon and Sunday morning paper, but its purchase bled the *Post-Gazette*. Only two years later, in a reluctant act of self-preservation, the *Post-Gazette* negotiated its joint-operating agreement with a longtime rival: the *Pittsburgh Press*.

The agreement was sealed only after U.S. Attorney General Robert F. Kennedy, convinced that it was important to preserve two distinct editorial voices in Pittsburgh, granted the newspapers a dispensation from antitrust laws. Under the agreement, the *Post-Gazette* and the *Press* remained independent editorially but combined their business operations in one building on the Boulevard of the Allies. The *Press* handled all the advertising, production, and circulation work. The *Post-Gazette* retained control only of its own reporters and editors. The arrangement continued for three decades—until 1992, a pivotal year in Pittsburgh journalism.

Contract talks between Scripps Howard and the unions that printed and distributed both papers had dragged on without progress. Unions, led by the Teamsters, finally walked out when Scripps Howard tried to impose new working conditions. Because of its business relations with the *Press*, the *Post-Gazette* was forced to cease publication as well.

After many months of on-again, off-again negotiations interspersed with a short-lived attempt to resume publication without unions, Scripps Howard threw in the towel. The Cincinnati-based corporation announced on October 2, 1992, that the *Press* was for sale.

"Our family had been involved with the *Post-Gazette* since 1927. There was a great deal of sentiment connected with the decision [to buy the *Press*] as well as a challenge and...an opportunity," Mr. Block said.

Blade Communications eventually did make its offer for the *Press* and, after the bid was accepted, managed to meet Scripps-imposed deadlines for reaching agreements with the Teamsters and other unions, arranging financing and obtaining U.S. Justice Department approval. The *Press* was closed in the process, although much of its staff was hired by the newly dominant *Post-Gazette*. The Block family ceded its paper in Monterey, California, to Scripps Howard as part of the deal.

Patron of the Arts

Mr. Block lightheartedly described the image he held for himself and his paper on a 1986 evening that united two labors of love: the *Post-Gazette* and the Pittsburgh Symphony. The occasion was the world premiere of "Classical Variations on Colonial Themes," a work by the composer Morton Gould, commissioned by the Blocks to commemorate the 200th year of the *Post-Gazette*. The paper, which long promoted itself as the "First Newspaper West of the Alleghenies" traces its lineage to the *Gazette* that John Scull published not far from the present printing plant of its corporate descendant.

From the Heinz Hall stage, Mr. Block gazed around at dignitaries from politics, business, and the arts and observed, "To avoid philosophical implications, you will note that the Republicans are seated on your left, the Democrats on your right, and I, like the *Post-Gazette*, am smack in the middle."

The symphony hall was a natural venue for the party. Mr. Block, a former vice president and for many years a board member of the Pittsburgh Symphony Orchestra, took a deep interest in that organization. He was a member of the search committee that lured conductor Andre Previn to the PSO in the mid-1970s.

One of the extracurricular duties of which he was most fond was his role as a founder and president of Gateway to the Arts, originally Gateway to Music, a program that started in 1957 to introduce students to classical music and the performing arts. Over the years, the program has expanded to add ballet, singers, and visual arts.

Mr. Block also had an enduring interest in abstract art. He donated several works to the Carnegie Museum of Art including *Feb 18—54 Azure*, a 1954 oil-on-canvas by well-known English painter Ben Nicholson, and *Two Figures*, a 1962 oil by Pittsburgh-born abstractionist Raymond Saunders, in 1974.

Mr. Block had helped Saunders attend the Pennsylvania Academy of the Fine Arts in Philadelphia and saw him become an important California painter. The Blocks acquired a half-dozen of Saunders' paintings, as well as a number of works by other Pittsburgh artists.

In later years, Mr. Block began collecting contemporary glass art, a passion that put him on the path to creating another cultural institution in Pittsburgh. In 1996 he and his wife gave four glass sculptures to the Carnegie Museum of Art, and, a year later, his vision and financial support helped lay the groundwork for what was to become the Pittsburgh Glass Center. The center, in Friendship, Pennsylvania,

opened in 2003 and has helped re-create Pittsburgh as a center for glass, this time through a public-access studio. A board member since the organization was formed, Mr. Block was named the first emeritus member of the center's board this month. "Once we got started, it almost became an obsession," he said of his fascination with the medium.

Mr. Block had been an avid baseball fan since childhood, an enthusiasm fanned when his father bought the Newark Bears of the International League in 1929. Though Paul Block Sr. later sold the Newark club, the circle of Mr. Block's interest in the game came round again when he approved the family's purchase of a small interest, later sold, in the Pittsburgh Pirates as part of the syndicate organized by current Pirates owner Kevin McClatchy. The interim investment was the Block family's answer to the perennial question of whether the Pirates had a future in Pittsburgh.

For all of his professional successes and interests, however, Mr. Block said his greatest achievement was his six-decade marriage and "the fathering of four great children."

In addition to his wife, Mr. Block is survived by his children: William Jr., chairman emeritus of Block Communications; Karen Johnese, of Marshall, executive director of the Pittsburgh Glass Center; Barbara Block Burney, an actress and music teacher in Mill Valley, California; and Donald, of O'Hara, the executive director of the Greater Pittsburgh Literacy Council.

He also is survived by eight grandchildren and two great-grandchildren.

Last month, on a day that Pittsburgh city council had proclaimed "Bill Block Sr. Day," Mr. Block was recognized at a reception at the Andy Warhol Museum for his decades of support for Gateway to the Arts. In a voice halting with emotion, his wife, Maxine, beside him, he told the appreciative crowd: "If you live long enough, good things happen."

MONDAY, DECEMBER 19, 2005

Bill Lenhart, 66
Cab-Driving Ambassador

By Gary Rotstein, *Pittsburgh Post-Gazette*

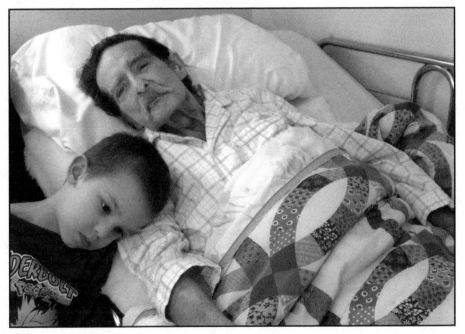

Beloved Yellow Cab driver Bill Lenhart with his grandson, Nickolas Thomas, age six. *Photo by Martha Rial.*

Sharon Hillier, a medical professor and researcher, remembers how dog-tired she felt upon arrival at Pittsburgh International Airport after a red-eye flight one morning in 1995. She'd recently moved to Pittsburgh. She'd been on a succession of professional, no-fun trips. She was cranky, bleary-eyed, and dying to get home to Fox Chapel, Pennsylvania, as soon as she could.

Then she stepped into Bill Lenhart's yellow taxi. He began chatting after explaining the flat $45 fare. He asked about her background. He mentioned some of Pittsburgh's special sights and attractions. She began perking up. Before she knew it, she was getting her first tour of Mount Washington. It was out of the way, but so what? Dr. Hillier was starting to feel the appeal of her adopted city, while being captivated by the mustachioed man driving her in the spotless cab.

"By the time I got to my house, I was laughing and happy, and I thought: 'What a guy, who can take someone sleep-deprived and make someone so comfortable and happy to be there. It's like a miracle.'"

Multiply Dr. Hillier's story by similar ones from dozens of other Pittsburgh newcomers in the course of Mr. Lenhart's 26 years of taxi driving. Then add in hundreds of other passengers touched by the everyday, common-man graciousness of a person performing a very basic transportation service in the most exceptional of ways. And there you have the impact of Bill Lenhart, "taxi driver extraordinaire," as he is touted in a pamphlet produced by coworker Harry Striplin, who rounded up comments from those who evolved from customers to friends over a quarter-century.

Mr. Lenhart, aged 66, died of cancer Saturday at his home in Stowe, Pennsylvania, leaving behind his wife, the two children they had together, five other offspring they had separately, 15 grandchildren, one great-grandchild, and a widespread adopted family whose members rode in his cab.

After Mr. Lenhart's bout with rectal and colon cancer a year ago curbed his driving, dozens of people who had been cushioned in his back seat over the years were happy to write remembrances and best wishes.

"Traveling with you always makes our trip so much more enjoyable, wondering what new jazz CDs and stories you'd have to share," wrote one rider identifying herself as Dorie. "You have redefined the cab ride as the superlative part of any trip."

"I believe there may be more than one employee that you helped us recruit because of the Pittsburgh they saw through your eyes and your cab window," said a Seagate Technologies Inc. official.

On and on such comments go about a man with a ninth-grade education who charmed a succession of research scientists, medical doctors, business executives, professors, and others among his regular clientele. Many were from Seagate, many more from Carnegie Mellon University—especially its Software Engineering Institute—as Mr. Lenhart's network grew by word of mouth.

Like other Yellow Cab drivers he was an independent contractor rather than an employee of the company. He paid a daily lease fee covering costs of the vehicle and the calls he received from a central dispatcher, when he hadn't booked his own rides. His bread and butter involved the stable of riders contacting him directly on his own line, using the business cards he passed out.

Mr. Striplin said his pal was known among cabbies as a classic "closer," a legend to them for the legions of faithful customers who wanted him. And if he was overscheduled, other drivers might feel honored to be chosen as a substitute.

It seems that many people prize a reliable cabdriver, guaranteed to pick up and drop off on time, always cheerful, ready with a cup of coffee or tea or a newspaper, with Windex and sanitized wipes forever at his side to keep the vehicle pristine. "That was my house," he explained recently, lying in bed in his living room, where friends and hospice nurses and volunteers checked in on him regularly and assisted his wife, Shirley.

He knew which customers preferred blues, jazz, or new age music to play in the car, from among a massive CD collection, and he was likely as not to shove one they liked into passengers' hands as they exited. Mr. Lenhart would bring Christmas gifts for customers' children he had watched grow by chauffeuring their families frequently to the airport. When customers had difficulties in life, such as hospital trips, he frequently refused to accept payment from them. And during the good times—weddings or christenings or other celebrations—Mr. Lenhart would make it onto customers' invitation lists.

"He became like extended family for many of us who don't have family in Pittsburgh," said Jane Siegel, a research faculty member in CMU's School of Computer Science. He accepted her invitation to her daughter's bat mitzvah seven years ago. For years before then and since, she and others made sure Mr. Lenhart was the one transporting key visitors to the university.

"He was like a local ambassador, getting a sense of people's interests, putting their musical tastes on his CD player," she said. "He was an incredibly astute human being in the sense of other people's needs and his response to them."

Mr. Lenhart was no saint. He exchanged cross words with other drivers he felt didn't conform to his standards. His daughters remember many times when he missed family events because of work, though they say they don't hold it against him. He fathered two children out of wedlock. He divorced and remarried his wife, who blames her former heavy drinking for breaking them up the first time.

A part-time home aide, his wife has been caring for him for the past year, receiving help and visits from the very people Mr. Lenhart had been driving around for all those years, during 12-hour to 18-hour days away from home.

"I always knew how important his work was to him," said his daughter, Aimee Lenhart Meadows, of Greensburg, Pennsylvania. "I never knew till now how important he was to all these people. Now that I see how much he affected other people, I'm floored."

His heart, more than anything, made the man. Dr. Hillier made a late-night return to the airport two Decembers ago from her father's funeral in Washington state. Mr. Lenhart couldn't be the one to pick her up that night and sent a trusted stand-in whom he had coached. "When he dropped me off, he said, 'Bill says your money's no good tonight. This one's on us. We're very sorry about your dad,'" she recalled. "Of all the gestures made when my father died, I think that was the most special."

She visited Mr. Lenhart regularly over the past year in his small home crammed with drawers of CDs, native American folk art, and porcelain salt-and-pepper shakers of all kinds he'd acquired for his wife's collection. As he far outlived the anticipated length of survival with the disease, piles of good-will cards also filled the home, which he had been unable to leave since September.

In addition to his wife and daughter, he is survived by two other daughters, Valerie Connors, of Industry, and Lori Lenhart Thomas, of Greensburg; a son, William Lenhart Suder, of McKees Rocks; two stepdaughters, Donna Bayura and Lisa Fox, both of Greensburg; a stepson, Anthony Koller, of Irwin; a brother, Wade Lenhart, of Esplen; two sisters, Patricia Connolly, of Denver, and Helen Klutch, of McKees Rocks; nine grandchildren; six step-grandchildren; and one step-great grandson.

FRIDAY, MARCH 24, 2006

Wayne Rotstein, 49
A Brother Lost in Life and Found in Death
By Gary Rotstein, *Pittsburgh Post-Gazette*

Wayne Rotstein was a kid from Oakland who struggled at school, rebelled at home, and never backed down from a fistfight on the streets.

Vishwamitra was a young man searching for spiritual enlightenment while wrestling with the pull of gambling, drinking, and pot-smoking.

Banyan was a serene, self-taught, self-sufficient Hawaiian who shunned material goods. His plantings made the earth more nourishing and beautiful than those around him imagined possible.

My brother went by all three names in a half century of evolution until his freakish death 10 days ago. A dam broke that morning at 6:00, and he was swept away, apparently to disappear into the Pacific Ocean forever. Six acquaintances lost their lives with him on Kauai, a tropical Hawaiian island nearly 5,000 miles from the asphalt Oakland neighborhood that he and I roamed as youths.

Back in our family's cramped apartment across from Forbes Field, Wayne, a year and a half older, was my best friend and worst bully. The distance between us grew ever since. By the time he died at age 49, I hadn't seen him in 10 years.

No Bank, No Possessions
It's hard to keep in touch with someone who doesn't have a phone much of the time. Or a permanent address worth writing in a book. Or a car, computer, furniture, or any of the other possessions billions of other people spend their lives hoping to acquire. Everything he owned fit into a duffel bag. Wayne didn't even have a bank account. Who the hell lives like that in 2006? He hadn't filed taxes in years.

I realize now that when he was carried tumultuously along a mile-long path between his one-room cabin and the ocean, the only personal items swallowed with him were probably a chess set, a bag of marijuana, and small icons of Hindu deities.

I didn't know any of that when the call came that Tuesday afternoon. I sat there, trembling at my keyboard, avoiding eye contact with colleagues as I scanned the Associated Press wire. My father in Las Vegas had phoned after getting a call from Wayne's landlord, who himself had lost three family members.

The first story from Kauai, known as the Garden Island for its unspoiled beauty, contained no names but confirmed the key details: "An earthen dam burst...a torrent of water 150 yards across...no warning about the dam's strength or the amount of water behind it...as many as seven reported missing."

Several weeks of steady, heavy rain filled a hilltop reservoir held back by the Kaloko Dam, built in the late 1800s for a sugar plantation.

After checking Hawaiian newspapers' reports online and wondering what pre-Internet people did in such situations, I called my mother and sister here in Pittsburgh. I then contacted authorities in Kauai to name my brother as missing and describe his features.

With the same phone I had used many times as a reporter to reach relatives who lost family members to war or local violence, I called newspapers in Honolulu to tell them about my brother. Call it professional courtesy. It might have taken them days to get the information through official channels.

The reporters expressed condolences before peppering me with the proper questions: how long had Wayne lived in Hawaii? Why was he in Kauai? Did he like it there? What were his interests? What were his future plans?

Too often, I stammered, guessed, and apologized. They must have wondered what kind of person couldn't describe the winding paths his own brother walked or even provide basic details of his life.

The past days have been spent trying to fill in the many blanks, to get some sense of the remarkable journey that was my brother's life. There has been nothing else to do, after all, but wait. Talk about Wayne, and wait.

A Nomad's Start

I knew plenty already about the first two decades of Wayne's life. He grew up in a four-brothers-to-a-bedroom home dominated by financial difficulties and a mother and father who spent many unhappy years together before divorcing.

The third of six children, Wayne got in more trouble than the rest of us, and his parents let him know it. School was a challenge he didn't much care for, right through his 1975 graduation from Allderdice High School after our family moved to Squirrel Hill.

My mother says if he'd been a child today, he'd probably have been diagnosed with dyslexia and attention deficit disorder and received proper support. Instead, he struggled alone at school.

But Wayne always had plenty of friends. He was smooth, even charismatic in an understated way. As a teenager he worked hard at jobs, had cash in his pocket, and enjoyed party-ing. Girls seemed to adore him, much to a shy younger brother's envy.

After school, we separated. I took the conventional route to college and steady employment, marriage, mort-gage, and three kids.

Wayne became a nomad, with feet in two worlds. He thought nothing of living alone, without electricity or run-ning water, for seven months in a tent in the Arizona desert. He loved being outdoors, building a wiry, muscular body from working the land.

Untrained, this city boy made him-self an accomplished gardener. He became a vegetarian, and, in a succes-sion of places, he turned barren ground into long rows of organic vegetables, feeding himself and dozens of others who lived communally with him.

At other times he lived in Las Vegas, working in restaurants, spending nearly all his off-hours gambling in glitzy casi-nos where no one noticed or cared if the sun was shining.

Much of his life reflected this yin-yang existence. Along with his gambling, which wobbled between passion and compulsion, his occasional carousing could lead to trouble. He had at least two arrests, for petty crimes. He fathered a child who died young, whom he never saw because the pregnant mother returned to Thailand.

Search for a Center

When you follow a swami, as Wayne began doing in his twenties, you are assigned a new name. He became Vishwamitra, or Vish, at a spiritual cen-ter in California and an ashram in the Poconos. He showed up unexpectedly in the mid-1980s at my apartment in Harrisburg. He had been kicked out of the ashram for disciplinary reasons I can't recall. Still, he was committed to finding a spiritual core. I can't recall what led him to Eastern religions we never heard of growing up. My guess is he knew the first decades of his life were essentially an unpleasant waste, and there had to be a path to something better. His search took him to the New Vrindaban Hare Krishna community in Moundsville, West Virginia, where an immense golden temple is a tourist shrine. He built one of his fabulous gardens there, stocking the communal kitchen.

He lived there off and on for several years, though he never became a full-fledged Krishna, which forbids vices such as gambling and smoking. Wayne was never a shaved-head devotee bang-ing a tambourine in public, though those around him were.

But my brother, the son of mixed-faith parents who never practiced religion, enjoyed being part of the extended Krishna family in West Virginia, the Southwest, and Hawaii. He embraced chanting, meditation, yoga, vegetarianism, self-sufficiency, and other aspects of the simple life. Even during periodic stays in Las Vegas he would keep to the rituals. Friends said he developed a personal religion, blending Eastern philosophies with aspects of Christianity, but he wasn't drawn to organized services.

Whatever it was, it centered him, gave him refuge from whatever demons he wrestled with otherwise.

In 2001 it drew him to Hawaii, where Krishna friends encouraged him to grow crops for their spiritual retreat center. He flourished amid the natural beauty, hard work, friendship, and sense of purpose. He helped serve travelers from around the world visiting the 42-acre property known as the Hamakua Ecology Center, overlooking the Hawaiian coast.

Something made him leave the name Vish behind and take "Banyan," in honor of a tree considered sacred in India. He played chess when not working, a hobby he had taken up years earlier.

Numerous people from Hawaii told me in recent days about the peaceful karma he gave off. Many sought to emulate his serenity. They make it sound as if my brother—whom my sister remembers sitting on my chest one time, his hands squeezing my neck in a death grip—could have been a guru if he'd wanted. They didn't sound like they're saying it just because he's gone.

The Challenge of Grieving

My family members have spoken with one another more in the past week than at any time since the 1970s, when we all began moving in different directions. The reactions, however, varied.

My father chatted comfortably with numerous reporters from Hawaii and Las Vegas, putting out the message that Wayne had a kind, loving spirit.

My more introverted mother politely rebuffed interview requests or ignored them altogether, as she did with the television crew that knocked on her door at 8:00 on the morning after her son disappeared.

With my brothers and sister, I exchange emails and phone calls and electronic photos of Wayne sent by friends and links to stories from Hawaii. Authorities on Wednesday gave up the search for any of the missing individuals amid mud and debris. That's fine. At this point, to us, Wayne's body itself has little relevance.

One night last week my wife and I gathered our three adolescent children to discuss what happened to an uncle they met once but can't remember. "It's okay if you don't feel sad for Uncle Wayne; he didn't suffer," I told them, explaining it's their grandparents who are most in pain. And I made them promise not to lose touch with one another the way Wayne and I did. "That's the bad part for me, that we weren't together very much when we had the chance, and it's too late now," I said.

The 12-year-old daughter sniffled and said in a small voice, "But I feel sad now," as though it were some alien, puzzling emotion. Looking to dab her eyes, she wiped them on the closest available cloth: the shorts on the two legs beside her. Her brother, of course, recoiled. We all laughed and felt better.

The truth is it's hard to grasp just how to grieve for this unusual brother who died in unique fashion half a world away. So I retreat to what a reporter does: I research, I interview, I write.

I become able to confidently tell reporters who are still interested that Wayne was in the place he wanted to be, making a living from the earth to satisfy his meager needs; that he would have preferred dying by nature's force to a more conventional car wreck or disease; that he would have trusted reincarnation to return him someday on a higher evolutionary scale. He had already evolved on earth, of course, in a more dramatic way than 99 percent of humanity.

And if the reporters remain interested, I would explain that a month and a half before his death, Wayne spent long hours in the casinos again while visiting his Las Vegas relatives. He risked every cent he owned in card games before winning $900 playing Texas hold 'em at the Mirage. Among his last acts, he used that to repay old debts to a friend and a brother.

That was the old Wayne, reckless and impulsive. But once back in Hawaii, he began making plans to help a Krishna veterinarian friend develop an animal shelter. He was to plant fruit trees for her, build a large garden, sell the extra produce at market.

That would be Banyan. I never knew him, but if my brother was carrying Banyan's karma when the water came, there's much reason to take comfort.

SECTION
VI

In the Arena

Looking to start a fight in a bar, a restaurant, a living room, or (in this case) a newsroom? You might attempt to put together an assortment of obituaries of a city's leading citizens. Then try to figure out which sports figures belong in a collection like this. We debated, we bickered, we fought. Even now there is no agreement about who should be in and who should be out. But, happily, this chapter includes such figures as Roberto Clemente, Honus Wagner, Lloyd Waner, Fritzie Zivic, Dick Stuart, Herb Brooks, and Marshall Goldberg.

TUESDAY, JANUARY 21, 1947

Josh Gibson Sr., 35
Great Negro League Slugger
By the *Pittsburgh Post-Gazette*

Josh Gibson, one of the greatest distance hitters in the history of baseball, died at the home of his mother yesterday. The great Negro League slugger was the victim of a stroke.

For many years Gibson, as a member of the Homestead Grays, was called the "Babe Ruth of negro baseball." He hit some of the longest balls ever to clear the fences at Forbes Field during his tenure as the top slugger of the Negro National League.

Was Outstanding Catcher
The 35-year-old Gibson was a product of the north side sandlots, where he played with the Pleasant Valley Grays and the Gimbel Brothers Browns. He was picked up by the Pittsburgh Crawfords in 1930 and immediately blossomed into one of the outstanding negro catchers and sluggers.

He didn't spend much time with the Craws, moving to the Grays late in the same season. He replaced Buck Ewing when the latter was injured and became the regular backstop.

He went back with the Crawfords in 1931, remaining with them for five seasons. Returning to the Grays in 1936, his slugging aided them in winning eight straight national loop pennants. He was the top home-run producer during that time.

Hit 513-Foot Homer
His best day with the bat was in 1938, against the Memphis Red Sox, when he connected for four circuit drives. The game was played in Zanesville, Ohio. He is credited with a 513-foot homer at Monessen, Pennsylvania, the same year, against the same club.

In his last season with the Grays, 1946, he led the league in batting with a mark of .354 for 33 games. His 40 hits were good for 101 bases, driving in 42 runs.

Besides his mother, he is survived by his wife; two children, Josh Jr. and Helen; and a brother and sister.

WEDNESDAY, DECEMBER 7, 1955

Honus Wagner, 81
Baseball's "Flying Dutchman"
By the *Pittsburgh Post-Gazette*

Honus Wagner, baseball's immortal "Flying Dutchman," who died early yesterday in his home in Carnegie, Pennsylvania, will be laid to rest Friday afternoon in Jefferson Park Memorial Cemetery.

Death came to the 81-year-old stalwart of the baseball world after he had been bedfast for almost 10 weeks following a fall in his home. For the last 10 days Wagner had been in a semi-coma, and it was thus that the end came—with immediate relatives in attendance—at 12:56 AM yesterday. In failing health in recent years, Wagner suffered bruises and shock in the fall, which hastened the end.

As the family prepared for services, tributes to the high character and amazing ability of the great athlete came from persons in all stations of life. For Wagner, an inspiration for many a young diamond hopeful, was as well-known for his clean living off the field as for his alert, winning play on the field. That was summed up concisely by Mayor David L. Lawrence.

"All of us who knew and loved Honus Wagner, who played with him and watched him play," the mayor said, "realize fully how great he really was, both as a ballplayer and as an example of good sportsmanship for his fellow men. We will all miss him but we will never forget him."

And in Chicago, where Major League executives now are meeting, leaders of the baseball world paused to pay similar tribute to Wagner—acclaimed in life as in death by many as the greatest player of all time.

18 Years with Pirates

In his 21-year career as a Major League player—18 years with the Pittsburgh Pirates—Wagner amassed National League records that still stand after 40 years. His smashing bat and near-perfect fielding led the Pirates to two pennant victories—in 1903 and 1909—and to a World Series win in the latter year.

Wagner was born February 24, 1874, in Mansfield, now Carnegie, the son of John Peter and Catherine Wolfe Wagner, immigrants from Germany.

He was christened as John Peter Wagner but playmates soon contracted "Johannes," which is German for John, to Honus, and the name stuck to him throughout his career.

Baseball was his early love—for he often said he would have been willing to play for nothing. He began his sand-lot career in 1889 when he was only 15, then moved into minor leagues, and in 1897 he made his Major League debut with the Louisville club.

Achieved Hall of Fame

Three years later Wagner was brought

to Pittsburgh by the late Barney Dreyfuss, and it was with the Pirates that he went on to amass the records that put him in baseball's Hall of Fame. In 1933 he returned to the Pirates as a coach and retired finally from the game only three years ago.

Aside from baseball, Wagner's chief hobbies were hunting and fishing, but he had a keen interest in sports of all types. And he was especially fond of helping young players and encouraging young boys to follow the game.

He was a member of the Carnegie Lodge of the Masons, the Carnegie Lutheran Church, and the Carnegie Elks Club.

Surviving him are his wife, Bessie Smith Wagner; two daughters, Mrs. Harry Blair and Virginia Wagner, both of Carnegie; a sister, Mrs. Charles P. Gallagher, also of Carnegie; and a brother, William Wagner, of Danville, Ohio.

FRIDAY, MARCH 17, 1972

Harold Joseph "Pie" Traynor, 72 Bucs Great Third Baseman
By the *Pittsburgh Post-Gazette*

Harold Joseph "Pie" Traynor, who came out of New England's baseball sandlots to endear himself to Pittsburgh as one of its greatest Pirates, died yesterday. He was 72.

Traynor, who had been acclaimed the greatest third baseman in baseball's first 100 years, was found on a couch in an apartment at 250 Melwood Street in Oakland, police said. Oxygen was administered by police who rushed him to Shadyside Hospital, where he was pronounced dead as a result of "a respiratory arrest." "Pie had been doctoring for a lengthy time at Allegheny General Hospital," said acting sergeant Robert Conroy, of No. 4 police station, which received a call at 5:20 PM.

Harold Joseph Traynor became a Hall of Famer in 1948, but baseball began for him more than 40 years before, when he was a youngster growing up in Framingham, Massachusetts, and other New England towns. He used to frolic with sandlot teams on the historic Boston Common and later in public school fields.

When Traynor played baseball in Somerville, Massachusetts, he was befriended by a priest who used to direct sandlot baseball games. After the games, the priest would treat the youngsters to almost anything they wanted. Most all of them used to request ice cream—but not Harold Traynor.

His inevitable response was "I'll take pie, Father."

So the priest began calling him "Pie." The moniker stuck like plaster.

Professional baseball became part of Traynor's life in 1920, when he had his first tryout with Portsmouth of the

Virginia League. The tryout was brief. Traynor impressed in a matter of minutes. He won a job as the club's regular shortstop and batted .270 as a 20-year-old fresh out of New England.

The Pirates paid the Portsmouth club $10,000 for Traynor in late August of 1920. It was a record price for the Virginia League at the time.

Bill McKechnie, who later was to manage the Pirates, was injured late in the 1920 season, and Traynor was rushed to Pittsburgh to play. In his first big league at-bat, Traynor won a game with a ninth-inning single. It was a signal of greatness to come.

As the years rolled by Pie Traynor became a familiar name in every household in Pittsburgh. He won friends both on and off the field. He wound up a brilliant 17-year career with a .320 average. In 1969 he was named the greatest third baseman in the first 100 years of baseball.

He played with the 1925 and 1927 pennant-winning Pirates and, as a manager, came close to leading the Bucs to a pennant in 1938. The 1938 Pirates were short pitching, but Pie drove them down the stretch. His best pitcher was a reliever named Mace Brown, and it was Brown who threw a home-run ball in the darkness at Wrigley Field in Chicago on a September afternoon to rob the Pirates of a pennant.

"I could never blame Mace," Pie once said. "He got us as far as we were in September."

Pie managed the Pirates from 1935 through 1939. In more recent seasons—in spring training—Pie would spend a few weeks talking to the young Bucs. They all liked and respected him.

It came as no surprise that young Pirates liked Pie Traynor. This was a man who made friends easily. He spent many afternoons strolling the streets of Pittsburgh, always smiling, willing to talk baseball—or any sport—with anybody.

Pie Traynor traveled with the elite. "The working man is the elite of this world," Pie Traynor once said. "They're my kind of people."

Pie could tell a joke and he was a good listener. And you know something, Pie Traynor had his faults. He used to like to tell people about them. "When I'm in Florida I like to go to the dog races," Pie Traynor would say. "And I like the horse races, too. I guess it is a bad habit."

Ask Pie Traynor's friends—he had thousands of them—and they will tell you that Pie Traynor didn't have a fault. He was a kind man, full of enthusiasm for the game that made him a celebrity.

He used to love to talk about the Waners, Arky Vaughn, and the present day Bucs, too—Bill Mazeroski, Gene Alley… "The ballplayers have changed," Pie would say, "but the talent is always there. I guess I have a soft spot in my heart for the old-timers, but I respect the kids playing today."

The baseball record book says Pie Traynor was born in Framingham, Massachusetts, on November 11, 1899. Once he had brown hair. He was handsome when he was young and distinguished as he grayed and grew older.

In 1931 Pie left the bachelor ranks when he married Eve Helmer. He is survived by his wife.

Pie Traynor is gone, but the memory of Pie Traynor will never fade. Ask the people who used to see Pie strolling down Grant Street. Ask the people who went to Gustine's pub in Oakland.

You didn't have to be a baseball fan to like Pie Traynor. He won friends among people in all walks of life. Pie Traynor didn't have to die to be called a nice guy. Pie Traynor was called a nice guy when he was the greatest third baseman in the game playing for the Pirates. He was called a nice guy when he managed the ballclub and later when he was not in uniform. Pie Traynor's "uniform" was a pleasant smile for everybody—both young and old.

There will always be substitutes at third base for Pie Traynor in Pittsburgh. Nobody will ever replace him.

Pie also built a supplemental career as a broadcaster, having served as sports editor of KQV radio for many years, in addition to delivering commericals for a heating firm on both Channels 4 and 11.

The Pittsburgh chapter of the Baseball Writers Association of America honored him at a testimonial last November 20 at the William Penn Hotel. And only last Saturday he was inducted into the Fraternal Order of Eagles Hall of Fame. Surviving is his widow Eve.

TUESDAY, JANUARY 2, 1973

Roberto Clemente, 38
"The Great One"
By Gabriel Ireton, *Pittsburgh Post-Gazette*

Pittsburghers—many of them bleary-eyed from New Year's celebrations—awakened yesterday to the shock: Roberto Clemente, "the Great One," is dead.

Some heard snatches of the news on radio and television. Some murmured in disbelief when a eulogy was said from the pulpit at a New Year's Day mass. Many of them wept.

Close friends who knew Clemente and his family, and those who knew the baseball "superstar" only from their view from "peanut heaven," wept the same tears.

Hundreds could not believe the news, and they telephoned the *Post-Gazette* and the Pittsburgh Baseball Club

for confirmation. Politicians and commoners here—Clemente treated them the same—expressed their shock at reports that the Pittsburgh Pirates' greatest outfielder had died with four other men when a DC-7 cargo plane in which they were flying crashed into the Atlantic Ocean at 9:22 PM Sunday. Clemente was coordinating a massive airlift of food and supplies to help the people of earthquake-stricken Managua, Nicaragua.

"It seemed fitting that Roberto Clemente had died when he was doing God's work of relieving the suffering," a Pittsburgh priest told his shocked congregation yesterday.

"The tragic death of Roberto Clemente has saddened Pittsburgh and

Roberto Clemente acknowledges cheers on his 3,000ᵗʰ hit. *Photo by Morris Berman.*

the entire nation," Mayor Flaherty said in a statement. "He died at the height of a great career while performing a valuable service for his fellow man. Mrs. Flaherty and I extend our deepest sympathy to his wife and children."

County commissioners Leonard C. Staisey and Dr. William R. Hunt expressed their regrets. "It is tragic," Hunt said, "to lose a person like this who has become such a hero for everybody. What a contribution he has made to the successes the Pirates have had— and then to lose him at the very peak of his career is just tragic."

"The Pirates lost a superstar," Staisey said, "but the world has lost a super guy. When someone tells me, 'Happy New Year,' it will seem to be a hollow wish."

In a telegram to Clemente's widow, Commissioner Thomas J. Foerster said, "Please take comfort in the fact that your husband was more than a complete baseball player; he was a 'complete man.'"

Among those who knew him best was Phil Dorsey, a postal worker who became Clemente's friend when he came to Pittsburgh as a rookie. Dorsey cried when he heard yesterday that Clemente was missing and presumed dead. "One of his brothers called me last night from Puerto Rico and told me Roberto was on the plane," Dorsey said, choking back the sobs. "I've been up all night. I'm so shocked, I can't think."

Dorsey, who served Clemente as a personal friend, chauffeur, business manager, and babysitter for the right fielder's three boys, said that Clemente was looking forward to next season. "He and I already made plans for his apartment, and I was sending some mail to him," Dorsey said.

When Clemente was a rookie, Dorsey said, "We used to go to movies and things together. I even remember when he first met his wife down in Puerto Rico. I used to go with them as a chaperone before they were married."

In an odd coincidence, the lead letter to the editor in yesterday's *Post-Gazette* praised Clemente's efforts in the earthquake relief and took the view that Clemente had not received the public acclaim he deserved. The letter, written by Trudy Labovitz of Pittsburgh, said: "Amid this world of bombings, murders, and overall destruction, it seems an anachronism to find a person such as Roberto Clemente, filled with pride, strength, determination, and love.... His is an example it would do us all good to follow."

Among those who befriended him when he first began playing for the Pirates were Mr. and Mrs. Henry Kantrowitz of Squirrel Hill. They left the Clemente family's suburban San Juan home last Tuesday to help set up a Pittsburgh-based fund drive for Clemente's relief airlift. "We curtailed our visit there for this very thing he was doing," Mrs. Kantrowitz said. "And I thought the very best thing was to come to Pittsburgh and see if we could find a way to help him raise money."

Kantrowitz said Clemente had devoted himself to making aid available to Managua's earthquake victims. "He was putting in 14 hours a day just working with his committee," Kantrowitz said. "As a matter of fact, when I brought him some food to eat, he wouldn't stop to eat it."

Clemente had made appeals on radio and television for food, clothing, and drugs, Kantrowitz said. Himself a state campaign chairman for the March of Dimes for five years, Kantrowitz called the response "unbelievable" as donations came "in carloads" to Hi Bithorn Stadium in San Juan, used as a depot to store and package goods headed for Managua. "The stadium parking lot was almost as filled as when there's a ballgame. There was enough food and clothing to fill Three Rivers Stadium, sections A and B, on the outside perimeter of the stadium."

"People came down there with Christmas gifts which had been unopened," Mrs. Kantrowitz said.

"As great a ballplayer as he was," Kantrowitz said, "he was a greater human being. In spite of his earnings, in spite of everything else, he was a down-to-earth human being who would spend as much time talking with the common man as he would with a captain of industry."

Clemente was a family man devoted to his children, his "adopted" Pittsburgh "parents" said. "The public will never know what a family man he was for his children," Mrs. Kantrowitz said. "He adored those kids. Those children adored him. Seeing him alone with them, feeding them…is unbelievable. One day last week," she continued, "he looked at his oldest son and he said that Roberto Jr. would be the next Pittsburgh Pirates' right fielder. 'Robertito' plays ball like his father—he stands like his father."

The Clemente household was an open house to nearly any Pittsburgher who visited San Juan.

Rabbi and Mrs. Moshe Goldblum yesterday recalled a recent visit with the Clemente family after an introduction before a game at Three Rivers Stadium. "He was so very gracious to us," Rabbi Goldblum said. "In his discussions with us, he showed he had a fine understanding of what was going on in San Juan. He talked about his own personal hopes, in terms of his own home and developing his own weekend retreat. He's a national hero there, and I'm sure that the whole population won't know how to accept it."

Clemente's death has left another service to his own people planned, but yet undone, according to Dr. Charles W. Murray, a McKees Rocks, Pennsylvania, chiropractor. Murray, who takes credit for relieving pain in Clemente's back and numbness in his legs, said Clemente had planned a chiropractic clinic near San Juan.

FRIDAY, DECEMBER 3, 1976

Danny Murtaugh, 59
Pirates Manager
By Charley Feeney, *Pittsburgh Post-Gazette*

Danny Murtaugh is dead.

The former Pirates manager, one of the most popular men in baseball, died at 8:50 last night in the Crozier-Chester (Pennsylvania) Medical Center after falling into a coma earlier in the day.

Murtaugh suffered a stroke in his home in Woodlyn, Pennsylvania, early Tuesday afternoon and was taken to the medical center. A spokesman for the medical center said the condition of the 59-year-old Murtaugh became critical yesterday after he had an uncomfortable night.

Murtaugh's wife, Kate, one of his two sons, Dan Jr., and a daughter, Kathy, were at his bedside when he died. Another son, Timmy, was en route from the Dominican Republic, where he had been relieved of his duties as manager.

Murtaugh announced his retirement as Pirates' manager on September 30, three days before the 1976 season ended. At the time he said he had periods during the season when he didn't feel well.

Joe L. Brown, who retired as Pirates' general manager on September 27, was deeply shocked by Murtaugh's death. Speaking from his home in Mt. Lebanon last night, Brown said: "He was like my brother. I loved him. I feel I've lost a second brother." Brown's brother was killed in World War II.

Brown spoke to Murtaugh's wife on the phone shortly after he died. "Kate said he died peacefully," Brown said in a low voice. "He never woke up."

It was Brown who first hired Murtaugh to manage the Pirates in the summer of 1957. Murtaugh retired four times during his career, but always said that he loved managing best. "Sometimes," Murtaugh would often say, "my health just can't take it."

Joe O'Toole, an assistant to Brown until he was named a vice-president of the club in early October, last night called Murtaugh "Mr. Pirate." "It is a terrible loss," O'Toole said. "He really will be missed. Not only by the people in the Pirates organization, but by all the people in all sports."

Murtaugh, a tobacco-chewing, quick-witted Irishman, always seemed to look older than his years. He was a tough competitor on the field and led the Pirates to world championships in 1960 and 1971.

Murtaugh's patience with his players was one trait that made him successful, many baseball people said. "He had ultra-patience," Pirates relief pitcher Dave Giusti said.

One of Murtaugh's favorite players was ElRoy Face. Murtaugh often said: "ElRoy made me look like a smart manager."

Face, an outstanding relief pitcher, heard the news of Murtaugh's death on television. "The man always said that I made him," Face said. "It was the other way around. He made me a pitcher, and he gave me the opportunity to make a name for myself. He was just one fine human being."

Baseball commissioner Bowie Kuhn described Murtaugh as "a wonderful mixture of basic professional toughness and reverence. He had a wonderful pixie quality about him."

Murtaugh was a non-drinker. "I may have had three glasses of wine in my life," he once said. "Maybe on New Year's Eve. I prefer malted milk."

When he traveled with the Pirates he enjoyed joking with waitresses and airline stewardesses. He found it difficult to hold late-night bed checks on his players because, as he used to say, "I can't stay up that late."

Murtaugh was probably the only manager in baseball who had a special rocking chair in his office inside the clubhouse. He used to rock, spit tobacco in a spittoon, and tell baseball stories.

He always wanted to be particularly close to his five grandchildren. When he retired for the last time, he said: "In my younger years, I don't think I spent enough time with my children. I'm going to kind of make it up with my grandchildren."

Murtaugh, the son of a shipyard worker, grew up in Chester, Pennsylvania, an industrial town with a population of 100,000. As a frail 5'9", 150-pounder, Murtaugh entered pro ball in 1937 in Cambridge, Maryland, in the Eastern Shore League. He reached the majors with the Philadelphia Phillies in 1941, playing both second base and shortstop.

He was in the army in 1944 and 1945 and spent most of the 1946 baseball season with Rochester in the International League. He was a late-season recall by the Boston Braves in 1947.

On November 18, 1947, Murtaugh and outfielder Johnny Hopp were traded to the Pirates by the Braves for pitcher Al Lyons, catcher Bill Salkeld, and outfielder Jimmy Russell. Murtaugh remained with the Pirates through the 1951 season, and the following year he became a player/manager at New Orleans in the old Southern Association. It was in New Orleans that Murtaugh first came in contact with Joe L. Brown, who was general manager of the New Orleans club.

Murtaugh left his job in New Orleans after the 1954 season, and in 1955 he started as manager of the Charleston club in West Virginia. In the summer of 1955 Murtaugh was fired at Charleston. It was the only time in his managerial career that he didn't leave a job of his own free will.

Murtaugh wasn't unemployed for too long a period. His old friend Brown had replaced Branch Rickey in November 1955 and hired Murtaugh to coach under Bobby Bragan.

On August 3, 1957, Brown fired Bragan, and, after Clyde Sukeforth, a coach, refused the job, Brown appointed Murtaugh as an "interim" manager.

The Pirates, who finished seventh in an eight-team National League in 1957, played .500 ball (26–26) under Murtaugh, who was rewarded with a one-year contract for the 1958 season. He had eight one-year contracts before he quit as manager near the close of the 1964 season.

Failing health was the reason for Murtaugh's first retirement. He remained with the Pirates as a scout until July 1967, when, as a favor to Brown, he returned to manage the Pirates. Brown fired Harry Walker, and Murtaugh handled the team for the remainder of the 1967 season.

Brown sought Murtaugh's advice on his selection of a new manager. They met in Bradenton, Florida, in early October 1969, and Murtaugh asked Brown if he would consider him.

Murtaugh led the Pirates to two straight Eastern Division titles and a world championship before he retired after the 1971 World Series

It was thought to be his last retirement, but in September 1973 Brown fired Bill Virdon, the man who had replaced Murtaugh almost two years earlier. Brown's new man was old. Danny Murtaugh remained the Pirates manager through the 1976 season.

"This is my final retirement," Murtaugh announced during a news conference on September 30 at Three Rivers Stadium.

FRIDAY, JULY 23, 1982

Lloyd Waner, 76
Little Poison
By Regis Stefanik, *Pittsburgh Post-Gazette*

Lloyd James Waner, who teamed with his brother to give the Pirates the famous "Big Poison and Little Poison" tandem, died yesterday in Oklahoma City, Oklahoma, of complications related to emphysema. He was 76.

Waner and his older brother, Paul, both members of baseball's Hall of Fame, formed one of the greatest brother combinations ever to play the game. The Harrah, Oklahoma, natives sparked the Pirates' attack during the late 1920s and throughout the 1930s.

Lloyd, known as "Little Poison," was elected to the Hall of Fame in 1967. The 18-year veteran had a lifetime batting average of .316 and had 2,459 career base hits—2,3176 for the Pirates.

His brother was elected to the Hall of Fame in 1952 after compiling a 20-year batting average of .333 and winning three National League batting titles, an honor that eluded Lloyd. Paul died on August 29, 1965.

Lloyd, recommended to the Pirates by his brother, joined the club in 1927 and set a then-Major League record with 223 hits, while batting .355. Paul, who had joined the Pirates the year prior, hit .380 in 1927, as the Waners led the Pirates to the World Series, where they lost in four straight games to the New York Yankees and their vaunted "Murderer's Row."

That was the only World Series appearance for either Waner.

Lloyd again hit .355 in 1928 and led the National League in singles for the second straight year. He hit over .300 his first six years in the majors. He was known as one of the best leadoff hitters of his era. He had exceptional speed and a good eye at the plate, striking out only 173 times in his career.

Waner played with the Pirates through the 1940 season, the year his playing time diminished. He was traded to the Boston Braves after three games of the 1941 season and played 19 games for the Casey Stengel–managed Braves before being traded to the Cincinnati Reds.

Waner was released by the Reds after the 1941 season and signed with the Philadelphia Phillies, where he played in 1942. He was traded to the Brooklyn Dodgers in the spring of 1943 but decided to retire.

In 1944 he rejoined the Dodgers, who released him after 15 games. Waner then signed again with the Pirates, where he batted .321 in 1944 and .263 in 1945, mostly as a pinch-hitter both years.

Waner, who played primarily in center field alongside his brother in right, long contended that their "Poison" nicknames had nothing to do with their baseball skills. He said the nicknames started when a New York sportswriter with a Brooklyn accent called the brothers "a big person and a little person."

Al Lopez, who roomed with Waner at the start of the 1941 season and later became a Hall of Fame manager, said that "Lloyd had unbelievable speed for those days."

"Lloyd was just a fine individual and an outstanding ballplayer," said Frank Gustine, a Pirates infielder who played with the Waners. "He and his brother were just good Oklahoma boys."

Gustine said Lloyd introduced him to chewing tobacco. "I was in spring training in my rookie year, and Lloyd asked me if I was chewing gum. He said I had to chew tobacco to be a big leaguer," Gustine recalled. "After the third inning of an exhibition game, I got sick. It was the last time I ever chewed tobacco."

The Waners were on their way out of Pirates baseball after the 1940 season when management became youth-oriented. "Lloyd and Paul were benched," Gustine said, "and I remember neither one of them complained. That's the way they were. I don't think either one of them ever got thrown out of a ballgame. They would have never kicked dust on the umpires' shoes."

After retiring as a player, Waner worked as a Pirates scout from 1946 to 1949 and scouted for the Baltimore Orioles in 1955. He worked as a field clerk with the Oklahoma City government from 1950 until retiring in 1967.

Waner, who attended East Central Oklahoma State College with his brother, was a member of the National Association of Intercollegiate Athletics Hall of Fame.

Lloyd is survived by his wife, Frances Snyder Waner, formerly of Oakland; a son, Lloyd Jr., and a daughter, Lydia Freeman, both of Oklahoma City; a sister, Ruth Formby; and five grandchildren.

FRIDAY, MAY 18, 1984

Fritzie Zivic, 71
Former World Welterweight King

By John Golightly, *Pittsburgh Post-Gazette*

Ferdinand "Fritzie" Zivic, who held the world welterweight boxing title for nine months and 25 days, died Thursday in the Veterans Administration Hospital, Aspinwall, Pennsylvania.

Mr. Zivic, 71, a native of Lawrenceville and former resident of Scott, had been confined in the VA hospital since February 24, 1981, when a stroke left him unable to speak except on rare occasions.

Although he was increasingly confused and disoriented during the last year, his wife, Helen, who lives in Scott, visited him daily and said yesterday he was in marvelous physical condition. "He could speak a little when the blood was circulating," she added.

Many of his friends and admirers had preceded Mr. Zivic in death. The others would have been surprised to confront a silent Fritzie, who not only had been a compulsive talker, but also a fast one. During World War II he was invited to speak at a war bond rally in old Forbes Field in Oakland, but refused to prepare a text. When called upon, he said: "I'm no public speaker. In fact, people tell me I talk too fast. But I don't talk too fast. People just listen too slow."

Shortly after the Civic Arena opened in the Lower Hill, Zivic told all his friends the structure obviously was erected in his honor, but the sponsors misspelled the name.

When he entered a ring to fight during his 18-year pro career from 1931 to 1949, fans were guaranteed action. Consequently, he was a popular fighter even in defeat, which was often. He lost 65 fights.

But if the referee was not a stickler for rules or became disgusted because both fighters were fouling and told them, "Go ahead, fight it your way," Fritzie generally was the winner. One of his favorite attacks was to flick out a long left, loop it behind his opponent's neck, draw him close, then bash him with several quick right uppercuts. He used his thumb to rip out his opponent's mouth piece or to grind it into the opponent's eye. If he missed with a right, in drawing back his arm, he made sure his elbow poked the opposing fighter in the ear, eye, or another section of the face. His knees and elbows were terrific weapons.

"He never broke clean in his life," said Jack Henry, a stockbroker who once managed fighters and covered sports here for the old *Pittsburgh Sun-Telegraph*. "If he was allowed to fight his way, he was unbeatable. But when the rules were invoked, he was an ordinary fighter but a willing one. His best punch was a left hook."

Despite his brawling tactics, Mr. Zivic was very friendly with old ring foes after he retired. Several of them stopped by to see him at the hospital when they passed through Pittsburgh, even though he didn't recognize them.

Mr. Zivic won the 147-pound welterweight title from Henry Armstrong on October 4, 1940, in a 15-round decision at old Madison Square Garden in New York City before 12,000 fans. The referee, exasperated with the fouling by both fighters, let them fight their way.

Armstrong had been the first fighter in history to win championships in different classes. He had held the featherweight, lightweight, and welterweight titles.

The Zivic-Armstrong rematch drew a record 23,170 fans to the Garden on January 17, 1941. Fritzie knocked out Armstrong in the 12th round. The two victories over Armstrong were probably his most notable in 155 victories—80 of them by a knockout.

He lost the welterweight crown to Freddie "Red" Cochrane July 29, 1941, in a decision.

Mr. Zivic said he earned his biggest purse of $25,000 from the second Armstrong fight. For beating Perfecto Lopez in 1934, he told a friend that he received $7.40. He once estimated that he earned $500,000 from boxing and frittered most of it away. Friends quarreled with his estimate but agreed with him on his often misplaced generosity.

He was the youngest of five brothers born to Croatian immigrant parents. Two brothers preceded him in the ring.

After leaving boxing in 1949, Fritzie tried promoting; managing; working in a steel mill; selling wine, whiskey, and beer; bartending; and laboring on a county work crew before settling into boilermaking.

Surviving, in addition to his wife, are a daughter, Jan of San Francisco; two sons, Ferdinand "Freddy" Jr. of Litchfield, Connecticut, and Charles of New York City; four grandchildren; and two brothers, Pete, a former Olympic boxer who resides in a nursing home, and Eddie of Lawrenceville.

TUESDAY, JUNE 11, 1985

Bob Prince, 68
Bucs Broadcaster
By John Golightly, *Pittsburgh Post-Gazette*

Bob Prince, who used a distinctive voice, a large vocabulary, and a usually unrestrained imagination to inform and entertain millions of Pittsburgh Pirates fans for more than 29 years, died at 5:35 pm yesterday in Presbyterian-University Hospital of complications following cancer surgery.

Mr. Prince, 68, of 2620 Fairgreen Drive, Upper St. Clair, Pennsylvania, had worked in radio and television here since 1940 as a play-by-play football, boxing, and hockey announcer and commentator on sports.

Post-Gazette employee Ray Burnett and Pirates broadcaster Bob Prince (left). *Photo courtesy of the* Pittsburgh Post-Gazette.

His partisan play-by-play accounts of Pirates baseball games on KDKA radio and television from 1947 through the 1975 season were by design and free choice. "A broadcaster has to be a shill," he insisted during a recent interview.

"He has to sell tickets, be factual and entertaining. There may be things you don't like about a club, but you better sell the product. A broadcaster can help attendance by making the game interesting enough that listeners will come out to the ballpark."

His controversial firing in 1975 angered thousands of Pirates fans. He rejoined the club's broadcast team last month, four weeks after surgery to remove cancerous growths from his mouth. "You've given me back the only thing I love in the world, besides my family," Mr. Prince said April 18, when his rehiring was announced.

Joe L. Brown, the Pirates interim general manager who was general manager during much of Prince's tenure, said last night, "There is no doubt of it now, 10 years later—it was a colossal mistake to fire Bob Prince. I was part of it. It was a flat-out mistake."

"I'm wondering how I'm going to get through this game tonight," KDKA's Jim Rooker said last night from the Buc broadcast booth. "He did so many favors for me when I was a player. And even after I got this job, he made it a point to call me and wish me well."

There was a moment of silence for 30 seconds at Three Rivers Stadium in honor of Mr. Prince before last night's game between the Pirates and the St. Louis Cardinals.

In his effort to increase interest in the Pirates, Mr. Prince coined such expressions as "we had them all the way," "a bug on the rug," "as close as fuzz on a tick's ear," "a game of inches," "the wind is a factor," "you can kiss it good-bye," "we need a Hoover," "by a gnat's eyelash," and "we need a bloop and a blast." And Green Weenies, those plastic noisemakers fans were told to "point at an opposing players [as a hex] and give 'em the green weenieeee sound," were his brainchild.

One of his several broadcasting partners, Jim Woods, began calling Prince "the Gunner" in the middle 1950s as a tribute to his speed in describing plays as they unfolded on the field below their broadcasting booth. Woods and his friends used the nickname until Prince's death.

The public Bob Prince never seemed to stop talking, wore outlandish sport jackets, and drove convertibles. He was out "to attract attention," and often strained the patience of listeners and viewers "to make the game more fun." But his popsicle-stick frame (6'1?", 170 pounds) accommodated another Bob Prince.

The less-public Mr. Prince was as sedate as a banker and thought a lot like one. "I'm a dyed-in-the-wool Republican. When I go to the Duquesne Club, I wear a dark, pin-stripe suit. I'm not seeking attention then," he said.

"I joined a lot of clubs over the years. I thought the best thing was to belong where the doers and shakers belong, and somewhere along the line they'll help you. I knew many of the company presidents and met socially the people who sponsored radio and later television shows. "I knew who they were. They know me. Nothing chummy. They just knew who I was. The association was valuable."

Mr. Prince had been having enormous success selling insurance as an independent contractor from 1940 to 1949 after coming to the district from his birthplace, Los Angeles, to live with his maternal grandmother. His success in sports broadcasting was modest. But he had plans. He coveted the $50-a-week, play-by-play job as assistant to Albert K. "Rosey" Rowswell, then the voice of the Pirates.

"No one knew this for a long time, but I got the Pirate job through my Harvard connection," Mr. Prince explained. "I graduated from [the University of] Oklahoma in business administration in 1938 and, let's face it, I was a ne'er-do-well. I didn't want to go to work. I had three uncles and a couple of cousins and an older brother who graduated from Harvard Law School. Why shouldn't I go? I did okay, but I gave it up after two years. I never intended to be a lawyer.

"One of my classmates was Tom [Thomas P.] Johnson. Uh huh, you get it. Tom Johnson became one of the Pirate owners in August 1946. He got the play-by-play job for me in 1947. Connections and associations are important."

Mr. Prince succeeded Rowswell in 1955 as the Voice of the Pirates. "From 1963 on I never earned less than $100,000 a year. My top pay for one year from broadcasting and all sources was $250,000," he said.

The money often went out as fast as it came in. Mr. Prince was near bankruptcy several times, generally because of business deals that misfired. But his friends always rallied and arranged intricate plans to enable him to pay off debts.

He complemented his play-by-plays with fund-raisers for organizations that looked out for handicapped children or provided opportunities for sports-minded youths. "I raised millions upon millions of dollars over the years," he said.

Mr. Prince was cofounder of the Allegheny Valley School for Retarded Children in Ingram. He was involved with the Verland Foundation, the Fred Hutchinson Cancer Fund, the Ham-Am Golf Tournament (now part of Bob Prince Charities), boys baseball, and numerous charitable organizations. He also participated in United Way and Salvation Army fund drives.

He contributed most of the fees paid to him as master of ceremonies or featured speaker at sports banquets to the charities he was urging others to support. He also contributed from his own pocket. He was indefatigable in trying to inspire others to support charities. This generous nature was really the cornerstone of Mr. Prince's character. He liked to help people.

His efforts on behalf of black and Latin American ballplayers after Jackie Robinson broke baseball's color barrier in 1947 were an extension of his generous nature. He treated the black player in his broadcasts with the same consideration accorded the white player. He was friendly with all ballplayers. "I suppose I would have to credit my mother for my feelings," Mr. Prince suggested. "In our family, no one ever told me a white person was better than a black person. I always try to treat everyone fairly. I wanted black athletes to have the opportunity to play."

Mr. Prince spoke Spanish, which enabled him to communicate easily with Latin American players. He was a close friend of Roberto Clemente, the great Pirates right fielder, who died in a plane crash in 1972.

Mr. Prince attended the University of Pittsburgh and Stanford before graduating from Oklahoma. He earned letters in baseball (first base), track (low hurdles and the 440), polo, and swimming.

His most remarkable and impromptu athletic feat occurred at the Chase Hotel in St. Louis during the summer of 1959. He and Dick Stuart, then a Pirates first baseman, were arguing one afternoon in Mr. Prince's third-floor room. "We were trying to top each other, and he didn't know I had been a swimmer," Mr. Prince explained. "I bet him $20 that I could jump into the hotel swimming pool [from the third floor] and that he couldn't. I did it, too, into nine feet of water. We measured the distance afterward—93 feet. I missed the side of the pool by a short foot." He said he never collected the bet.

Mr. Prince received his greatest tribute as a broadcaster at Three Rivers Stadium June 7, 1976, about seven months after he and partner Nellie King, a former Pirate pitcher, were fired as Pirate broadcasters by KDKA-TV and radio.

Mr. Prince was the play-by-play announcer that year for the Houston Astros, who allowed him to work Mondays with the ABC-TV Monday night baseball broadcasting team. When his name and the message "Welcome" were flashed on the scoreboard, "It stopped the ball game," Mr. Prince recalled.

"Bruce Kison was pitching, and he stepped off the mound. The Pirates and Cincinnati Reds came out of their dugouts and doffed their caps. The fans were applauding. Even the umpires took off their caps. That got me. I cried. I bowed. Then I waved a babushka, repeatedly. The fans went wild."

He was named Man of the Year in broadcasting or Sportscaster of the Year endlessly, it seemed. He was cited for his charitable activities and the example he set for others.

The fans sent him about 1,000 letters a week during the season when he was doing play-by-play. In general, the letter writers were complimentary. "I tried to respond to every signed letter," he said.

Unfortunately, his boss, Edward Wallis, then regional vice chairman of Group W, which included KDKA-TV and radio, did not share the views of the letter-writers. He wanted fewer long anecdotes and more concentration on play-by-play. He insisted Mr. Prince had been told before the season started in 1975 what was wanted and was warned he would be fired if he did not comply. First he called Mr. Prince on the telephone and fired him October 28, 1975. Then he let King go.

Almost 10 years later, long after Wallis had left the station, and during a period when the Pirates were in a serious decline, KDKA hired Mr. Prince for three years to do play-by-play for the middle three innings of the radio games and occasional television play-by-plays.

He was able to broadcast two innings of the May 3 game in which the Pirates swamped Los Angeles, 16–2, but he had trouble with his speech then. He had been taking radiation treatments.

He entered Eye & Ear Hospital May 20. He was transferred to the intensive care unit at Presbyterian-University Hospital two days later.

Survivors include his wife, the former Betty Casey; a daughter, Nancy Elizabeth of Green Tree; a son, Robert F. Jr. of Clarkston, Michigan; three grandchildren; and a brother, Frederick S. of Salt Lake City, Utah.

FRIDAY, AUGUST 26, 1988

Art Rooney Sr., 87
Steelers Founder and Owner

By Steve Halvonik, *Pittsburgh Post-Gazette*. Sportswriters Ed Bouchette, Gary Tuma, Paul Meyer, and Chuck Finder contributed to this report.

Art Rooney was against dual ownership. *Photo by Andy Starnes*.

Ed McCaskey was a love-struck college student singing in a smoky Philadelphia bar the night Art Rooney paid him a visit.

Rooney, the founder and owner of the Steelers, was in the company of Bert Bell, a cofounder of the Philadelphia Eagles, who had just become Rooney's right-hand man in Pittsburgh. The two men were in Philadelphia at the request of George Halas, their good friend and the owner of the Chicago Bears. Halas wanted them to get the skinny on this McCaskey, who was courting his daughter Virginia, a student at Drexel University.

Virginia was talking marriage, and Halas wasn't sure he liked his daughter dating a saloon singer, even if the kid was doing it only to pay his way through the University of Pennsylvania.

The year was 1941.

"As you know, George Halas was at his height then," McCaskey said. "I was walking on campus one day and two guys in double-breasted camel's hair overcoats, one with a cigar in his face, walked up to me.

"'You McCaskey? I'm Bert Bell, and this is Art Rooney. Halas sent us here to investigate you.'"

McCaskey said the two men left and caught up with him later that night at the saloon. They had been to see Bill Lennox, the ticket manager at Penn. "Bill Lennox said you're okay, and if you're okay with Bill Lennox, you're okay with me," McCaskey said Bell told him.

"Then Art took his cigar out of his face and said, 'If you're okay with Bert, you're okay with me. And whoever said Halas was an angel?'"

Rooney died yesterday morning at age 87, eight days after being stricken with a stroke. His many friends and admirers honored him in the way he would have liked most: with a good story.

"Cigars and stories. That's what I think of first when I think of Mr. Rooney," said Lynn Swann, the former Steelers receiver. "He was always telling stories. And the miracle of it is, he never told the same story twice."

Rooney was truly a legend in the National Football League: a larger-than-life figure who was blessed with the common touch. A man called "Chief" who never once acted the part.

"One time he was up in Canada, and he sent me a postcard right in the middle of the off-season," said Gary Dunn, the Steelers nose tackle who was released by the team this week. "I picked up this postcard and I'm reading it, and it says, 'Gary, how's your off-season going? I'm up here in Canada and just been thinking about you. Hope you're doing fine and hope your mother's fine, and we're looking forward to a good year this year, and I want to thank you.'

"I'm reading it, and I'm looking at the bottom and it says, 'Art Rooney.' And it just set me back. I just couldn't believe that someone like him would take the time, in the middle of a trip somewhere, to send me something like that. It really meant a lot to me."

Rooney, who formed the Steelers in 1933, was the last living link to the founding fathers of the NFL. He lived long enough to see his team shake off four decades of losing and become the dominant team of the 1970s, winning four Super Bowls in six seasons.

"Art Rooney led his beloved Pittsburgh Steelers for more than half a century in the NFL, but he was a man who belonged to the entire sports world," said NFL commissioner Pete Rozelle. "It is questionable whether any sports figure was any more universally loved and respected. His calm, selfless counsel made him a valuable contributor within the NFL. But he will be remembered by all he touched for his innate warmth, gentleness, compassion, and charity."

Rooney's death follows that of Mayor Caliguiri, who died May 6.

"The passing of Art Rooney has taken from us another civic and community leader who was the essense and embodiment of the spirit of our city," said Mayor Masloff. "There are very few men and women whose names are synonymous with their particular city, but Art Rooney will always mean Pittsburgh to all of us."

Rooney wasn's just the patriarch of the Steelers; he was a friend to the other sports franchises in the city. "The entire Pittsburgh Pirates organization is deeply saddened by the passing today of Art Rooney," said Carl F. Barger, president of the Pirates. "He was a devoted friend of the city of Pittsburgh and the Pittsburgh Pirates. Very rarely can the word 'legend' be properly attached to someone, but it is certainly appropriate in describing Art Rooney. Words cannot describe how deeply he will be missed."

"I think he symbolized the style of the Steelers and the style of Pittsburgh," said Edward J. DeBartolo Sr., the Penguins owner, who bought Randall Park in Ohio from Rooney and his associates. "He was respected by everyone. I know that's a trite expression, but everyone did respect him. He's going to be a big loss."

Two other members of Pirates management, general manager Syd Thrift and manager Jim Leyland, both recalled that Rooney seemed to know when a kind word was needed. "He always seemed to show up at the right time to give me encouragement and support," Thrift said. "I had a deep appreciation and love for this great human being who represented the true heart and spirit of Pittsburgh."

"I think the thing I'll remember most is that during the darkest hours for me when I took this job, Mr. Rooney would show up in my office," Leyland said. "I don't know how he figured it out, but he would always show up at those times. He knew what I was going through, and he was there to cheer me up and tell me to hang in there. I'll never forget that. In a short period of time, I think we became close friends, and I had a tremendous amount of respect for him."

"He's the kind of guy you wish would live 87 more years," said Joe L. Brown, the Pirates' former general manager. "He was one compassionate, caring guy. Particularly when things weren't going well—and there were years like that when I was there—Art would come around and just sit and chat a while. Without appearing to, he would make life seem happier and everything seem rosier. He cared about his city, and I think the city cared for him."

"He certainly is one of the most respected people in Pittsburgh, and probably is the singular most powerful force in this century when it comes to sports in Pittsburgh," said Paul Martha, the president of the Civic Arena Corp., who played for the Steelers from 1960 to 1965.

The Steelers moved from the old National Football League to the American Football Conference's Central Division in 1970, but Rooney remained close to his old friends in the other league. "I always root for the Steelers, the Chicago Bears, and New York Giants," he once told McCaskey, who became the Bears' chairman of the board in 1983, after Halas's death.

Rooney's granddaughter, Kathleen, is married to Chris Mara, the son of Wellington T. Mara, the Giants owner and president. "Mr. Rooney leaves a legacy of decency which he has contributed to the NFL for half a century," Wellington T. Mara said yesterday.

A mark of Rooney's greatness was that he earned the friendship and respect of some of the Steelers' greatest rivals. "He's one of the greatest guys in sports," John Madden, the former Oakland Raiders coach, told *USA Today*. "We had some giant battles with the Steelers, but Art Rooney was always above that. Win or lose, he would treat you the same. There's a saying: 'Shut up until you win, then talk like hell.' He was never like that."

"The Chief was a gentleman and a gentle man," said Art Modell, owner of the Cleveland Browns. "He was a true sportsman, a fierce competitor, and one of my dearest friends since the first day that he welcomed me to the NFL 28 years ago. Pat [Mrs. Modell] and I will miss him dearly."

Rooney touched the lives of many people, from his neighbors on the north side to national figures like James Michener, who wanted to do a book about him. He even left his mark on coaches he couldn't hire.

"There are few people you meet in your life that you respect any more than Mr. Rooney and his family," said Joe Paterno, the Penn State football coach, who turned down a chance to coach the Steelers in 1969. "He was my kind of guy," Paterno said. "Loyal.

Never took himself seriously. Always concerned about everybody but himself. He didn't make money just to make money. He was the easiest touch, I suppose, in the whole city, for the right kind of people. He's the kind of guy you just hope you have a little of in yourself."

Mike Gottfried, the Pitt football coach, said, "Our thoughts and prayers are with his family."

Although he never thought of himself as a big shot, Rooney was one of the most important and influential men in the NFL. He helped to hold the league together during World War II, and in 1960 he was among those supporting an expansion franchise in Dallas.

"He was one of the great men of the game," said Tex Schramm, the Cowboys' president. "He was one of the builders of our sport. He went through the tough times that too few of those today who are enjoying the success of the league had to go through. He was just a great individual, a great person, and a man I loved very dearly."

After Halas's death, Rooney grew closer to the McCaskeys, calling faithfully three times a week to find out how Ed and Virginia were doing. When the Bears returned recently from an NFL exhibition game in Sweden, Rooney called to ask about Virginia's health after such a long trip.

"If I had to be somebody else, I'd like to be Art Rooney," McCaskey said. "I've learned so many lessons from him. His religiousness, his sense of fair play, his decency. I think his greatest quality is his fairness with everyone. He's such a beloved figure to people in all walks of life. I've been with him in

Pittsburgh when people just walked up to him."

Despite his decreasing involvement with the Steelers, Rooney remained a popular figure in the NFL. At the league meetings last winter in Phoenix, he was given a standing ovation by the other owners when he entered a conference room one afternoon.

"You can't have any more respect for someone than I had for Mr. Rooney," said Don Shula, the Miami Dolphins head coach. "He's been like a father to this league. He's one of the reasons I'm proud to be associated with the NFL."

Besides football and his wife, Kathleen, Art Rooney's other great love was horse racing. Swann said he saw Rooney at the Kentucky Derby and Preakness this year while covering both events for ABC-TV.

Gerald Lawrence, the son of David Lawrence, the former Pennsylvania governor, is vice president and general manager of Churchill Downs. He said he keeps a football signed by Rooney near his desk. "The Rooney-Lawrence relationship spans four generations, all the way from my maternal grandmother selling whiskey to Art Rooney's father for the Rooney saloon," Lawrence said. "I would unequivocally say that Art Rooney was my father's closest personal friend. They had a great mutual admiration for each other that descended through our families to where I now have a nephew [Tom Donahoe] who works as a Steeler scout."

Mary Lib Miller, the wife of Del Miller, the harness-racing legend, recalled how Rooney used to bring his relatives, including his mother, to the Millers' farm in Washington County. And she remembered how it was Art Rooney who helped her husband build the Meadows, the harness-racing track in Washington County.

She said that Rooney once air-mailed a present to them in Florida—a Steelers football inscribed, "Happy 25th anniversary, Art."

"It'll be a different ballgame, won't it?" Mrs. Miller said.

Caesar's Casino in Atlantic City honored about a dozen people at its Legends of Racing dinner in June. Rooney was one of the scheduled recipients, but he could not be there because he had a blood clot removed from his arm in May. He asked Lawrence to accept the award for him.

Lawrence traveled to Pittsburgh on June 7 to give the award to Rooney personally. They sat in his office at Three Rivers Stadium and talked about racing and politics for three hours. "Next to sports, politics was his second love," Lawrence said. "I was in Ireland one time and ran into Tip O'Neill when he was the Speaker of the House, and the first thing he asked me was how Art Rooney was."

Unlike the owners of today's professional sports franchises, Rooney always enjoyed a special relationship with his players, although it evolved through the years from brotherly to fatherly to grandfatherly. Rooney was in his early thirties when he formed the Steelers and was not much older than many of his players. But he always commanded their respect. They always knew who was in charge.

"As far as I was concerned, he was the boss," said Bill Dudley, who joined the Steelers as a running back in 1942. "Bert Bell did most of the signing of ballplayers, but I got to know [Rooney] right from the start. "He did business different from any other businessman, but he had a way with him that commanded respect and admiration. My nickname for him was 'Bossman.'"

Dudley said he had lunch with Rooney at the Allegheny Club in Three Rivers Stadium last month—"one of the nicest one-on-ones I had with him in a long time."

"I don't think you're going to find a more loyal Pittsburgher than Art Rooney," Dudley said. "I'll miss him. He was an employer who became a friend."

"Many of us owe so much to Mr. Rooney," said Jim Finks, the New Orleans Saints' general manager, who played quarterback for the Steelers from 1949 to 1955. "My seven years as a player for Mr. Rooney were the most important years of my life. He was always for you, win or lose. The example he set for us is something I have never forgotten. He had the greatest people skills of anyone I've ever known."

John Henry Johnson, who played for the Steelers from 1960 to 1965, asked Rooney to present him at his induction into the Pro Football Hall of Fame last summer. "He was really a grand old gentleman, one of the nicest people I ever had the chance to work for," Johnson said. "I always had the feeling that if I was being treated unjustly, I could always talk to Mr. Rooney and he would adjust the situation."

Johnson said his reason for asking Rooney to introduce him at the Hall of Fame was very obvious. "Who had

more input into the football picture than Mr. Rooney?" Johnson said. "Who else could have done a better job than Mr. Rooney? I think he had a genuine liking for me as a person and as a football player."

George Perles, the Michigan State head football coach, said Rooney "was very good to me" when Perles was a Steeler defensive coach from 1972 to 1982. "He liked my sons and treated them very well," Perles said. "But that's not unusual. He was very good to many people. He was a grand old man. He used to tell my kids that I was the best knife-and-fork man because I like to eat."

Terry Bradshaw, the quarterback on the Steelers' four Super Bowl championship teams, said he would go into Rooney's office and steal cigars for everyone. "That's how he wanted it," Bradshaw said. "He'd give anybody anything he had."

Swann said that by the time he joined the Steelers in 1974, Rooney was no longer involved in contract negotiations or other player-management squabbles. Hence, his friendly relationship with the players. "There was never a threatening atmosphere between a player and Art Rooney," Swann said. "He wasn't the kind of owner who felt he knew more about the way the game should be played than the players and coaches, so you never felt threatened or intimidated. He'd ask you about your family, about your wife, your kids, and things like that. He never had anything negative to say. It was like talking to your grandfather."

Ray Mansfield, the former offensive lineman, said the thing he remembered most about Mr. Rooney—"that's what everybody called him; not 'Art' or something else"—was his sense of humor. "I used to tell stories about my early years with the Steelers in the 1960s, about how bad the facilities were," Mansfield said. "We used to practice at South Park. Some people didn't think it was funny, but Mr. Rooney did. He'd just roar."

Robin Cole, a member of the current Steelers, said, "There's going to be a hole in this team and this city without Art Rooney being here. Art Rooney was a pioneer of this football club, but he was more than that to the players. Before each game he would come around, shake everyone's hand, and

wish them good luck. He felt for the people. He could relate to people regardless of who they were or where they were from. He believed in each and every one of us. There will always be a place in my heart for Art Rooney."

Swann said that Rooney left a permanent mark on the city and on professional football. "We will lose his actual physical presence, but I don't think we'll ever lose the impact the man had on this city, the game of football, and the Steelers," Swann said. "He's like the foundation of a great building. You can change what's inside or paint the building, but you can't change the foundation. He'll always be a part of the NFL."

WEDNESDAY, NOVEMBER 27, 1991

Bob Johnson, 60
Coached Penguins to First Stanley Cup

By Tom McMillan, *Pittsburgh Post-Gazette*. The Associated Press and staff writer Ernie Hoffman contributed to this report.

Bob Johnson, the ever-optimistic Penguins coach who led the team to its first Stanley Cup championship last season, died yesterday in his home in Colorado Springs, Colorado, after a nearly three-month battle against incurable brain cancer. Mr. Johnson, 60, had been in a coma for about a week, Penguins spokesman Harry Sanders said.

Mr. Johnson, whose slogan "It's a great day for hockey" carried him from coaching jobs at the high school, collegiate, professional, and international levels, joined the Penguins in June 1990

and quickly became popular among players and staff members for his upbeat, energetic style.

"Everybody he crossed paths with— or touched—was very fortunate to meet the man. Bob…had such a great influence on a lot of people throughout his life," Penguins general manager Craig Patrick said yesterday. "He was so unbeat, so positive, and had so much enthusiasm for life. He created that atmosphere around our organization."

"He was kind of like a coach and father figure all wrapped in one," Winger

Phil Bourque said yesterday. "I know every day when I come to the rink I think about him rubbing his hands, rubbing his face, saying what a great day it was for hockey. He'd be out there on the ice before you'd be out there. His memory is forever."

The Penguins won the Stanley Cup with an 8–0 victory over the Minnesota North Stars in Mr. Johnson's hometown of Minneapolis on May 25.

"Bob's the reason we were able to win the cup, but he meant more to us as a person," defenseman Paul Coffey said. "I've never met a better man."

Mr. Johnson was inducted into the U.S. Hockey Hall of Fame in Minneapolis on October 12 for his contributions to the sport he loved. More recently, he was named Man of the Year in a unanimous vote by the Dapper Dan Club, the charity arm of the *Pittsburgh Post-Gazette*. The club will present the award posthumously at its annual banquet February 7 in the Pittsburgh Hilton and Towers Downtown.

The son of a Swedish immigrant who changed his surname from Olars, Mr. Johnson played major-college hockey at the universities of North Dakota and Minnesota. An outfielder and pitcher, he was good enough in baseball to sign professionally with the Chicago White Sox but chose hockey instead.

After serving in the U.S. armed forces in Tokyo and Korea, Mr. Johnson began his coaching career at Warroad High School in Minnesota in 1956.

He became known as "Badger Bob" during his 15 years as head coach of the University of Wisconsin Badgers. He revived a dormant program there and steered the Badgers to three National Collegiate Athletic Association titles.

During that period Mr. Johnson also coached the U.S. national team in 1973, 1974, 1975, and 1981 and the U.S. Olympic team in 1976 at Innsbruck, Austria.

Mr. Johnson joined the professional ranks as head coach of the Calgary Flames in 1982. After five seasons in the National Hockey League, which included one trip to the cup finals, he left the bench to become executive director of USA Hockey, the governing body for the sport, in Colorado Springs.

He served three years in that capacity, but Brad Buetow, coach of Colorado College in Colorado Springs, said he was like a "caged lion" in a desk job. "He belongs behind the bench, coaching a team," Buetow said.

Mr. Johnson got that chance again when his old friend Patrick offered him the Penguins job.

Johnson's task was monumental— sort through the egos to mold a complete, well-balanced team from a group of highly skilled offensive players. He did it.

He was at his best integrating new players into the program. Patrick made trades throughout the season, adding as many as 10 new faces, but Mr. Johnson refused to allow that to be a distraction.

"That's why the best acquisition we made was Bob himself," Patrick said.

Playing without star center Mario Lemieux for two-thirds of the season, the Penguins nonetheless won their first Patrick Division regular-season title, then eliminated New Jersey, Washington,

Boston, and Minnesota to win the Stanley Cup.

Mr. Johnson, a physical-fitness buff, enjoyed an active off-season. He traveled, spoke at coaching clinics, played in a tournament for senior players, and taught at hockey schools.

He was coaching Team USA in the Canada Cup tournament when he was stricken.

Mr. Johnson underwent emergency surgery to remove part of a brain tumor August 29 at Pittsburgh's Mercy Hospital. The next day, Paul Martha, then president of the Civic Arena Corp., said the prognosis was "not good."

Soon afterward doctors confirmed the presence of a second tumor but decided against further surgery. Mr. Johnson instead underwent a cobalt treatment in mid-September before returning to Colorado Springs, where he underwent radiation treatment. Throughout the ordeal, he kept tabs on the team, writing questions on a notepad when he was unable to speak. He asked about practice plans, suggested line combinations, and drew up strategy for the NHL season.

"He couldn't get enough information about the team," assistant coach Barry Smith said.

"When I visited him, the discussion wasn't about his condition," defenseman Paul Stanton said. "It was about who was playing well. It was about whether I was in top shape."

Mr. Johnson attended the Penguins' exhibition game against Calgary in Denver on September 19, watching the game with members of his family in a private box. He met with Penguins players before the game and gave them a "thumbs up" sign.

Mr. Johnson is survived by his wife, Martha; two sons, Mark—who played on the 1980 gold-medal U.S. Olympic team and later for the Penguins, and Peter—who played for his father in Wisconsin and is an assistant coach there; three daughters, Julie, Sandy, and Diane; nine grandchildren; and his mother, Myrna Johnson of Minneapolis.

SUNDAY, MAY 30, 1993

Billy Conn, 75
"The Pittsburgh Kid"
By Gene Collier, *Pittsburgh Post-Gazette*

Boxing Hall of Famer Billy Conn, a Pittsburgh treasure as an enduring symbol of the city's immense pride and toughness, died yesterday of complications from pneumonia after a long illness. He was 75.

Death came for "The Pittsburgh Kid" at 10:20 AM at the Veterans Administration Hospital in the East End. "The champ is gone," said Mary Louise Conn, his wife of 52 years and the beautiful woman with whom he spun a storybook life across most of the 20th century.

Like his friend and contemporary, the late Art Rooney, Conn dined with kings and presidents and loafed with shot-and-beer guys, and it was those guys he liked more to be identified with because, as Mary Louise explained: "Billy thought a lot of the other stuff was overrated. He loved Pittsburgh. We could be in Paris or London or Las Vegas, and he'd say to me, 'There's no place like Pittsburgh.' He always wanted to come back here. [Former middleweight champion] Jake LaMotta used to tell him, 'Billy, come up to New York. This is where the action is. There's something going on every night.' But Billy'd tell him there was no place like Pittsburgh."

Billy's Pittsburgh, in his later years, was the city as seen from places like Conley's, the saloon near Fifty-third and Butler. The outside of Conley's was dark yesterday, which is pretty much like the inside of Conley's, where the only harsh light radiates from a one-word slash of orange neon: "Conley's," but with that there is something implicit. Something like, "This ain't no bistro."

You and a buddy can sit down at the bar in Conley's and purchase an evening's worth of draft beer without dropping much more than a fiver between you, and all you have to do is listen to a couple dozen unsolicited opinions on the Clintons, the Pirates, foreign aid, and life in post-industrial Pittsburgh from the patrons sitting behind the drafts and the sticky shot glasses.

Until little more than a year ago, before his illness, you could often enough find yourself sitting here next to a man who fought 21 times against 11 world champions in three different weight divisions, who lost to only one of them—the great Joe Louis, and then only because he was probably too much like too many guys in too many city places like Conley's: too Pittsburgh, too Irish, too stubborn. This was Billy Conn.

He is remembered today most for that first Louis fight—the defining moment of a classically romantic Pittsburgh lifetime on the eve of World War II, and for perhaps the most famous tactical blunder in the history of the fight game, and perhaps even more for his explanations of it. At stations from 50 seconds to 50 years after that night, Conn would say his decision to stand and slug with the larger and more powerful Louis in the 13th round after stunning the champion with a left hook in the 12th was purely a case of having "too much Pittsburgh in me," or more plaintively, "What's the sense of being Irish if you can't be dumb?"

This, too, was Billy: blunt as a knuckle but funny and happy.

"It's tough for me now," said Joey Diven, the legendary street fighter and Conn contemporary. "He was a funny guy. He didn't like the notoriety of being who he was. He'd look for an excuse not to be put in front of people. And he did get tired of people askin' him what happened in the 13th. He'd say, 'You seen what happened; I got knocked on my ass.' I had a lot of fun with him. Many, many good times. He got the best out of life. He did everything he wanted to do."

Diven, like hundreds of his acquaintances, repeatedly felt the sting of Conn's acidic tongue. For this, Conn came to be regarded by those with the chance to study him as a kind of misanthrope, a conclusion that never quite reconciled with his passion for life and his humor, crippling as it often was.

Once upon a time, Diven and a writer were in a local bar. They were in there just long enough for some imprudent ideas to bear the potential of high comedy. Eventually, they conspired to phone Conn in Las Vegas with the grim story that Diven had been killed in an auto accident on the parkway. Just to see what he'd say. The writer made the call and told the tale, but immediately had an attack of conscience and handed the phone to Diven.

"Billy, it's me," Diven said.

"Of course it's you, Joey," said Conn. "I knew it was too good to be true."

Years later, attending the Muhammad Ali–Al Lewis fight in Dublin, Ireland, Billy was asked by his hosts about seeing his ancestral homeland for the first time. "All I can say about it is, I'm glad my mother didn't miss the boat."

After a benefit at the William Penn Hotel in 1971, where Conn and Louis watched the film of their classic fight, Conn trudged through the lobby with the film in a shopping bag. "Imagine this: I fought 11 champions 21 times, and I end up carrying a shopping bag. They kiss your ass to get the film, and when they're done, they throw it at ya." Coming upon Louis, he said, "Joe, you

shouldn't have knocked me out. You should have just killed me."

Conn played himself in the 1942 film *The Pittsburgh Kid*, which he absolutely hated. Offered the starring role in the life story of "Gentleman" Jim Corbett, he snapped, "No thanks; one stinkbomb is enough."

The often-cantankerous character that was Billy and his devotion to his stunning wife, with whom he eloped the month after the Louis fight, drew the rapt attention of the best sportswriters of the last 60 years and of several filmmakers.

The most celebrated slice of Conn journalism is Frank Deford's loving and incomparable *Sports Illustrated* piece titled, "The Boxer and the Blonde," which triggered more reader response than any story in the history of that magazine. "I'm as fond of that story as any I've done," Deford said. "I published a collection a while back, and I chose that to lead it off. I had an affection for Pittsburgh because it reminds me of my hometown, which is Baltimore. A lot of people don't like the smaller, gritty cities, but I love them.

"The thing about that story was the love interest. It was really two love stories. His wife—the whole family, really—and his mother. His mother was dying while he was falling in love and trying to win the heavyweight championship of the world while the world was falling apart. You just can't scare up that kind of thing. Against the whole tapestry of history, and of boxing, it was so compelling."

Conn's mother, Maggie, died in 1941, just after he left for New York and the Louis fight. The last time he saw her, he said, "The next time I see you, I'll be heavyweight champion of the world." "The next time I see you," she answered, "will be in paradise."

So Maggie got it right, but Louis wasn't sure about it until late on the evening of June 18, 1941. After the eighth round, Conn snapped at the champion, "You're in a fight tonight, Joe." "I know it," Louis said.

Louis had tried desperately to get his weight under 200 pounds for the fight because he did not want his size advantage to appear so glaring, with Billy expected to come in about 169. Louis never made it. He weighed 201, and Conn weighed 169 ?, but promoter Mike Jacobs announced Louis at 199 ? and Conn at 174.

Conn had started slowly as he always did, but by the ninth he had the fight in hand, with his exquisite left hook and typically stiff right hand landing often. In the 12th Conn caught the champion flush with a hook, and Louis staggered back, then came forward and hung on to Conn.

"It's simple," Billy would say. "I miss that punch, I'm the champion."

Pulitzer Prize–winning sports writer Red Smith of *The New York Times* called it "an indestructible myth" that Conn, with that punch, deluded himself into thinking he could knock Louis out, thus the decision to stand and slug in the fateful 13th. Billy, Smith contended, had lived on the edge the whole fight and just got caught. But Conn was ahead eight rounds to four and 7–5 on two scorecards (a third was even at 6–6) going into the 13th, and, in the

minute after he was knocked out at 2:58 of the 13th, said, "If I'd have kept moving, we'd have won easy."

Deford wrote that Conn lost, in part, because he envisioned himself running on the beach with Mary Louise in the coming days and didn't want people to merely say, "There goes Billy Conn, the man who beat Joe Louis," but rather, "There goes Billy Conn, the man who knocked out Joe Louis."

Conn acknowledged this with a wink toward poetic license.

Conn's most celebrated fight after that came not in the rematch with Louis, but in the kitchen of his father-in-law, "Greenfield Jimmy" Smith, an irascible former New York Giants bench jockey and a man who clearly did not feel his lovely daughter should be involved with a boxer.

"I didn't see it," Mary Louise remembered. "I was in the living room dancing. It was Timmy's christening, and we had the rug rolled up in the living room. It was catered; we had champagne, and I guess Billy was sitting out there on the stove with his legs dangling off of it. Pap liked to pick at Billy. Criticize him. I guess Billy had just had enough. I still remember Art Rooney saying, 'I can still see Billy coming off that stove.'"

Conn damaged his right hand and his face and his father-in-law in that well-documented dustup, and the hand damage cost both him and Louis hundreds of thousands of dollars because it postponed a rematch. World War II then postponed it until 1946.

"There was this sergeant, big southern guy, 6′4″ or something," Conn's son Tim said the other day. "He has them lined up, all the new privates, and he says, 'If any of you guys think you're tough, just step out of line right now, and I'll show you how tough you are, and that goes for every last one of you.' The others look at my father, and he kind of reluctantly steps out. The sergeant comes over to him, says, 'Who are you?' Dad says, 'I'm Billy Conn.' The sergeant turns to the rest and says, 'Like I said, that goes for every last one of you except this guy here.'"

"Billy called me from Staten Island when he was in the army," Mary Louise said. "He said, 'I've got bad news: I'm shipping out tomorrow.' I said, 'I've got bad news: I'm pregnant.' When he came back 18 months later, there was Billy Jr. standing in the entryway with long dark curls. 'Who's this kid?' Billy says. 'That's Billy Jr.' I told him. Billy looks at him and says, 'Cut that hair!'"

Mary Louise tells this story in the Squirrel Hill home Billy bought for them in 1941 for $17,500. They were recently offered $475,000. "Jesus, that's better than fighting Joe Louis," Billy would say.

Now the face of Billy Jr. is the image of the Pittsburgh Kid, with dark and baleful eyes that break into an easy laugh. In the club cellar, among the collected Conn archives, Billy Jr. flips the pages of the giant central scrap book and conducts a spontaneous tour of the hundreds of framed photographs with the expertise of a ring historian. "I hope you know," he says pridefully, "that my father and the fighters he fought were so much better than today's fighters it's not even funny."

The irony of Billy Jr.'s throbbing respect for his father, and that of Tim and their brother Michael, as well, is that their dad had little regard for athletes and made sure his sons knew it.

"He thought athletes were bums, a dime a dozen he'd say," said Tim. "He'd say, 'Never be an athlete.' He was no natural athlete. He never played baseball or football. He'd throw a baseball like a girl. He never did that stuff. He only wanted to be a fighter to make some money and get out of his circumstance."

Conn once estimated he made more than $1 million in the ring. He made $70,000 from the first Louis fight and $325,958.22 from the second (Lewis made a combined $779,821), in which he was knocked out in the eighth. Though he was ultimately best known for those losses, he was a hugely skilled and successful boxer who won the light-heavyweight title. "Of all my fights, the first one with him was my toughest," Louis once said.

Despite it all, Conn never felt particularly special. "He looked up to doctors and lawyers, writers and professionals—not athletes," said Mary Louise. "And he had great faith. The only autograph he ever asked for was Bishop Sheen. He used to say, 'This life is only a tryout for the big leagues.'"

Billy had what seemed extraordinary confidence, and he kept it a very long time. Coming across a robber in a convenience store on Beechwood Boulevard only three years ago, Conn floored him. "I interrupted him," Conn told the TV stations. "I guess he won't be robbing too many more stores. I hit him with a left. You've got to go with your favorite punch. These kinds of things happen once in a while."

And yet for all of these "things"—which included 74 professional fights among dozens of, well, unsanctioned matches—Conn led a life of unusual stability.

"He was living in the same house and the same community all those years, with the same wife," Deford said. "If I'd interviewed him, say, in Tampa, with some trophy wife or something, it wouldn't have been half the story. But he was pure Pittsburgh. I don't know if there's an athlete who is woven as much into any town as Billy is there. Some ballplayers might be, but usually they come from somewhere else and leave when they're done. Billy is absolutely Pittsburgh. He's not a tragic story at all. I can't think of an athlete who had a happier life."

Billy Conn is survived by Mary Louise and sons Tim of Point Breeze, Billy Jr. of Squirrel Hill, and Michael of Basking Ridge, New Jersey; by three brothers, Frank Conn of Morningside, and Ronnie and Jimmy Conn of Edgewood; by two sisters, Mary Jane Cunningham of Swissvale and Peggy McKenna of Edgewood, and by eight grandchildren. Billy and Mary Louise's only daughter, Suzanne of Lake Forest, Illinois, died of cancer in February.

TUESDAY, APRIL 10, 2001

Wilver Dornel "Willie" Stargell, 61
Seven-Time All-Star
By Gene Collier, *Pittsburgh Post-Gazette*

Willie Stargell, whose great menacing bat and gentle patriarch's compassion were the hallmarks of his singular 21-year career with the Pittsburgh Pirates, died of a stroke shortly after midnight yesterday. He was 61.

The Pirates organization, already at the brink of emotional overload with the opening of its new ballpark just hours away, got the news from Wilmington, North Carolina, where Stargell lived. Stargell had been in New Hanover Regional Medical Center since February 23, when he underwent gall bladder surgery.

A stirring four-minute video presentation on the new PNC Park's electronic scoreboard moments before the Pirates' afternoon game with the Cincinnati Reds showed Stargell in a series of quirky highlights from his playing career—slapping a pie in the face of teammate Tim Foli during a TV interview, coming up short on a slide into second base and calling timeout, and, finally, stroking a two-run homer in Baltimore to push Pittsburgh ahead in Game 7 of the 1979 World Series.

Chins Quaked from Foul Pole to Foul Pole
"When we heard about [Roberto] Clemente's death at 4:00 in the morning,

I went to Willie's house," said former teammate Steve Blass, now a Pirates broadcaster. "I'm not sure where to go this morning."

Some thought they knew where to go. They flocked to the statue of Stargell on Federal Street, unveiled only Saturday. Thick portions of the opening day crowd reached to touch it and laid flowers at Stargell's feet.

"Willie battled," said Pirates owner Kevin McClatchy, standing nearby. "He was pretty sick, but he battled, and Willie Stargell made it to Opening Day." "He was really touched when we announced that we were going to build this statue. Willie knew how much everyone in Pittsburgh loved him."

In a sport forever enslaved by its statistical minutiae, Stargell's impact on the Pirates was far greater than the production that made him only the 17th player in baseball history to be elected to the Hall of Fame in his first year of eligibility. His numbers were dwarfed by his humanity.

For the record then, he was a seven-time All-Star who hit 475 homers and drove in more than 1,500 runs. No Pirate in the 115-year history of the franchise posted greater numbers or had more extra-base hits. He was the Most Valuable Player in the 1979 National League Championship Series against Cincinnati and the MVP of the 1979 World Series, the last in which the club competed. His seven extra-base hits in that series remain a record.

And None of That Begins to Explain Him

Former Reds great Joe Morgan told an ESPN television audience last season, shortly after it first became widely known that Stargell was ill: "When I played, there were 600 baseball players, and 599 of them loved Willie Stargell. He's the only guy I could have said that about. He never made anybody look bad, and he never said anything bad about anybody."

There were times when that must have been difficult, for there was a period in the modern history of the game where it seemed that no one had its physical and psychological demands calculated so precisely as Wilver Dornel Stargell. At the height of his powers, in the fall of 1979, his wisdom and the windmilling mischief of his bat combined to write history.

In the next-to-last game of the regular season that year, Stargell made a throwing error that cost the Pirates the game in extra innings—and with it a one-game lead on Montreal in the standings. In a deadly quiet locker room, Stargell regarded a flock of writers advancing and yipped, "Hey, you guys are always sayin' that [Terry] Bradshaw is the only guy who can throw a down-and-out like that. Well, Bradshaw couldn't have thrown that ball I just threw!"

His teammates smiled. One got up and turned on the stereo. The Bucs rocked on. Stargell homered the next afternoon, and the Pirates won the Eastern Division title. Stargell and Bradshaw, the stars of Pittsburgh's two championship franchises, shared the cover of *Sports Illustrated* as the magazine's Sportsmen of the Year.

"To learn how to win, you've got to

learn how to lose," Chuck Tanner said yesterday. "I'd always find things that I liked in a loss, and Willie would help me."

In the 1979 playoffs, pitching to Willie Stargell was the baseball equivalent of playing Russian roulette. He lashed two homers and drove in six runs, and the Reds were gone in three straight. In the World Series, a cauldron of anxiety after Baltimore raced to a three-games-to-one lead, Stargell not only ripped that critical homer in Game 7, but steadied reliever Kent Tekulve as Teke tried to seal it in the Maryland darkness.

"Eighth inning of that game, and I'm pitching to Eddie Murray with the bases loaded," Tekulve remembered once. "Willie comes over to me from first base and says, 'If you're scared, you play first and I'll pitch.' I figured if he can stay calm, so can the rest of us."

Murray Flied Softly to Right

"The thing about him I'll remember most," Teke said, "is how he could take all the guys, all different personalities, and simply bring them together."

Even more pointedly, Stargell's baseball pedigree was not exactly framed in harmony. A native of Earlsboro, Oklahoma, he grew up in the projects near Oakland, California. Stargell's first professional experiences were laced with the constant indignity of segregation. In minor league towns like San Angelo, Texas, and Roswell, New Mexico, Stargell suffered what he called "aches and pains mentally" because he was forced to live apart from the white players.

Stargell told Roy McHugh, the sports editor and columnist for the *Pittsburgh Press*, that living on the road in those leagues was like living like a tramp, that housing in "the colored sections" of those towns was nothing more than shacks.

He once told of having a gun put to his head in Roswell and of being advised by the man holding it, "N——, if you play in that game tonight, I'll blow your brains out."

"We had some Latin players, but they didn't speak English. There was no one to talk to. Nothing to do. Nowhere to buy a square meal. The only time I saw the rest of the team was at the ballpark."

"He internalized all of that," McHugh said yesterday about Stargell's tour of late 1950s racism. "He didn't talk much about it, and he didn't reveal his feelings in his behavior."

Stargell thought about quitting but kept getting inspirational letters from Bob Zuk, the scout who somehow signed him for $1,500 when it was said the Yankees were ready to offer $20,000.

So rather than an acquired bitterness, Stargell brought a purely joyous approach to Pittsburgh when he finally stuck in the big leagues in 1963. After a bad day at the plate, he once buried a bat in the dirt of a tunnel between the clubhouse and the dugout at Forbes Field. He called it the legendary sword of Kumasi and claimed it was planted there 2000 years earlier by an Ashanti sorcerer. Players tried to pull it out, but none could budge it. Finally, Cubs third baseman Ron Santo pulled the sword from the stone one day with minimal effort, and both he and Stargell were amazed to find that Pirates teammate Donn Clendenon, tiring of the ritual, had pried the bat loose with a crowbar.

Though Pirates manager Harry Walker occasionally would keep Stargell out of the lineup against left-handed pitching, other managers were relieved when he did. Former Phillies manager Gene Mauch once said, "I'd go across the street to Frank's Bar to get three left-handers just to keep that big guy out of the lineup."

During spring training, Stargell took to writing his offensive goals for the coming year inside his cap. In 1967 he wrote 30-100-.300 (homers, RBI, batting average). His actual numbers that year were 20-73-.271. For a while, Willie had bigger numbers in his March hat than on his baseball card, but he eventually sculpted some monster summers, like 48-125-.295 (1971) and 44-119-.299 (1973).

By then he was known throughout the game for Titanic homers, including the first one ever to leave Dodger Stadium, and a fistful of the longest hits at Three Rivers Stadium and in parks throughout the National League. Stargell routinely shrugged at that stuff. "They don't pay you any more for distance," he said.

As the prototypical left-handed power hitter, Stargell was sometimes underrated as a fielder, but never by the players who'd seen his entire career. "When he played left field and he wasn't very heavy, he threw as well as Clemente," former teammate Nellie King remembered last night. "He had as good an arm as Roberto, and he ran pretty decently, too."

As Stargell grew to embrace Pittsburgh and his leadership and natural people skills became evident, the greater potential of his persona became evident to people outside the game. He visited Vietnam and reported, "They're sick of the war. They just can't wait until that thing is over, and I'm on their side. I wish they'd get out of there."

He was named one of Pennsylvania's outstanding young men by the Jaycees for his work in founding and serving as president of the Black Athletes Foundation, a group dedicated to fighting sickle-cell anemia. He served on the board of directors of United Mental Health Inc. He was invited to the Nixon White House in 1972 as part of an athletes-against-drugs effort. He narrated Aaron Copland's *A Lincoln Portrait* from the lawn of the U.S. Capitol on July 4, 1983, and did it again last fall at Heinz Hall.

He sobbed during the first Willie Stargell Day in July 1980, when members of the Los Angeles Dodgers lined up to shake his hand.

Former teammate Dock Ellis once said, "He was a friend to one who had no friends, a constant reminder that once a Pirate, always a Pirate."

On October 3, 1982, the final day of his final season, he went first to third on a hit-and-run single by Omar Moreno. Doug Frobel then ran for him. When he came off the field, players in the Pirates' dugout wept, as did some of the 14,948 on hand at Three Rivers.

In Willie Stargell's Pirate afterlife, however, there were occasions that strained his mammoth credibility and even his relationship with the organization. In September 1985, former teammates Dale Berra and Dave Parker, testifying in highly publicized drug trials, said they got amphetamines from Stargell and Bill Madlock. Though Stargell and Madlock immediately called a press conference to deny those charges, suspicion lingered until March of the following year when Peter Ueberroth, then commissioner of baseball, absolved both of any wrongdoing.

"And I mean *any* wrongdoing," Ueberroth said.

Another awkward public moment came in 1988 after Stargell joined Tanner's staff with the Atlanta Braves. Before a game at Three Rivers Stadium, Stargell's name was announced, and boos from the crowd were more prominent than cheers.

The response grew out of the cancellation of Willie Stargell Hall of Fame Night. Stargell, still suspicious of new Pirates management for dismissing Tanner as manager and having already been honored in two such ceremonies since 1980 in the same stadium, resisted a third.

But, in time, with another changing of the Pirates ownership and administration, McClatchy helped to bring Stargell back to the Pirates family as an assistant to General Manager Cam Bonifay. Stargell loved the opportunity to evaluate and instruct young players, especially at spring training in Bradenton, Florida. It was there a little more than a year ago that he first revealed the genesis of his medical problems in an extended chat with *Post-Gazette* sports columnist Ron Cook.

"Something distracted me on TV, and I looked up [while chopping meat in his apartment]," he said. "I ended up doing a better job on my finger than I did on the meat."

Stargell didn't think much of it—just dressed his wound and had dinner. But a resulting infection spread throughout his body. He was in intensive care and eventually developed kidney disease, undergoing dialysis three times a week for more than three years.

In his last public appearance in Pittsburgh, on October 1, 2000, for the final game at Three Rivers Stadium, he threw a depressingly feeble ceremonial pitch, its bounces telegraphing his growing weakness.

The next time the Pirates lined up to play for real in Pittsburgh, Willie would be gone.

"It was thundering really, really hard last night, and then all of a sudden it stopped," said catcher Jason Kendall in the Pirates clubhouse before the game yesterday. "I guess it was right around then... It's really strange now. Three Rivers gone. New season. You just know 'Pops' is watching us."

Blass brought a plaque Stargell once presented him to the park. "This is going to be our 12th opener together," he said. "I don't know what happens when you die, but if where he's goin' has some kind of ballteam, they just got one helluva first baseman."

Stargell is survived by his second wife, Margaret Weller-Stargell; a son, Wilver Jr. of Atlanta; four daughters, three of whom—Wendy, Precious, and Dawn—live in Atlanta, the other, Kelli, in Herndon, Virginia. He is also survived by his mother, Gladys Russell; a sister, Sandrus Collier, and five grandchildren.

SUNDAY, FEBRUARY 24, 2002

Willie Thrower, 71
Opened Door for Black Quarterbacks
By Chuck Finder, *Pittsburgh Post-Gazette*

One hundred fifty folks crammed into Mount Calvary Missionary Baptist Church in New Kensington yesterday for a funeral. They came to celebrate a brief legacy as much as a long life. They sang, they praised Willie "the Pro" Thrower, and they heard mention of the NFL quarterbacks who followed the trail he blazed: Joe Gilliam, Doug Williams, Michael Vick, so many others.

There were two wooden pews with empty seats near the front of the Fourth Avenue church, the place with a 50-yard-long sanctuary and a high-peaked roof perfectly suitable for a passing quarterback. Williams should've sat in one of those pews. James Harris should've sat with him. Warren Moon and Randall Cunningham and the Steelers' Kordell Stewart and Steve McNair and Donovan McNabb and Daunte Culpepper and Vick should've been there, too.

They owed him—the NFL owed him—as much.

The late Willie "the Pro" Thrower was at the front of their color line.

Yesterday's funeral program told the tale: Going Home Service for Willie T. Thrower—First Black Quarterback NFL. His accomplishment of October 18, 1953, has been commemorated in the Pro Football Hall of Fame. His mitt-sized passing hand has been immortalized in plaster by Ripley's Believe It or Not. All because he was the first black quarterback, his was the first black hand, to toss an official NFL pass. "I was like the Jackie Robinson of football," he used to say.

Almost until the day he died—Wednesday, after a prolonged illness, at age 71—Thrower had to convince people in his own hometown that he made history. They called him a liar. They doubted. So he hardly talked about it.

"It was like a nothing, like a void," said Vince Pisano, a longtime friend and backfield mate from their days at Ken High in New Kensington and Michigan State, where Thrower was likewise credited with being the Big Ten Conference's first black quarterback, in 1950. "It didn't come up too much."

Even this reporter was guilty of ignorance, mentioning Thrower in an August piece about Stewart and Tee Martin without ever realizing how nearby such a treasure resided.

Too many fail to realize it still. A long line of African American quarterbacks neglected to pay some sort of respects yesterday. Michigan State sent flowers in honor of the backup quarterback from its 1952 national championship team, but not the Chicago Bears, for whom he carved a piece of NFL history. The Steelers sent Jim Rooney, Dan's young son, who spoke not only on behalf of his family and the hometown club, but the NFL as a whole.

Rooney spoke eloquently, all right. He talked about the late Gilliam being the first black quarterback to start the season for an NFL team, his family's own Steelers, in 1974. He talked about Williams being the first black quarterback to win a Super Bowl, in 1988. He talked about Vick being the first black quarterback to become the league's first-overall draft choice last spring. Shoot—even the self-proclaimed America's Team, the Dallas Cowboys, began training camp last summer with African Americans as their first-, second- and third-string quarterbacks.

"It never would have reached this status if it weren't for Willie to lead that way," Rooney said.

Because 11 African American quarterbacks started at some point this past NFL season, because nearly half of the 2000 season's playoff teams relied on a McNabb or a Culpepper or a McNair or an Aaron Brooks or a Shaun King, we tend to forget the sordid history. That the league didn't begin integration until 1947. That Thrower was one of just two blacks on the Chicago Bears' 1953 roster, so no wonder he felt animosity, no wonder he thought he heard a snicker every time he ducked into a huddle.

That on a forgotten October day in 1953, Thrower completed three of 8 passes for 27 yards and directed the Bears to the San Francisco 5-yard line, whereupon owner/coach George Halas promptly reinserted starter George Blanda.

Later that same season, the Baltimore Colts switched halfback George Taliaferro to quarterback and started him in two games. In 1955 Green Bay sent Charles Brackins into seven games, in which he attempted just two passes. Then...nothing.

It wasn't until 1968, nearly a decade and a half later, that another black quarterback was given a fleeting pro chance: Marlin Briscoe for the American Football League's pathetic and injury-riddled Denver franchise.

The Steelers' Gilliam begat Harris in that 1974 season. Harris begat Williams, a 1978 first-rounder. Williams begat Moon and Cunningham, who begat the current generation.

Then again, the road remains pock-marked. Shrieks of fan protest surrounded Stewart until deep into this past season, calling into question the glacial progress of civil rights and right-thinking Pittsburgh.

This line all started with that first, giant step by 5'11", 182-pound Willie "the Pro" Thrower, whose two-time WPIAL Class AA championship team skipped a 1947 Orange Bowl prep classic because organizers objected to the pigmentation of its quarterback's skin.

"He was by far the best passer you'll ever see," Pisano remembered yesterday of the quarterback who lasted one year with the Bears and three Canadian Football League seasons before a shoulder injury caused him to retire. "Oh, if he played today? He would have fit right in there. Doug Williams. McNabb. Definitely. Definitely."

In yesterday's eulogy, the Reverend Mildred C. Taylor stood at the flower-adorned pulpit and read from the biblical passage about David and Goliath. How fitting a parable: the ogre that cast a frightening, dark shadow over sports, if not all America, was small-minded racism. The kid who slung the first rock for black quarterbacks was the aptly named Thrower.

With only a few days left in Black History Month, it's a shame the dozens who followed him didn't come to the Fourth Avenue church yesterday and celebrate the man who made black-quarterback history. The Pro who proudly begat a long line of pros.

FRIDAY, DECEMBER 20, 2002

Dick Stuart, 70
Dr. Strangeglove
By Robert Dvorchak, *Pittsburgh Post-Gazette*

Bill Virdon can see the play yet. It was a one-hop smash that Dick Stuart, a first baseman so noted for his defensive shortcomings that he came to be known as "Dr. Strangeglove," fielded with uncharacteristic prowess. "He picked it clean," said Virdon. "But when he went to tag the bag to get the out, he dropped the ball."

Then there was the time when Stuart, known as much for his prodigious power as his balky mitt, launched a home run over the scoreboard in Crosley Field in Cincinnati to win a Sunday game in the ninth inning. As it happened, the Steelers were playing at home, and almost everybody at a Steelers game in those days carried transistor radios to keep abreast of baseball.

The news of Stuart's heroics brought a spontaneous cheer just as the Steelers were getting thrown for a 10-yard loss. "When Stuart was told about it later," Virdon recalled, "he said, 'Darn, the first time I was ever cheered in Pittsburgh and I wasn't there to hear it.'"

Teammates from the 1960 championship team were saddened by the news that Stuart, age 70, died of cancer Sunday at his Redwood City, California, home. But they remembered him fondly in uproarious anecdotes that immortalize him as one of the game's true characters and lovable rogues.

"You couldn't help but love Dick Stuart," said Dick Groat, the National League MVP in 1960. "All of us thought the world of him. He could make fun of anybody, including himself."

Groat recalled a play against the Dodgers in the Coliseum. In the tenth inning, pinch-hitter Gil Hodges smote a ball that glanced off Dick Hoak's glove at third. Playing in the hole, Groat tracked it down and wheeled to fire a strike to first. "Stu thought the ball had gone through, so he turned around and was talking to the umpire while the throw sailed right past his ear. If he had been standing on first base, I would've hit him right in the No. 7," Groat said, laughing. "Then he came into the dugout after the game, and the first thing he says was, 'E—six. Two-base error.'"

Groat, the National League MVP in 1960, also shared this nugget: "One time he was being shipped to the minors, but it didn't get him down. He told me, 'I hope you hit .300 this year—.150 the first half and .150 the second half.'"

Richard Lee Stuart played 10 Major League seasons, the first five with the Pirates. He hit 117 of his 228 home runs while with the Pirates. But he also struck out an average of once every 4.2 at bats, and he was charged with 90 errors in those first five seasons. He also played for the Red Sox, Phillies, Mets, Dodgers, and Angels.

When Stuart signed autographs as a major Leaguer, he wrote "66" next to his name. A free swinger and a free spirit, Stuart had drawn national attention in the minor leagues when he launched 66 home runs in 1956 while playing for Lincoln, Nebraska, of the Class A Western League. At the time, Babe Ruth held the major league record of 60 in a season. It was such a feat that *Life* magazine dispatched a photographer and reporter. "They called me an irrepressible egotist," Stuart told the *Post-Gazette* five years ago. "That hasn't changed any."

Bob Friend recalled a blast by Stuart that he swears "was one of the longest home runs I ever seen. It was at Forbes Field, which was so spacious they used to put the batting cage in right center because nobody thought anybody could reach it with a ball. It sailed over the cage, over the wall. It must've gone 525 feet. It came off Glenn Hobbie of the Cubs."

Stuart also hit a winning home run that allowed Friend to notch his 20th victory in 1958, and Friend still has a picture of that moment. But he got a chuckle recalling Stuart's fielding. "He could have been a great fielder, but he never worked on it. He liked to hit," Friend said. "One time there was a throw over to first that bounced in the dirt in front of him. He lost it and was looking around when he looked up at the umpire and said, 'Don't just stand there. Help me find the SOB.'"

The myth is that Bob Prince hung the "Dr. Strangeglove" nickname on Stuart. But Stanley Kubrick's "Dr. Strangelove" didn't come out until 1964, after Stuart had been traded. He said it was Henry Aaron who gave him the moniker. During his first two seasons, the Pirates had a slugger named Ted Kluszewski, and Prince called them "Big Stu" and "Big Klu."

ElRoy Face, the relief pitcher extraordinaire, almost always came into games with the outcome in the balance. The route from the bullpen brought him into proximity with first base. "He'd be over there kicking the dirt with his spikes, and he'd say, 'Don't throw it to me. I don't want to screw it up,'" Face said.

The boos hurled at players from Dave Parker to Derek Bell never reached the decibel levels of the catcalls aimed at Stuart, who reveled in his relationship with fans.

Long before his days as a broadcaster, the noted writer Myron Cope, who always had a fondness for characters, profiled Stuart in a magazine piece that became a part of Cope's book, *Broken*

Cigars. "He was a delightful fellow, and he toyed with the fans," Cope said. "During infield practice, he used to drop balls on purpose to get the fans going. And he'd laugh and say, 'When they start throwing Coke bottles, that's when I know it's time to go to the dugout.'"

A sliver of Pirates trivia has Stuart in the on-deck circle when Hall of Famer and defensive wizard Bill Mazeroski hit the home run that beat the Yankees in the 1960 World Series. And it has been speculated that Stuart was the only Pittsburgher not jumping up and down—because he had wanted to hit the historic shot.

"We were in spring training the following year, and everybody on the bus was razzing Maz about waving his arms and his helmet while he was running around the bases," Groat said. "Stuart said, 'You should have seen what I had planned.' That's how confident he was."

For every ball he ever booted, he was swinging at another for the fences. Go easy, Big Stu.

TUESDAY, AUGUST 12, 2003

Herb Brooks, 66
"Miracle on Ice" Coach
By Chuck Finder, *Pittsburgh Post-Gazette*

It's a grim day for hockey. A grieving day. In the Penguins organization, across America, and all over the puck planet, Herb Brooks is being mourned.

He was John Wayne in skate boots. He was Babe Ruth with a twig of a stick. He was Knute Rockne with a whistle and Casey Stengel with the media. He was a legend of the game who loved it so deeply that anybody who stopped him would get an earful of hockey talk. He was such the stuff of American folklore that Hollywood was working on its second movie about him and his daring 1980 U.S. Olympic team, this time with Kurt Russell offering a far more handsome and hockey-knowledgeable alternative to Karl Malden. Do you believe in miracle workers? We lost one yesterday.

Brooks died yesterday at the ominous age of 66 and six days. He was apparently driving home from a U.S. Hockey Hall of Fame celebrity charity outing at Giants Ridge Golf Resort in northern Minnesota. His Toyota minivan veered into the grass off Interstate 35 just north of his native Minneapolis. As the van rolled over, he was ejected and killed.

For the Penguins, it was the loss of their first-year director of player development, a man set to work with the club's number of burgeoning young prospects, not to mention a scout for much of the eight previous years and an interim coach for most of one season—1999–2000—that nearly ended in storybook fashion before one overtime defeat followed by a quintuple-overtime defeat spelled the playoff end against Philadelphia.

For the country, it was the loss of the stoic visage behind the U.S. Olympic bench, the taskmaster who shoved a bunch of college kids and minor-league bums to a gold medal and the Miracle on Ice triumph over hockey's Big Red Machine—all at a time when Americans were held hostage in Iran, and the Soviet Army was invading Afghanistan and a fuel crisis gripped the land.

For hockey, it was the loss of a coach who not only succeeded on many levels of the game, but planted plentiful seeds in Lake Placid, New York, ice.

Sports Illustrated dubbed it the greatest sports moment of that century. Folks of that generation remembered where they were when John F. Kennedy was shot, when man walked on the moon, and when Mike Eruzione scored the eventual game-winner. American kids grew to become hockey players thanks to Brooks and the boys of 1980, kids named Modano and Hatcher and Roenick and Olczyk.

The number of American-based NHL teams swelled by one third since then, from 15 to 22. Professional rosters went from dotted by the occasional U.S.-born oddity to dumping entire American lines onto the ice. And these red, white, and blue bloods come from half of the states.

Division I college hockey has grown by 25 percent since 1980, growing to include such places as Mercyhurst and possibly soon Robert Morris. High school hockey has doubled, and junior hockey has trebled in the states. Girls' hockey has multiplied by 25 times in size.

"Herb Brooks is synonymous with American hockey," Penguins general manager Craig Patrick was quoted as saying in a statement released by the club last night, while Patrick was likely as emotional as he was while tearing up in filming a television special about the coach and the team he helped to run. "He loved the game, he lived the game…"

"This is a great loss for the Penguins," Mario Lemieux added, "and for the entire hockey world."

The same as American hockey in his wake, Brooks was a success at every stage of the game. He was the last cut of the 1960 team that was the first bunch of Americans to win Olympic gold and, even though his insurance salesman father, Herb Sr., wanted his son to ditch those silly puck dreams, the kid made the 1964 and 1968 U.S. teams, too. As a coach at the University of Minnesota, he won three NCAA titles, including one with an all-American-born lineup. He won the 1980 gold. And, after a 1998 try with France, he returned to the U.S. bunch for a reunion-tour 2002 campaign that ended with a silver, losing in the final to Lemieux's Canada.

He also coached various NHL stops with the Rangers, Devils, Minnesota North Stars, and the Penguins, and the Rangers were interested again last summer, but Brooks and his wife preferred the Minnesota life. He was to U.S. hockey what television was to the NFL, what the pharaohs were to pyramid construction, what Elvis was to rock 'n' roll. King-maker and king all at once.

"He was a true, legendary American character," Penguins announcer Paul Steigerwald said. "He loved to talk about hockey and tell you his philosophy. It was like he was spreading the gospel, trying to convert you to his way of thinking."

He was a John Wooden walking around the Penguins offices, last appearing there in the late July orientation sessions with young prospects. He was a funny guy who joked of the Penguins under Kevin Constantine, whom he replaced in December 1999: "These guys skate backward more than Peggy Fleming."

Burial arrangements were incomplete last night. Yet on October 18, in Eveleth, Minnesota, the entire 1980 team will be inducted into the U.S. Hockey Hall of Fame, and the coach—inducted there in 1990—will be fondly remembered.

Bow your heads and bang your stick blades and get misty, boys and girls. There is crying in hockey today, and for several more days. Tears won't melt a miracle, just some of the ice.

FRIDAY, APRIL 29, 2005

John "Red" Manning, 76
Former Dukes Coach and Athletics Director
By Phil Axelrod, *Pittsburgh Post-Gazette*

John "Red" Manning, a link as a player, coach, and athletics director to the glory days of Duquesne University basketball, died Wednesday of pancreatic cancer at his home in Bethel Park. He was 76.

Mr. Manning had a 247–138 record as the head coach from 1958 to 1974, guiding the Dukes to four National Invitation Tournaments and two NCAA tournaments.

"He was a very good game coach who always had his teams prepared," said John Cinicola, who was Mr. Manning's assistant from 1960 to 1974 and the head coach from 1974 to 1977 with Mr. Manning as the athletic director. "He believed in discipline. Red was a no-nonsense guy. It was his way, and the record proved it was the right way."

Cinicola said he thinks one of Mr. Manning's favorite teams was the 1962 squad of Mike Rice, Billy Stromple, Clyde Arnold, Paul Benec, and Willie Somerset, which was ranked as high as number three in the country by the Associated Press. That squad finished 22–7 and reached the third round of the NIT. "That probably was his best team," Cinicola said. "He also had a special feeling for the teams that had the Nelsons—Garry and Barry—Billy Zopf, and Jarrett Durham in the 1960s and early 1970s."

Durham, who played for Manning from 1969 to 1971, is now an associated athletics director at Duquesne. "Red was definitely the father figure. When he spoke, you listened," Durham said. "He always let you know where you stood. He was a guy who knew how to win. He had a knack of putting people in the right positions."

Mr. Manning was often a coach of few words. "He was sort of intimidating to me as a young player," Durham said. "When I first came to Duquesne, I learned that if you didn't make this guy happy, you will never see the game. Red always let us know we couldn't do anything he didn't know about.

"His practices were pretty tough. You had to be physical. You had to be tough in practice."

Like most young players, Durham didn't fully understand or appreciate Mr. Manning's coaching style. "As soon as I started coaching, I really began to appreciate him as a coach and how he managed people," said Durham, who coached at Community College of Beaver County, Robert Morris, and Duquesne. "Red was the boss. No one questioned that. You were afraid if you didn't do what he wanted, you'd have to pay the consequences."

Mr. Manning grew up in the Homeville section of West Mifflin and helped Homestead High School win two state basketball championships. He played for Chick Davies at Homestead and Dudey Moore at Duquesne.

Mr. Manning graduated from Duquesne in 1951 and spent the next two years coaching at St. Canice High School while earning his masters degree at Duquesne. He returned to Duquesne as an assistant under Moore in 1954 and succeeded him in 1958.

Mr. Manning was an assistant in 1955 when Duquesne, led by All-Americans Sihugo Green and Dick Ricketts, won the NIT championship, which at the time was widely regarded as equal or superior to the NCAA tournament.

"Red and I were close," Cinicola said. "Every day we had lunch together. Every day I went to work was enjoyable."

After Mr. Manning retired as basketball coach he served as the athletics director until 1978. He was a salesman in the Trust and Real Estate Department of Pittsburgh National bank until his retirement 12 years ago.

Mr. Manning is survived by three sons, John, Patrick, and Michael, who all live in Peters Township; two brothers, Richard of Greer, South Carolina, and Edward of Lancaster; and a sister, Margaret Micka of Canonsburg.

THURSDAY, APRIL 6, 2006

Marshall Goldberg, 88
Legendary Pitt Back
By Paul Zeise, *Pittsburgh Post-Gazette*

Marshall Goldberg, a University of Pittsburgh All-American running back in the 1930s and a member of Pitt's "Dream Backfield," died Monday. He was 88.

Mr. Goldberg, a native of Elkins, West Virginia, led Pitt to back-to-back national championships in 1936 and 1937. He was runner-up for the Heisman Trophy, awarded to college football's best player, in 1938. The Panthers were 25–3–2 during his three years of eligibility.

Mr. Goldberg died at a Chicago nursing home after spending several years battling the effects of brain injuries caused by numerous concussions during his playing days, his wife, Rita Goldberg, said yesterday.

Mr. Goldberg's high point as a professional player came in 1947 when he intercepted a pass against the Philadelphia Eagles that clinched the NFL title for the then-Chicago Cardinals.

As a high school sophomore, Mr. Goldberg weighed just 110 pounds and was dubbed "Biggie" by his friends.

"*Sports Illustrated*'s Dan Jenkins, one of the greatest college football writers ever, once wrote an article looking back at all the Heisman Trophy winners and tried to figure out who should have won it each year," said Beano Cook, a college football historian and former sports information director at Pitt. "He believes Marshall should have won it in 1937 [he finished third in the balloting] based on the season he had. But that tells you how great he was for his time and in comparison to players of his era.

"Tony Dorsett was Pitt's greatest runner, but Marshall was one of the greatest football players because he played at a time where he played on both offense and defense, and he also threw the ball," Mr. Cook said.

Pitt coach Dave Wannstedt, who played for the Panthers from 1971 to 1973, said Mr. Goldberg was "one of the crown jewels of both Pitt and college football. He will be missed, but his legacy will live on for a very long time."

Mr. Goldberg played for the Cardinals from 1939 to 1942 and again from 1946 to 1948. His football career, however, was interrupted while he served in the Navy during World War II.

After his football career, he worked in the insurance business and a heavy-machinery business in Illinois. In 1965 he took over a machine parts company and became a millionaire as head of the Marshall Goldberg Machine Tools Ltd., of Rosemont, Illinois.

His career rushing yards of 1,957 stood as a school record for 36 years, until Mr. Dorsett became the leader in 1974.

Mr. Goldberg played from 1936 to 1938 and was named an All-American halfback in 1937 and All-American fullback in 1938, the only Pitt player to be named to the honorary team at two positions. In his three years at Pitt, Mr. Goldberg, who weighed 185 pounds, also was a defensive standout.

Before the 1938 season, Mr. Goldberg moved from left halfback to fullback to make room for a talented player named Dick Cassiano. The two, with quarterback John Chickerneo and right halfback Curly Stebbins, formed the Panthers' "Dream Backfield," which is considered one of the greatest compilations of talent in one backfield in college football history.

So talented was that group that Fordham coach Jimmy Crowley, who was one of Notre Dame's legendary "Four Horsemen," was once quoted as saying the Dream Backfield was even superior to the Irish's quartet.

In addition to the 1936 and 1937 national championships, Goldberg-led Pitt teams won a Rose Bowl and two Eastern championships. He was later named to *Sports Illustrated*'s College Team of the Decade for the 1930s.

Mr. Goldberg's coach at Pitt, the late Jock Sutherland, called Mr. Goldberg "a football player's football player." Mr. Sutherland said Mr. Goldberg was one of the finest running backs he had seen and once commented on his toughness by saying, "He has been knocked out only once…and he ran to a touchdown on the next play."

Mr. Goldberg had his No. 42 jersey retired at halftime of Pitt's 21–17 win against Miami on September 18, 1997. He is one of only eight Pitt football players to receive that honor.

In Pitt's final home game at Pitt Stadium, Mr. Goldberg presided over the closing ceremony in which he "captured the spirit of Pitt Stadium" in a wooden chest. Pitt beat the Irish, 37–27, that game, which was November 13, 1999. Two years later he released the spirit at Heinz Field when the Panthers played host to Miami September 27, 2001. That chest is on display in Pitt's football practice facility.

"I walk past his retired jersey every day," Mr. Wannstedt said. "It is a reminder of the high standards he set both on and off the field. He was not only an outstanding player, but also a true professional and gentleman."

Mr. Goldberg was inducted into the College Football Hall of Fame in 1958. He is a member of 14 other Halls. Of his success in football, Mr. Goldberg said in a 1982 interview, "I don't like to live in the past…and talk about my athletic accomplishments all the time. I prefer to live in the present. I'm more proud of my accomplishments off the field. To me, playing sports should be a stepping stone to a career. It's not an end in itself."

Mr. Goldberg remained an active fund-raiser for Pitt and headed the Corporate Alum Drive. He was a member of Pitt's board of trustees in the 1980s and became an emeritus member in 1986. While on the board he served on the athletics committee, the student affairs committee, the academic affairs committee, and libraries committee. He was also on Pitt's school of information sciences board of visitors

"Marshall was a Pitt sports legend, a devoted member of the university's board of trustees, and an outstanding human being," Pitt chancellor Mark A. Nordenberg said. "We feel privileged to have played a role in Marshall's life as he was learning, growing, and building the foundation for all of the good things that followed his many contributions to Pitt athletics. We are saddened by the loss of a good friend."

In addition to his wife, Mr. Goldberg is survived by a son, Marshall; a daughter, Ellen Tullos; and two grandchildren.

In the Pulpit

Archbishop Canevin, Father Cox, Cardinal Wright, Rabbi Freehof, Sister Michele, Monsignor Rice—these are names of people who have touched the hearts and the souls of Pittsburgh over the years. In the region's churches, synagogues, and, in more recent times, mosques, there breathes a community of the spirit that has sustained, comforted, and inspired the people of Western Pennsylvania since the earliest days of settlement.

WEDNESDAY, MARCH 23, 1927

Regis Canevin, 73
Former Bishop
By the *Pittsburgh Post-Gazette*

The body of J.F. Regis Canevin, titular archbishop of Pelusium and former bishop of the Pittsburgh diocese of the Catholic church, will be taken at 9:00 this morning from Mercy Hospital, where he died early yesterday, to the residence of Right Reverend Bishop Hugh C. Boyle, at 114 North Dithridge street.

Tomorrow morning at 9:30 the remains of the former bishop, whose death came after seven years of failing health, will be taken into St. Paul's Cathedral on Craig Street, where he officiated for many years, to lie in state until 10:00 Saturday morning when the first funeral mass for an archbishop in Pittsburgh will be sung with 200 diocesan priests, dignitaries of the Catholic church in America, and civic and state leaders present.

Pupils to Attend

Representatives from every parochial school in Pittsburgh will attend the solemn requiem high mass to be sung at 10:00 tomorrow morning in the cathedral. Tomorrow and Friday nights at 7:30 there will be the recitation of the Divine Office by 50 priests in the church.

While messages of tribute and condolence came yesterday, plans were made for the funeral of the first bishop since 1904. Two committees were appointed by Bishop Boyle to make the necessary arrangements. The committee on laymen's activities members are: Right Reverend Monsignor Martin Ryan, Very Reverend E.P. Griffin, and Very Reverend Stephen Schramm. The committee appointed to make arrangements for the visiting prelates members are: Very Reverend Monsignor P.C. Danner and Rt. Reverend Monsignor John Gorzynski.

Bishop Boyle probably will officiate at the solemn requiem high mass Saturday. The names of his assistants had not been announced last night. These arrangements were tentative, but it is possible they will not be changed. The bishop's secretary was busy yesterday sending messages notifying dignitaries of the church of the death and tending to business necessitated by the death, which came unexpectedly.

Last night the bishop was receiving messages from church officials who expect to be here for the funeral and burial in St. Mary's cemetery in Lawrenceville.

To Sing Mass Today

Reverend Thomas F. Coakley, who for 10 years was secretary to Archbishop Canevin, will officiate at 9:00 this morning at a solemn requiem high mass for the dead archbishop in the new Sacred Heart Church, of which

Father Canevin some years ago was assistant priest under the pastorate of the late Monsignor Keane. Reverend Carl H. Demorest will be deacon. Reverend Victor I. Kennedy will be sub-deacon, and Reverend Raymond Mulvehill and Reverend Thomas J. Gillen will be masters of ceremonies. Nine hundred children of the Sacred Heart High and grade schools will sing under the direction of Earl Scanlon.

James Francis Burke, former congressman, who as a boy studied Latin and Greek under the late archbishop when he was a young priest, paid him the following tribute:

Western Pennsylvania has been a nursery for great men. Many of their names are known around the world. Other less widely heralded have wrought results that long will reflect credit upon their earthly careers.

When the Right Reverend Regis Canevin passed away this morning, Western Pennsylvania gave to eternity a real man of God whose life was given to teaching his fellow men how to live and die. His career as a young clergyman and a bishop of a great diocese and archbishop included the period of Pittsburgh's architectural transformation. From old St. Paul's, whose spires rose above Grant's Hill at the crest of Fifth Avenue, where the Union Trust building now stands, to the graceful pillars and classic contour of St. Paul's that sets like

an architectural jewel surrounded by the hills of Shadyside, represents a story of toil as well as transformation. The gentle, kindly Christian leader of his flock was the beloved center of it all. To him hatred was a stranger, and the love of his fellow man was the gospel of his life.

As he was my boyhood friend, let me drop this flower of memory upon his grave.

J.F. Regis Canevin, who was bishop of the Pittsburgh diocese from December 20, 1904, when he succeeded the Right Reverend Bishop Phelan upon the latter's death, until he retired because of ill health in December 1920, went to the hospital January 26 this year. The dying archbishop was conscious until midnight Monday and conversed with Reverend Michael Hegerick, hospital chaplain; Bishop Boyle; Fathers Hegerick and Bernadine, the latter of the Passionist order; and the archbishop's two nieces. Sisters Eulalia and Mary Regius and several other nuns from the Mercy order were at the bedside when death came at 3:20 in the morning.

Born in Westmoreland County June 5, 1852, Archbishop Canevin received his education in St. Vincent's Seminary in Beatty and was ordained to the priesthood in 1959. His first appointment was that of rector of St. Mary's Church in Pittsburgh. He remained there until 1881, when he became assistant at St. Paul's Cathedral. From 1886 to 1891 Father Canevin was chaplain of St. Paul's Orphanage in Idlewild and the Pennsylvania reform school and the Western penitentiary. In 1891 he became chancellor of the Pittsburgh diocese, a post that he held for two years. He then assumed the pastorate of St. Philip's Church in Crafton.

In 1895 Father Canevin became rector of St. Paul's, serving until 1902. February 24, 1903, he was consecrated titular bishop of Sabrata and named coadjutor bishop of the diocese of Pittsburgh because of the ill health of Bishop Phelan. The following year he became bishop. Six weeks after his resignation as bishop in 1920, he was made titular archbishop of Pelusium. About the same time he became chaplain to the Felician Sisters and resided in the convent of that order in the Fifth Avenue extension in McKeesport, until he was removed to the hospital.

While he was bishop, on the average one parish building was erected every 30 days throughout the diocese. Many of those structures were costly improvements. The number of nuns in the diocese trebled. The period marked the building of more Catholic hospitals and the increase of activities in each.

Reviews Life

Dr. Thomas F. Coakley, who for many years was Bishop Canevin's secretary, briefly reviewed the bishop's life:

> Archbishop Canevin founded the first Catholic club for boys in the diocese, and it has left its influence upon a host of now-prominent Catholic business and professional men. Out of this club grew the Catholic Truth Society, which has since become international.
>
> He was the first to encourage retreats for women, and he brought the Passionist nuns to the diocese to erect a house for this purpose, their first foundation in the Western hemisphere. He did the same thing for laymen's retreats, which, annual affairs at first, are now carried throughout the entire year.
>
> Several years ago the archbishop opened a new house of retreats for laymen devoted exclusively to the purpose and presided over by Passionist fathers. He introduced into the diocese more communities of women than existed when he assumed the direction of affairs, and today there are no less than 24 communities of nuns engaged in almost every variety of religious, educational, and charitable work.
>
> The cry of the afflicted always reached his ear, and he founded here the DePaul Institute, one of the largest and finest private oral schools for the deaf in the country.
>
> He founded the Confraternity of Christian Doctrine to catechize the children of the sparsely settled districts of the diocese, and in 1921 there were two priests directing the work of 700 teachers of 18,000 children who otherwise

would be entirely outside the pale of religion. He began the diocesan band of missionaries to evangelize the rural districts and to give missions to the non-Catholics. The Missionary Aid Society was his idea, and the present national plan to reorganize Catholic missions in the country is based entirely upon the plan which the bishop of Pittsburgh put in force in this diocese many years ago.

And in the full tide of accomplishments he did a thing that in the opinion of many sagacious observers eclipsed all his other triumphs. He resigned. Resignation has not been the least of virtues possessed by the bishops of Pittsburgh, three out of five having laid down their office in this fashion. Having attained the crested wave of perfect achievement, Archbishop Canevin passed on to an uncommonly capable younger head and hands the ripened harvest of his more than 40 years in the priesthood and episcopate.

In accordance with his last request, there will be no eulogy at the funeral mass. That was the statement that came from Bishop Boyle's office last night.

WEDNESDAY, MARCH 21, 1951

James R. Cox, 65
Cox's Army
By the *Pittsburgh Post-Gazette*

Solemn pontifical high mass of requiem for the Reverend James R. Cox, age 65, pastor of Old St. Patrick's Church for nearly 28 years, will be celebrated at 10:00 Monday in Good Samaritan Chapel of the church. The Most Reverend John F. Dearden, bishop of the Pittsburgh Catholic Diocese, will be the celebrant.

Father Cox died early yesterday in Mercy Hospital, where he once was chaplain, after suffering a stroke in the rectory of the church.

His body will lie in state in the church at Seventeenth Street and Liberty Avenue from 6:00 tonight until 2:00 Easter Sunday afternoon. Then it will be translated into the Good Samaritan Chapel at Fourteenth Street and Penn Avenue. After an all-night vigil, the office of the dead will be chanted at 9:30 Monday morning, preceding the pontifical mass.

Father Cox will be buried in Calvary Cemetery, as he had wished, at the side of his late father and mother, James Cox and Julia Mason Cox.

Father Cox had collapsed Monday night in the rectory. As he was preparing to retire, he became faint and telephoned one of his assistants, the Reverend Walter C. Karaveckas, who was in another part of the rectory. He asked Father Karaveckas to hurry to the study, and he requested that his housekeeper, Mrs. Mary Spehar, remove his shoes.

A few minutes later Mrs. Spehar heard him fall in the bathroom. Father Karaveckas helped Father Cox to bed and called a doctor. Then he administered Extreme Unction, the last rites of the Catholic church, to the unconscious priest.

Father Cox was rushed to Mercy Hospital and was placed immediately in an oxygen tent. That was at 11:05 PM Monday. At 1:29 AM he was dead, the victim of a massive stroke, his third.

At his bedside when death came were the only two surviving members of his immediate family, his brother, Dr. Earl Cox, and his sister, Mrs. Dehnis Dwyer.

Also keeping vigil were Father Cox's assistants: Father Karaveckas, the Reverend Paul Lackner, the Reverend James Burke, and a former assistant, the Reverend Herman Baumann.

Father Cox had been working on a radio sermon when he became ill. Earlier in the evening he had visited his cousins, Mr. and Mrs. William Mason.

He had suffered previous strokes in 1943 and 1948 but had recovered, and he had appeared in good health.

Long Continuous Pastorate
Just the other day he told the Post-Gazette proudly that his pastorate at Old St. Patrick's was the longest continuous pastorate in the 143-year history of the church. He also said, laughing, that the present church rests on the site of what first was a cemetery, then a brewery, and how, before the church was destroyed by fire in 1935, one of the large brewery vats was discovered under the church and used as a little chapel for years.

Father Cox said that he had come to Old St. Patrick's on September 6, 1923, at the age of 37. He succeeded the late Father Thomas F. Coakley, who went to Sacred Heart Church.

Asked how many members he had in his parish, he said, "Oh, 15 families." He laughed. "That's right, only about 15 families are left. But of course the attendance at the six Sunday masses goes up into the thousands."

Thousands Hear Broadcasts
And that was not counting the thousands more all over the tri-state area who listened to the broadcasts over radio station WJAS, he said. "Through radio we take the church to people who can't get out of their homes or who live in areas where there are no churches and wouldn't ever get to hear a mass if it wasn't for us," Father Cox said.

Ruddy of complexion and stocky, Father Cox was a vigorous man and enjoyed good health most of his life. "I'll die here at St. Patrick's," he had said to intimates. "I want nothing more."

SATURDAY, FEBRUARY 21, 1976

Kathryn Kuhlman, 68
Radio Evangelist
By Thomas J. Porter Jr., *Pittsburgh Post-Gazette*

Evangelist Kathryn Kuhlman, who recently underwent open-heart surgery, died at 9:00 last night in a hospital in Tulsa, Oklahoma.

Miss Kuhlman, in her midfifties, according to a spokesman, died of pulmonary hypertension "having never really regained her strength" after the December 30 surgery at the Tulsa hospital.

Miss Kuhlman resided in Fox Chapel and was internationally known for her faith-healing services but disliked being called a faith healer and disavowed any credit for healing.

She was first hospitalized in Tulsa in July for what her physicians described as a minor heart flareup. She suffered a relapse last November in Los Angeles and decided to go to Tulsa when the need for open-heart surgery was indicated.

For more than 25 years the fundamentalist preacher, whose following was interdenominational, held sessions throughout the country, prompting "miracles" that she attributed to God—but which the skeptics called psychosomatic. In her books, *I Believe in Miracles* and *God Can Do It Again*, she quoted doctors to substantiate various claims of dramatic healing.

Miss Kuhlman was born in Concordia, Missouri, where her father, whom she revered, was mayor. She began preaching at the age of 16, following what she describes as a deep spiritual experience.

After studying the Bible on her own for two years, she was ordained by the Evangelical Church Alliance.

Although Miss Kuhlman retained membership in the Concordia Baptist Church, she considered herself nondenominational and said she had a special rapport with Roman Catholics. The evangelist viewed her healing ministry as secondary to that of salvation.

Miss Kuhlman restricted publicity for her appearances and was careful about financial matters. She took a yearly salary of $25,000 plus travel expenses, turning over all additional earnings to a nonprofit charitable foundation that bore her name.

The headquarters of the Kathryn Kuhlman Foundation is the Carlton House, where Miss Kuhlman taped half-hour programs heard daily on more than 50 radio stations. In Los Angeles, she prepared telecasts viewed on more than 60 stations.

In an interview in 1972 Miss Kuhlman said she had no idea how large her following was, but that it was greater then than ever. She attributed this to a general trend toward the spiritual. She stressed that God was doing the healing and that she merely served to remind people of their faith.

Miss Kuhlman smiled a great deal and her manner on and off stage was more often cheerful than reverent. But she was moved to tears occasionally during her services. "It is very easy for me to give myself to God because I had no talent. When you have nothing—it's easy," she was quoted as saying in 1972.

Acknowledging that many people with severe afflictions left her services unhealed, Miss Kuhlman said there was much she could not explain or understand. "I just don't know," she said, shaking her head. "I don't know. I don't know."

Her ministry reportedly brought an annual $2 million to the foundation. Through that organization she carried on a program of foreign missions drug rehabilitation and education of the handicapped.

She filled the 7000-seat Shrine Auditorium in Los Angeles to overflowing once a month. She always invited persons who were seeking healing at her meetings to bring their physicians.

Through her foundation she built more than 20 missionary churches and mission centers in 11 countries. On the 20th anniversary of her ministry, residents of the Philadelphia area raised $100,000 to complete, in her name, a project center in Indonesia. The foundation established a revolving loan fund for students at Wheaton College in Illinois and provided scholarships for students in many other universities.

MONDAY, AUGUST 13, 1979

John Joseph Wright, 70
Cardinal and Former Pittsburgh Bishop
By Bohdan Hodiak and Alvin W. Rosensweet, *Pittsburgh Post-Gazette*

He was the highest-ranking American in the Roman Catholic Church and bishop of the Catholic Diocese of Pittsburgh from 1959 to 1969. The death of Cardinal John J. Wright last Friday brought sadness to thousands of district residents, many of them non-Catholics.

The 70-year-old prelate died at 8:15 PM at the Youville Rehabilitation and Chronic Disease Hospital in Cambridge, Massachusetts. In the past year he had undergone several operations for cataracts and a neuro-muscular disorder that confined him to a wheelchair.

Hospitalization forced him to miss the first 1978 Vatican conclave to choose a pope. He did manage to attend the second conclave.

Pope John Paul II described him as a man "who lived an exemplary life dedicated to pastoral service." In a telegram sent to the diocese from Vatican City, the pope said: "May the memory of his diligent and zealous pastoral service to God's people be a constant incentive to charity on the part of all who knew and loved him as a friend and pastor of the flock."

Cardinal Wright. *Photo courtesy of the* Pittsburgh Post-Gazette.

Bishop Vincent M. Leonard, the cardinal's successor in Pittsburgh, will preach the homily at the 11:00 AM mass to be offered Friday in Holy Name Church in the Boston suburb of West Roxbury. The principal celebrant will be Cardinal Humberto Medeiros, archbishop of Boston.

"Our prayers and our affection are for John Joseph Wright, a dedicated and devoted priest of Christ who made the faith so real and so beautiful for so many of us," Leonard said. "He had endeared himself to all by his infectious humor, good nature, and love of people. May God grant him eternal rest, light, and peace."

A beloved cleric who left a major impact on this city's civic, cultural, and religious life, Cardinal Wright achieved a number of distinctions upon his appointment to the Vatican in 1969 by Pope Paul VI. He was the first American ever to be elevated directly from bishop to cardinal, bypassing the rank of archbishop, and he was only the third American in history to head a department of the Vatican. As Prefect of the Congregation for the Clergy he supervised some 350,000 priests around the world. Since 1969 he had been the only American cardinal in the Curia, the central administrative body of the Catholic Church in Rome.

A stocky man of great wit, intellect, and grace, Cardinal Wright generally was considered a social liberal and a theological conservative. Although he disliked such labels, he felt those designations to be entirely compatible. He was a loyalist on virtually every papal policy. He was vigorously opposed to the liberalization of abortion laws, against artificial birth control, and against a married clergy.

On priests leaving the priesthood he said, "What they need is to go to confession, and right away. They made a promise. They should keep it."

He was one of the first bishops to support the civil rights movement and to oppose the war in Vietnam, which he described as "a morally dubious mess."

During his 10-year stay in Pittsburgh, he was beloved among his parishioners and was highly regarded in the Protestant and Jewish communities. He was ecumenical before it was fashionable. The Pittsburgh Jaycees named him Man of the Year in 1967.

When he announced in 1968 his approval of a $12,000 grant to the United Movement for Progress, with $10,000 of that amount going to a black militant, adverse reaction was swift. Contributions to the Bishop's Fund dropped sharply, and an effigy of Cardinal Wright was draped across a treetop near St. Paul Cathedral in Oakland.

The New York Times once described him as "the American hierarchy's most brilliant orator, writer, and intellectual." He loved French culture and had been deeply influenced by such writers as Jacques Maritain, Henri de Lubac, and Cardinal Emmanuel Suhard. His library contained 4,100 books and artifacts about Joan of Arc.

A leading Catholic journal once devoted an entire issue to a discussion of his writings. But his intellectual achievements didn't detract from his sense of humor. Once on St. Patrick's Day he arrived at an interfaith breakfast in Washington, D.C., wearing a green skullcap. Even on his elevation to cardinal he couldn't resist saying: "I'm not sure what it means, but a lot of people had better do a lot of praying." He noted that a cherished Protestant teacher had introduced him to the Latin poem which he took as his motto—*Resonare Christum corde Romano*—to echo Christ.

Born in Boston, his mother was of Irish descent, his father of Scottish. He was the oldest of four sons and two daughters.

He helped pay his way through school by working in a library and as a copyboy for the old *Boston Post.* He decided he was not cut out to be a reporter when the city editor assigned him to go to the home of a girl who had committed suicide and ask the mother for a picture. "The tears were streaming down her face. How could I ask her for a picture?" he explained later. He never returned to the newspaper office.

But throughout his ecclesiastical career he had a rapport with newsmen, who delighted in interviewing him and exchanging banter. Although he always had a busy schedule, one reporter remembers calling the bishop to ask Wright if he could talk to a former alcoholic who was sliding into dispair. That same day Bishop Wright spent one and a half hours with the man.

Cardinal Wright graduated from Boston Latin School and received a bachelor of arts degree from Boston College. He started preparation for the priesthood at the American College in Rome, where he was ordained in 1935. He stayed at the Gregorian University in Rome for three years, earning a doctorate in theology with highest honors. There he continued his lifelong custom of seeking out unfortunate individuals to help. He was at the bedside of a notorious American gangster who had been deported to Rome when the man died.

For a time he took nonsalaried parish jobs in Scotland, England, and France before returning to this country. In 1939 he became professor of philosophy at St. John's Seminary in New Brighton, Massachusetts, then was appointed secretary to Cardinal William O'Connell and Archbishop Richard J. Cushing in Boston. In 1947 he was appointed auxiliary bishop of Boston and in 1950 was assigned as bishop of Worcester, Massachusetts, holding that position until he came to Pittsburgh. In 1957 the Worcester B'nai B'rith, a Jewish service organization, named him its Citizen of the Year.

Cardinal Wright was the author of several books on catholic social teaching. His works include *National Patriotism in Papal Teaching,* which was the subject of his doctoral dissertation, and *Words in Pain.* He was fluent in Italian and French.

"I love the Catholic Church as I love nothing else," he once said. "I don't think of the church as an organization, an institution. To me, it's the personal presence of Christ in history."

Cardinal Wright is survived by three brothers, Richard of Milton, Massachusetts, Robert W. of Cleveland, Ohio, and Alfred of Duxbury, Massachusetts; and two sisters, Harriet Gibbons of Milton, Massachusetts, and Margaret Haverty of Brighton, Massachusetts.

WEDNESDAY, JUNE 13, 1990

Solomon B. Freehof, 97
Rabbi at Rodef Shalom
By Alvin Rosensweet, *Pittsburgh Post-Gazette*

Dr. Solomon B. Freehof, who served as rabbi of Rodef Shalom Congregation in Shadyside for 32 years and was one of the world's foremost Reform Jewish leaders, died yesterday in Montefiore University Hospital. The cause of death was not released.

Rabbi Freehof, age 97, was elected president of the World Union for Progressive Judaism in 1959, the first American granted that honor, an acknowledgement of his stature in world Reform Judaism. But after retiring to the status of rabbi emeritus, he continued the studies that brought him recognition in his field. In 1981 he completed the writing of *New Reform Responsa*, a volume of Jewish law answering the most recent questions and problems posed by members of the Jewish community.

Rabbi Freehof had a commanding presence on the platform. He was a solidly built man of medium height with a handsome shock of white hair he retained all his life.

On his 89th birthday on August. 8, 1981, he delivered a sermonette in Rodef Shalom Temple. "We treasure our memories, but we live by our hopes," he had said at that time. His retirement in 1966 had been in name only; until his death, he spent his time among his books, continuing the contemplation and reflection that marked his life.

His knowledge was shared in public lectures that attracted thousands of Pittsburghers. During the greater part of his tenure at the temple on Fifth Avenue, the city's leading Reform Jewish congregation, he shared his love of books in his modern literature classes, book reviews that attracted thousands of people. For many years, his knowledge of the works of Shakespeare was reflected in a series of radio lectures.

Rabbi Freehof was born in London in 1892. He recalled that at age 9, he sat on a London curb watching the funeral of Queen Victoria go by. He chuckled that when he told that to a small girl in his congregation, she asked, "Why, rabbi, did you know George Washington, too?"

He came to this country with his parents in 1911, living first in Baltimore, where he was bar mitzvahed, the Jewish ceremony in which a boy of 13 passes into manhood, and he graduated from high school with honors. The family then moved to Cincinnati, where he attended the University of Cincinnati while also studying at Hebrew Union College, graduating with honors and becoming a rabbi at age 22.

He taught at Hebrew Union College for several years, then served as a Jewish chaplain with the American Expeditionary Forces in Europe during

World World I. After the war he was named rabbi of Kehillath Anshe Mayriv Temple in Chicago, before joining Rodef Shalom Temple in 1934.

In 1935 he married Lillian Simon, who had been his secretary in Chicago and who went on to write more than 20 books of Jewish legends and children's stories. The walls in their apartment in Park Plaza on North Craig Street in Oakland and in his study at Rodef Shalom Temple held a 9,000-volume library, including one of the world's greatest collections on Jewish law, on which he was a respected authority.

Rabbi Freehof's hobby was bookbinding, and he said of it, "Handling old books is play. Books keep me busy." At his apartment he would spread out newspapers and work with cloth, leather, and paper, mending ancient volumes.

When a Hebraic library owned by another Pittsburgh rabbi was struck by fire, an insurance company asked Rabbi Freehof to estimate its value. He and an assistant helped to sort 2,000 volumes describing life in the Jewish ghettos of Europe during the Middle Ages.

Rabbi Freehof was a baseball fan and often followed the Pirates at old Forbes Field, a few blocks from his home.

He was president of the Central Conference of American Rabbis and a member of the executive board of the Union of American Hebrew Congregations. On his 85th birthday, Rabbi Freehof was described as "a teacher of rabbis," and in 1979 he was honored by the National Conference of Christians and Jews.

On the eve of his retirement, reflecting on his career, he said: "It's a happy profession provided that a man is suited for it, and to whom public life is not a trial."

Rabbi Freehof enjoyed expensive cigars but noted that after breakfast he smoked a pipe. When someone commented that he looked younger than his age he replied, "If that's true, it's because I don't waste my time exercising."

He is survived by his wife.

SUNDAY, SEPTEMBER 11, 2005

Sister Michele O'Leary, 70
Cofounder of Ireland Institute
By Dennis B. Roddy, *Pittsburgh Post-Gazette*

Michele O'Leary, a diminutive nun who spent a quarter of a century as head of an innovative program to bring the children of Northern Ireland's feuding Catholics and Protestants together in Pittsburgh where they were trained for jobs back home, died yesterday of cancer. She was 70 years old.

The child of an immigrant Irish father, she joined the Sisters of Mercy in 1951 and, after 30 years as a teacher, grade school principal, health care administrator, and director of an antidrug program, began a new career as cofounder of the Ireland Institute of Pittsburgh, a project to divert young people in Ulster from violence.

Her work began in the mid-1980s, when "the Troubles," as they were called, seemed beyond resolution. After rounding up funds from Irish American business leaders—Steelers owner Dan Rooney and Heinz chairman Anthony O'Reilly were major benefactors—Sister Michele set out to Northern Ireland to recruit young people to come to Pittsburgh for training.

Mel Madden, a social worker who cofounded the institute and designed its curriculum with Sister Michele, died in 1999.

When she first began recruiting students for the institute, Sister Michele kept her religious affiliation a secret for fear of frightening off Protestant civic leaders who doubted Catholic Americans could be impartial in the province's religious struggle. "I probably got away with that for two years," she said in a 2003 interview.

By the end of her dealings, Sister Michele had not only won the trust of Protestant leaders in Northern Ireland, she was fêted by one of the most prominent, Reg Empey, a onetime leader of the militant vanguard movement, who had gone on to become lord mayor of Belfast. "I looked out and realized the limousine was pulling up to city hall," she recalled. "Reg told me I must have been the first Catholic nun ever to be given an official dinner at Belfast City Hall." Two years ago, the University of Ulster in Coleraine, an overwhelmingly Protestant town, added an honorary

doctorate to go with Sister Michele's bachelor of science from Mount Mercy College and her master's in education from Duquesne, both Catholic schools.

Sister Michele's office in the Pittsburgh Regional Enterprise Tower Downtown was studded with photographs of her alongside the major figures in Northern Ireland's strife and the peace process that followed. Her dealings brought her alongside such pivotal figures as Gerry Adams, the head of Sinn Fein, and Martin McGuinness, a longtime leader in the Irish Republican Army, as well as figures from pro-British paramilitary organizations from the Protestant community. Her wall included photos of her with John Hume and David Trimble, two men who would later win the Nobel Peace Prize for their work hammering out the Good Friday Agreement, the pact that set the stage for a Protestant-Catholic power-sharing government, easing the way for an eventual end to the Troubles.

Sister Michele played a part in linking Pittsburgh to the process in 1996 when she essentially hijacked a White House conference to promote trade and development in Ulster, and had the conference moved from Philadelphia to Pittsburgh. Attendees included then–Northern Ireland secretary Patrick Mayhew and White House special envoy George Mitchell, who flew in to confer with attendees.

"She was the spirit of the Good Friday Agreement long before we got a Good Friday Agreement," said Davy Kettyles, a trade union leader in Enniskillen, Northern Ireland, where city leaders recently named its reconciliation center in honor of Sister Michele. "I think it's the American Indians who have a saying that you never really die as long as someone remembers you. I don't think Michele will be dead for a very long time."

For a peace advocate, Sister Michele was not always identified as "peaceable" in her style, breezing into the offices of major executives, often with a set of instructions. Ted Smyth, chief administrative officer for H.J. Heinz Co., remembered how she appointed him to the institute's board—and then informed him of it. "I said 'I'm on too many boards.' She said, 'Well you have to go on this one. You're on it,'" Smyth said. He remains on the board to this day and credits the institute with offering a practical model that convinced the largely segregated population of Northern Ireland that decades of bloodshed and distrust could be put aside.

It was one of the building blocks to hold out an example of how Protestants and Catholics could come together," he said.

Rooney, the Steelers owner, credited Sister Michele's work with saving lives that would otherwise have been directed toward the paramiltary groups that recruited from Ulster's unemployed, working-class youth. "She put people on a path for success," Rooney said. "She just kept you going and made you feel this was the most important thing

you had to do at this particular time," he said.

Yesterday, hours after Sister Michele succumbed in her room at the Sisters of Mercy Convent on the Carlow College campus, staff arrived at the institute's headquarters to begin the transition to a post-O'Leary era. "We're going to continue to pursue the mission of the institute in the spirit of Michele O'Leary," said James Lamb, the institute's vice president.

Raised in a neighborhood along the bluff on which Duquesne University and Mercy Hospital have grown, Michele O'Leary joined the Sisters of Mercy in 1951. Her closest friend in the order, Sister Margaret Hannan, remembered her as a no-nonsense character with great warmth toward friends and a skill with school children that only once seemed to miss the mark.

When a student at St. Regis Elementary School, where she worked as principal, failed to come in from recess promptly, Hannan said, "Michele told him, 'Mr. Marino, you need to get back to math class. You'll never make a living throwing a football around.'"

Dan Marino went on to quarterback the Miami Dolphins. He was paid rather well and occasionally enjoyed telling the story himself.

Sister Michele is survived by a brother, Terry O'Leary, a former Pittsburgh detective, of Brookline, and a sister, Kathleen O'Leary, of Mt. Lebanon.

MONDAY, NOVEMBER 14, 2005

Charles Owen Rice, 96
Labor Priest

By Nate Guidry and Jon Schmitz, *Pittsburgh Post-Gazette*. Staff writers Jan Ackerman and Jim McKay contributed.

Monsignor Charles Owen Rice at a prepublication party for his new book at the Heinz Regional History Center on July 11, 1996. *Photo by Tony Tye.*

Monsignor Charles Owen Rice, known as Pittsburgh's "labor priest" for his decades of activism on behalf of working people, died yesterday at Vincentian Home in McCandless. He was 96.

Monsignor Rice marched on picket lines and led labor protests starting in the 1930s, joined arms with Martin Luther King in the civil rights movement of the 1960s, and was an early opponent of the war in Vietnam. His forceful and opinionated writings appeared for years in the *Pittsburgh Catholic* newspaper, and Bishop Donald Wuerl once joked about the volume of mail the columns generated.

A series of small strokes had left Rice frail in recent years, but he was able to attend a celebration of his 70th anniversary as a priest in July 2004 at St. Anne in Castle Shannon, his home church. He was given a standing ovation during the mass, which was celebrated by Bishop Wuerl and more than 40 priests, some of whom worked with Monsignor Rice through the years.

"Monsignor Rice was a priest's priest," said the Reverend Robert Cedolia, current pastor at St. Anne. "He gave his entire life to the church. For 71 years he was dedicated and committed to the church. He loved God and he loved people, and everything he did flowed from that. Everything he did was for the good of the people."

"It's like the passing of an era," said the Reverend John Rushofsky, director of clergy personnel for the Pittsburgh Catholic Diocese. "He was the oldest priest in the diocese. He really loved being a priest and enjoyed having priests around. He used to say that being a priest was the best job in the world."

Monsignor Rice was born in New York City in 1908, the son of Irish immigrants. After his mother died when he was four years old, he and a brother were sent back to Ireland to be raised by his grandmother. By age 11, he returned to the States with an Irish brogue and a vocation. He was ordained into the priesthood in 1934, following studies at Duquesne University and St. Vincent Seminary. Three years later, he helped found the St. Joseph House of Hospitality in the Hill District, a shelter that still operates under the umbrella of Catholic Charities. He and two older clergy also organized the Catholic Radical Alliance, which later became an important adjunct of the Catholic Worker movement in America.

During World War II, Monsignor Rice was rent-control director for the city of Pittsburgh. In the 1940s he became a leader of anti-Communist forces inside the labor movement, a role about which he later expressed regret.

He marched arm in arm with Martin Luther King at the United Nations in 1967, addressed antiwar rallies in the 1960s, and wrote in the *Pittsburgh Catholic* in 1972 that "Vietnam is a dirty and dangerous business and we have to get out."

As a young priest, he joined his first picket line at the H.J. Heinz Co. factory on the north side during the Depression in 1937, a year that was a turning point in the movement to organize industrial workers. His appearance at the Heinz plant along with two other priests caused an uproar. He was denounced from pulpits, particularly by clergy whose parishes had been helped by Heinz. It also drew the attention of the Steel Workers Organizing Committee, which invited him to visit a picket line in Ohio during a strike called to organize Youngstown Sheet and Tube and other "little" steel companies.

He is remembered as one of the few clergy in American mill towns to take the side of the union. "I got the other two priests in my little Chevy, and we hit the picket line there," Monsignor Rice wrote in one of his columns. "We all spoke, but mine was a rip-roaring, no-holds-barred denunciation of the steel magnates and the infamy of great wealth."

Once back in Pittsburgh, Monsignor Rice, by his own account, became involved in every labor struggle and every strike—and there were many of them over the years. Some called him a publicity hound, others a great friend.

In January 1948 the Reverend Charles Owen Rice (center) joined the picket line of striking American Federation of Labor restaurant employees at the Downtown Rodgers Dairy Co. stores. Here he is shown at the Wood Street store. *Photo courtesy of the* Pittsburgh Post-Gazette.

A year after Heinz, Msgr. Rice delivered the invocation at the founding convention in Pittsburgh of the Congress of Industrial Organizations, a forerunner of the AFL-CIO.

He protested steel plant shutdowns in the 1980s and joined striking workers of the *Pittsburgh Press* in 1992.

"He was the most important Catholic social activist in 20th-century Pittsburgh," Charles McCollester, a labor relations professor at Indiana University of Pennsylvania, said in 2004 at the reception honoring the 70th anniversary of Monsignor Rice's ordination. Dr. McCollester was editor of *Fighter with a Heart*, a collection of Monsignor Rice's writings.

In 1998, at a celebration of his 90th birthday, Monsignor Rice said, "I've only been a parish priest, and I haven't tried to be anything else, but as far as labor is concerned and the poor and the blacks, I kept the faith. I tried to help the downtrodden."

In his seven decades as a priest, Monsignor Rice was pastor of numerous churches, including St. Joseph in Natrona; Immaculate Conception in Washington, Pennsylvania; and Holy Rosary in Homewood.

In 1976, at the age of 68, he was named pastor of St. Anne at his request. He remained a part of that parish as retired emeritus pastor up until his death, which was announced at the evening mass at St. Anne yesterday.

SECTION

VIII

Music and All That Jazz

The soundtrack of Pittsburgh is jazz. The soundtrack of Pittsburgh is classical music. The soundtrack of Pittsburgh is the popular song. The soundtrack of Pittsburgh is all of these things, from the great heritage of Stephen Collins Foster to the songs of Perry Como to the strains of Billy Eckstine and Stanley Turrentine. If music be the food of love, then Pittsburgh has never been underfed.

FRIDAY, JANUARY 22, 1864

Stephen Collins Foster, 37
Songwriter
By the *Pittsburgh Post-Gazette*

An Eastern contemporary thus speaks of the late Stephen C. Foster:

His taste for music was early developed, his first and one of his most popular songs, "Uncle Ned," having been composed at the age of 18. This was about 20 years ago, and from that time until within the last two or three years, a flood of song music has flowed from his pen and has met with a popularity almost unrivaled.

His productions have furnished entertainment and solace to men and women in all quarters of the globe, though but few know or acquired to know to whom they were indebted for the pleasure they experienced. To mention a few of his songs most familiar to the popular bar will give an idea of Mr. Foster's industry and will call attention to his merits as a maker of ballads that are said to be more potent than even government itself.

His first were, like "Uncle Ned," written for the negro minstrels, which were so much the rage 15 or 20 years ago. Among that class were his "Oh! Susannah," "Nelly Bly," "Nelly Was a Lady," "Mama's in the Cold, Cold Ground," "My Old Kentucky Home," "Camptown Races," "Oh! Boys Carry Me 'Long," and most famous of all, his "Old Folks at Home."

His later compositions were chiefly ballads of a sentimental order, among which were such as "Gentle Annie," "Mollie Do You Love Me," "Come with Thy Sweet Voice Again," "Little Ella," "Jennie with the Light Brown Hair," "Farewell My Lillie Dear," "Willie We Have Missed You," "Ellen Bayne," "Maggie by My Side," "The Spirit of My Song," "Happy Hours at Home," "Come Where My Love Lies Dreaming," "I See Her Still in My Dreams," "Willie My Brave," etc.

As an instance of the popularity of his "Old Folks at Home," it was stated by a correspondent at the time of the Crimean War that in the English camps around Sebastopol that that song and "Annie Laurie" were heard in every tent to the exclusion of almost all others. Anyone will recognize in the list we have given the airs which are perhaps the most familiar to his ear and which he has heard sung, played, and whistled by most people in all the variety of places and styles which evince popularity.

Mr. Foster died in New York City on September 13, 1864, at the age of 37 years. His remains were taken to Pittsburgh to be interred in the family burying ground near that city.

Stephen C. Foster was a brother of the late William B. Foster Jr., who was so long and well known in Pennsylvania in conjunction with its public improvements, and who was at the time of his death the popular vice president of the Pennsylvania Railroad Company.

WEDNESDAY, MAY 17, 1978

William Steinberg, 78
Symphony Musical Director
By Tom Hritz, *Pittsburgh Post-Gazette*

William Steinberg. *Photo by Morris Berman.*

William Steinberg, a foremost figure in the ranks of the great musical minds of the 20th century under whose direction the Pittsburgh Symphony Orchestra achieved international fame and recognition, died yesterday in Lenox Hill Hospital in New York.

Steinberg, 78, who once characterized himself as being "too closely wed (to his beloved symphony) to contemplate any divorce," had been a patient at Lenox Hill for two weeks.

He had been a resident of Atherton, California, since 1976, when he resigned his position as musical director of the Pittsburgh Symphony Orchestra and was named director emeritus of the symphony. He was succeeded by Andre Previn in the 1976–1977 season.

Music was Steinberg's life, and although ill health during his final years forced him to conduct while seated and ultimately led to his resignation as director of the Pittsburgh Symphony, he continued to pursue his art, returning to concert stages here and in New York as a guest conductor.

His final appearance in Pittsburgh was last December 8, when he conducted the orchestra in a performance of Mahler's Symphony no. 1.

About two weeks before his death Steinberg had appeared as guest conductor with the New York Philharmonic. The featured work was one of his favorites: the Brahms Violin Concerto. Isaac Stern was soloist. Shortly after the performance, Steinberg was rushed to Lennox Hill Hospital.

Steinberg was born in Cologne, Germany, on August 1, 1899. Music came to him as naturally as speech comes to the average child. At the age of four he was picking out tunes on the piano and learning to read music before being introduced to the alphabet.

"My very gifted mother invented a clever system in which she took colored pencils and coded each note a different color," he related to *Post-Gazette* music critic Robert Croan in a 1976 interview. "This is how I learned to read music."

Steinberg told how, as a child, he came home from school one day and informed his mother that his teacher was a liar. "He told us the alphabet starts with A," said the boy. "This is not true. The alphabet starts with C."

Steinberg was an accomplished violinist at the age of 10, and the idea of becoming a conductor rarely entered his mind as a youth. He related how after returning from his first opera, *Der Freischuetz*, he asked his mother, "What is that man doing who waves his hands in front of the orchestra? He disturbs me."

"This was my first impression of a conductor," he said.

Steinberg studied at the School of Higher Musical Studies in Cologne, conducted at the Cologne Opera House at the age of 21, and was opera director. in the German Opera House in Prague, Czechoslovakia, from 1925 to 1929.

In 1925 he moved to Prague as the principal conductor of the German Theater and later became opera director. He held those two posts and was a regular guest conductor at the Berlin Symphony when the Nazis forced him to resign in 1933.

Being Jewish, he was forced underground by the Nazis and for two years gave concerts before Jewish audiences using leading unemployed Jewish musicians. When the Nazi pressure mounted, Steinberg and violinist Bronislav Huberman fled Germany in 1936 and founded the Palestine Orchestra, which is now the Israel Philharmonic.

Arturo Toscanini conducted the symphony's inaugural concert, marking the beginning of a strong friendship between himself and Steinberg. Toscanini talked Steinberg out of returning to Berlin and convinced his friend in 1938 to go to the United States, where Steinberg was ultimately selected as associate conductor of the NBC Symphony.

After several seasons with the NBC symphony, Steinberg appeared as guest conductor with several American orchestras and became music director of the Buffalo Philharmonic in 1945.

Steinberg's reputation as a "builder of orchestras" in the musical world brought him to Pittsburgh in the fall of 1952.

The Pittsburgh Symphony Orchestra, formerly conducted by Fritz Reiner, had fallen into musical doldrums.

Steinberg didn't realize it then, but he was on the threshold of a blazing love affair with symphonic orchestra, which over a quarter of a century he would mold into one of the finest in the United States.

"When I was invited to come to Pittsburgh in 1952, I did not know what I would find," he told Croan. "I was very much surprised that it was an orchestra of good qualities, with a basic knowledge of what orchestral playing means. I looked for the reasons why, if this was so, the orchestra had not grown more before I came.

"My predecessor, Fritz Reiner, was a man of great intelligence who had a strange idea about orchestra education. Every year he had engaged 50 percent new men, and fired them as soon as he found they were not satisfactory. He must have been a poor auditioner.

"Every year he had a new ensemble, which is not the way I thought one builds an orchestra. I made it my task from the beginning to keep the orchestra together as well as I could and make what was to be made of the material. This seemed to me the secret for the growth of the orchestra.

"Little by little the Pittsburgh Symphony grew, through my own unified concept, well-planned repertory, and many tours up to the present day, when the orchestra is in very good shape. It is without doubt the sixth of the great American orchestras; and abroad, only the Berlin Philharmonic can compare.

In 1964 Steinberg and the Pittsburgh Symphony Orchestra were selected by the Cultural Presentations Office of the State Department to resume overseas exchange tours of major symphony orchestras. A three-month tour of 14 European and Near Eastern countries followed.

In May 1968, William Steinberg became the first conductor in American concert history to be named director of two major orchestras—the Pittsburgh Symphony and the Boston Symphony.

The appointment was made from 1969 through 1972. At the request of the Pittsburgh Symphony's board of directors to give more of his time here, Steinberg refused to renew his Boston contract through 1972, although he did appear with the Boston Symphony Orchestra as a guest conductor.

Though Steinberg had previously served in dual positions, the Pittsburgh Symphony always came first. From 1958 until 1960 he commuted between Pittsburgh and England, where he was musical director of the London Philharmonic. In 1964 he was principal guest conductor of the New York Philharmonic while remaining in his Pittsburgh position.

The dual positions often led to rumors that Steinberg was ready to leave Pittsburgh. He scotched them once and for all in 1968 when he declared, "We are too closely wed, the Pittsburgh Symphony and I, to contemplate any divorce."

William Steinberg was a shy, sensitive, serious man not incapable of humor. He was not given to false modesty and would never deny his own greatness. A young reporter was once assigned to write a story on what famous Pittsburghers would do were they given the opportunity to live their lives over again. Steinberg gave it to the young writer straight from the shoulder. "Young man," he declared flatly. "I would do nothing different. I have achieved my destiny."

John Edwards, former manager of the local symphony who left to become manager of the Chicago Symphony, once explained why the maestro was held so highly in his profession. "Steinberg commands colossal respect because of his musical and personal integrity. He commands loyalty because he never connives. He never plays favorites. He's friendly but impersonal, sympathetic when players ask for help. He's a manager's dream."

Although he knew individual scores of musical programs completely, members of the symphony never considered Steinberg to be a narrow specialist. But he did have a decided preference for the German romanticists, especially Wagner, Mahler, Beethoven, and Bruckner.

Those who knew him well said he made music in an atmosphere of good will. He had the respect and admiration of the public as well as his musicians. Yet he could be brusque and sarcastic on occasion and had little patience with small talk. One of his aides once proudly told the maestro that he had to stand in the crowded hall during an entire concert by the Pittsburgh Symphony Orchestra.

"So did I," returned Steinberg.

He could be a warm conversationalist but was bored with people with whom he found no rapport. His wife, Lotti, who died in 1967, once remarked that she felt sorry for her husband. "He's so one-minded in all he does," she said. "He's lonely. So consumed with music he excludes everybody, everything.… But his personal shortcomings are more than balanced by his talent."

"I am one of those lucky men whose profession is also his hobby," the maestro once said. "I work at music 26 hours a day."

Despite the artistic forces which drove him from conformity, Steinberg retained the ability to laugh at himself. He often said he spoke four and a half languages—the half being English. He once suggested that because the conductor usually distracted the audience, the concert should be conducted from behind a screen.

Steinberg was not always contented with the times in which he lived. "We are not too fortunate to be living in an era like this when ugly things are taken over into the realm of human feeling and thinking and do not serve beauty anymore. And this is where I stop. If social revolution today is depicted in things that are ugly and against the nature of art, it is just too bad, in my opinion."

In 1965 Steinberg was named Man of the Year by the Pittsburgh Jaycees. "In a city known for science and industry," he said, "it is fitting that this award be made to a man of the arts. The award actually should go to the members of the orchestra. The conductor stands up in front of the band, the only member of the orchestra who does not play."

In 1964 Steinberg received an honorary doctorate of music from Duquesne University.

He is survived by a son, Arthur; a daughter, Mrs. Silvia Tennenbaum; and five grandchildren.

TUESDAY, MARCH 9, 1993

Billy Eckstine, 78
Jazz Vocalist and Trombonist
By Ernie Hoffman, *Pittsburgh Post-Gazette*

Billy Eckstine, the Pittsburgh-born singer and jazz trombonist whose romantic ballads made him one of America's most popular vocalists of the post–World War II era, died of cardiac arrest yesterday morning in Montefiore University Hospital. He had entered the hospital about a month ago after complaining of chest pain.

Since July, Mr. Eckstine, age 78, had been staying with a niece, Carole A. Watson, and her husband, Common Pleas Judge J. Warren Watson, at their home in Schenley Heights.

Mr. Eckstine had an aneurysm of the heart that resulted in clots that caused two strokes, Judge Watson said. The first occurred in April shortly after he had performed in Salina, Kansas.

Eckstine was known as "the Great Mr. B," and his long list of hits from 1945 to 1951 included "Fools Rush In," "Everything I Have Is Yours," "A Cottage for Sale," "Prisoner of Love," "I Surrender, Dear," "Blue Moon," "My Foolish Heart," "Caravan," "Body and Soul," and "I Apologize." In all, he had 11 gold records.

Singer Nancy Wilson said Mr. Eckstine was a warm man who overcame racial stereotypes to succeed. "He was a man of great character, of courage. He came along at a time when it was difficult to survive. His blackness kept him from being as big as he could have been," Wilson said.

Nevertheless, he was one of the country's most popular vocalists in the late 1940s and early 1950s and was the first black singer to become a national sex symbol.

Mr. Eckstine appeared on the cover of Life magazine, and he was a role model for youths, black and white alike. Many young men in the 1950s emulated his style of clothing, including the rolled-up "Mr. B" shirt collar and jacket draped off the body.

"The most important thing to me as a jazz musician is that Billy Eckstine, from a historical point of view, had one of the most revolutionary big bands in jazz," said Nathan Davis, a saxophonist who is professor of music and director of jazz studies at the University of Pittsburgh.

"There were four big bands that changed jazz—Earl "Fatha" Hines, Billy Eckstine, Dizzy Gillespie, and Woody Herman," Davis said. "[Mr. Eckstine] had

Billy Eckstine performs at the 1986 Pittsburgh Jazz Festival, which was dedicated to him that year. *Photo by Bill Wade.*

all those great innovators who left their marks in jazz."

In his band at one time or another were Gillespie, Fats Navarro, Miles Davis,

Gene Ammons, Dexter Gordon, Charlie Parker, Sonny Stitt, Art Blakey, Lucky Thompson, and Sarah Vaughan.

"As a vocalist...he was—and most people will say this—in the same class as Sinatra and Tony Bennett," Nathan Davis said. Davis, who last performed with Mr. Eckstine last year, said the Pitt Jazz Seminar in November was dedicated to Mr. Eckstine and Gillespie, but that both were unable to attend to accept plaques prepared for them.

Mike Taylor of Bridgewater in Beaver County was Mr. Eckstine's bass player in Pittsburgh for 12 years. He said Mr. Eckstine was a "true artist who meant everything" to jazz. "Everybody who came up in that era came through him."

Mr. Eckstine, born William Clarence Eckstine on July 8, 1914, was raised in East Liberty and graduated from Peabody High School. He first sang publicly at a church bazaar when he was 11. Seven years later his singing was good enough for second prize in a Washington, D.C., amateur show. A week later, he won the first prize by singing "Stardust." He went to New York to compete for the grand prize in the contest and won it by singing the same song, beating out a young female vocalist named Ella Fitzgerald.

He started working smaller night clubs and in 1940 joined Hines's orchestra, sharing the singing chores with Vaughan for a while. During his four years with Hines he recorded "Skylark," his first big hit.

Mr. Eckstine, whose instrumental specialty was valve trombone, put his own band together in June 1944 with the help of Hines, Count Basie, and Duke Ellington. It was the first bebop band. A few years later, however, the band was beset by financial problems, and Eckstine decided to concentrate on vocals. In 1948 he began to string together hits like "Caravan," "A New Shade of Blue," "Temptation," and others.

Despite his advancing age, Mr. Eckstine continued to perform until suffering his first stroke. He was featured in July 1991 along with Freddie Hubbard, Stanley Turrentine, and Nancy Wilson in a concert billed as a "jazz explosion" at Hartwood Acres in Hampton. The event drew a crowd of 10,000.

The East Liberty Chamber of Commerce saluted Mr. Eckstine at a homecoming celebration October 6, 1991, in East Liberty Presbyterian Church, at which his good friend and fellow jazz musician Jerry Betters also performed. That was his last public appearance here.

He is survived by two ex-wives, June and Carolle; seven children, Kenny, Ronnie, Billy Jr., Ed, Guy, Charlotte Carolle, and Gina; four grandchildren; and a great-grandchild.

SUNDAY, OCTOBER 13, 1996

Johnny Costa, 74
Musical Director of Mr. Rogers' Neighborhood

By Timothy McNulty, *Pittsburgh Post-Gazette*. Staff writer Mike Bucsko contributed to this report.

When pianist Johnny Costa, the longtime musical director of *Mister Rogers' Neighborhood*, went into the studio to record a Christmas album last fall, he had been sick with aplastic anemia for six years. Studio engineers looked at the man, frail with a blood disease, and wondered if he could still play.

One session he began playing "Christmas Time Is Here," the theme of the *A Charlie Brown Christmas* cartoon special. Then he bridged into the Charlie Brown theme music and from there to "O Christmas Tree" because he somehow knew that the Christmas special was about finding a tree. Finally he went into Beethoven's "Ode to Joy"—because Schroeder, the pianist in the *Peanuts* gang, was, of course, a big Beethoven fan.

The engineers were amazed. Costa, the consummate improviser and student of music, hadn't even planned to do the song—he made it up as he went along. And in one take.

The New Kensington native, age 74, died of aplastic anemia Friday afternoon at Longwood at Oakmont Health Center, said his brother, Alex Costanza.

Costa collaborated with Fred Rogers for 31 years. "I saw him a couple days before he died, and he remembered so many of the songs that we did together," Rogers said yesterday. During the visit

Costa repeated to Rogers a line from an opera they did together called *A Granddad for Daniel*: "The darkest hour comes before the dawn."

"He had some dark hours just before he died. He had a good deal of pain," Rogers said. "But now he has his dawn, his eternal dawn, and he certainly deserves it."

Costa was born January 18, 1922, in Arnold, a small town near New Kensington. His father, an Italian immigrant, didn't want his son to follow him into the coal mines, where he worked. So when Johnny showed promise as a musician at age 10, his father sold his house to buy a $500 accordion.

Though he was good at the instrument, it was too heavy for him to carry. After Arnold High School music teacher Frank Oliver watched Johnny's father carrying the accordion for his son during a high school assembly, he told the youngster to try piano.

Costa played with a New York City band for a year after high school but returned to Pittsburgh after the bombing of Pearl Harbor. He got married to Helen Zamperini then went to war. He spent three years in Europe, landing with the 90th Division on Normandy. After the war, he went to Carnegie Tech (now Carnegie Mellon University) and studied music composition.

Guitarist Joe Negri met Costa 40 years ago on a KDKA radio broadcast and went to the school on Costa's suggestion. He said a music composition instructor there referred to Costa as "the savage" because "he had this kind of wild streak in him, a totally uninhibited way of playing and writing."

Costa went into TV after college. He played piano for a small station called WDTV, which was bought by KDKA in 1951. He hosted his own show on the network, *The Wonder World of Johnny Costa*, and played a piano-playing character called Indian Mary on the children's show *Funsville.*

Costa was also on the road at the time, playing with his trio and appearing several times on *The Tonight Show* with Steve Allen.

Jazz pianist Walt Harper said jazz greats Duke Ellington, Count Basie, and Cannonball Adderley would frequently ask him what Costa was up to. Ellington once sneaked into New York's Embers club to hear Costa play, Harper said, and left shaking his head.

Fred Rogers asked him to arrange, conduct, and play music for his new children's show in 1965.

"At first I thought, 'A children's show?' But I started to realize the worth of this man and this program," Costa told the *Pittsburgh Post-Gazette*'s Nancy Anderson last year.

Rogers would usually suggest a line of melody or some chords, people familiar with the show said, and Costa would take it from there. He never looked at the piano keys—he'd wear headphones, look at a TV monitor, and make up the music as he went along.

Bobby Rawsthorne, who has played percussion and vibraphone on *Neighborhood* since 1970, said the tune at the end of the show, which Costa, Rawsthorne, and bassist Carl McVicker played under the credits, was never the same. "It sounded like we rehearsed this for a week, but we didn't for a minute," Rawsthorne said. "It was completely spontaneous."

"Any musician who ever worked with him or listened to him would tell you the same thing—they shared a common idea that nobody can play like this guy," he said.

Musicians marveled at Costa's quick hands, particularly his left-hand stride, which could hit bottom bass notes and chords in time, freeing up his right hand to embellish notes on top. His fingers reached across 13 keys.

Harper remembered getting ready for a duet he was about to play with Costa on KDKA and worrying about the pianist's quick style. "I told him my style was more laid back and asked him to play some blues," Harper said. "We hit a hell of a groove. He came up to me after we were done and said 'I like that laid back stuff—I think I'll stay away from going all over the keys.'"

"I hope Pittsburghers realize what a gem they had among them," Harper said.

Costa was sitting in the green room at the Manchester Craftsmen's Guild in December waiting for Marion McPartland to perform. McPartland, host of National Public Radio's *Piano Jazz* show, a concert pianist and recording artist, asked Costa to come on stage. Costa walked on, to a standing ovation, thinking he would sit at the piano with

McPartland. She told him to sit by himself. "I want to watch you play," she said.

"He was a combination of a jazz musician and storyteller," she said yesterday. "He had a very fleet, elegant style but sublimated all those things to be whatever he had to be for the show—a butterfly, someone in big boots, an elephant. Not everyone can do that."

Tony Mowad, jazz host on WDUQ and president and founder of the Pittsburgh Jazz Society, said Costa "had the capabilities of performing any kind of music" and called Costa's solo piano recordings "among the most unique piano CDs in the world."

"He was one of the most kindest and gentlest persons you'd want to meet," Mowad continued. "He would think nothing of devoting his time and talent to help other musicians."

"He always paid me more than what we'd agreed on," Rawsthorne said, "or he'd be sending you notes saying how well you'd played."

Costa wasn't only admired by other musicians. Former Republican National Committee chairwoman Elsie Hillman, a friend of Costa's for 30 years, often had him play at parties. She called his music "unbelievably beautiful."

"We gave him to ourselves for birthday and anniversary presents," Hillman said yesterday. "He was so at ease at the piano, he set everyone else at ease."

Len Meledandri, Costa's assistant for 17 years and the voice of Prince Tuesday on *Neighborhood*, said Costa didn't know where his song ideas came from. He thought his talent was simply God-given. "Where did that come from?" Meledandri would hear Costa say after getting up from the piano. "Wasn't that wonderful?"

Costa is survived by his wife, Helen; a son, John Costa of Lower Burrell; a daughter, Deborah Elwood of Fox Chapel; two brothers, Alex Costanza of Apollo and Victor Costanza of Washington Township; two sisters, Clara Nelson of New Kensington and Viola Marino of California; and four grandsons.

WEDNESDAY, SEPTEMBER 13, 2000

Stanley Turrentine, 66
Hill District–Born Jazz Giant
By Rick Nowlin, *Pittsburgh Post-Gazette*

Jazz giant Stanley Turrentine, the tenor saxophonist who grew up in the Hill District and whose hit "Sugar" established him in the popular mainstream, died in Manhattan yesterday after suffering a stroke. His agent, Robin Burgess, said Mr. Turrentine died at a Manhattan hospital two days after he was stricken.

Jack Kreisberg, a friend, said Mr. Turrentine collapsed at a hotel Sunday evening, just hours before he was to close

Stanely Turrentine. *Photo by V.W.H. Campbell Jr.*

out a week-long engagement at the famed Blue Note jazz club in New York City. He was rushed to New York Weill Cornell Center of New York Presbyterian Hospital, where he had a second stroke early Monday morning, Kreisberg said.

Mr. Turrentine was 66 and lived in Fort Washington, Maryland, outside Washington, D.C.

He often blurred boundaries with his saxophone playing, mixing jazz with blues, rock, rhythm and blues, and pop. "His impact on jazz was just astonishing," Burgess said.

Another in a long line of Pittsburgh jazz musicians who would embrace the international stage, Mr. Turrentine began playing saxophone at the age of

11, following in the footsteps of his sax-playing father. His late brother Tommy, who played trumpet, became a jazz star in his own right.

He was surrounded by music growing up. The piano player Ahmad Jamal lived nearby and often visited to practice on the Turrentine family's upright piano. Mr Turrentine and his brother Tommy played at the Perry Bar in Pittsburgh, their first professional gig, while they were still in high school.

Mr. Turrentine's first professional gig took place with Lowell Fulsom's blues band, which included a blind pianist named Ray Charles. "I guess my sound started back then," Turrentine said. "I couldn't avoid the blues."

Mr. Turrentine received his big break when drummer Max Roach's band fell apart while touring Pittsburgh in 1958. Roach ended up hiring both Turrentine brothers.

And Mr. Turrentine never abandoned his Pittsburgh roots. One of his albums from the mid-1980s, *La Place*, was named for a Hill District street, and in the credits he mentioned the names of several dozen people, some of them musicians he grew up with.

"He was one of the great tenors of our time—he was as big in the 1950s and 1960s as he is today," said pianist and bandleader Walt Harper. "He mesmerized you…. He would blow everybody off the stand when he was playing, but his style endured time. He had a style that everyone enjoyed."

In 1970 Mr. Turrentine, then recording for Creed Taylor International Records, released the album *Sugar*. Not only did the title track become a major hit, but it also introduced the music world to several up-and-coming musicians, such as bassist Ron Carter, trumpeter Freddie Hubbard, and especially guitarist and fellow Hill District–native George Benson.

Mr. Turrentine also enjoyed a sterling reputation among his peers in the jazz world. Marty Ashby, executive producer of the Manchester Craftsman's Guild jazz concerts, called Mr. Turrentine "one of the greatest musicians in the history of jazz…every single tenor saxophonist that is out there playing today has some Stanley Turrentine in them. That's the kind of impact that Stanley has. You can listen to the young lions, to the Michael Breckers of the world, and say, 'Ah, that's T—that's Stanley coming out.'"

Mr. Turrentine went solo in the 1960s. His blues-influenced riffs brought him commercial success with albums such as *Stan "the Man" Turrentine*, *Up at Minton's*, and *Never Let Me Go*.

He said he preferred mixing genres to being boxed in by one label. "One day my stepson and I were alphabetizing my albums over the years, and I noticed that they categorized me as a rock-and-roll player on certain albums, a bebop player on other albums, a pop player, a fusion player," he once said. "And I'm just saying, 'Gee, I'm just playing with different settings, but I'm still playing the same way.'"

SUNDAY, MAY 13, 2001

Perry Como, 88
Never Forgot His Roots
By Jonathan D. Silver and Mark Belko, *Pittsburgh Post-Gazette*

In Canonsburg, the barbershop where Perry Como got his start was located in a building owned by Mike Pihakis that also housed a Greek coffee shop. One day when Como was still a teenager he got a rude shock: the barber had died.

"[Como] came to work the next day, and my dad said, 'Perry, this is your shop now. You're on your own,'" Mike Pihakis's son, Manuel, recalled last night just hours after the crooner's death.

Greek grooms who stopped in at the barbershop for a shave and haircut followed tradition and gave the young Como a gold coin. "He got rich," Pihakis said. "He used to take the money home, and his parents thought he was a millionaire."

It wasn't Como who got rich, though. It was his friends back home, all the people in Canonsburg he never forgot.

Years after leaving the barber's life, when Como's celebrity was soaring, he returned to Canonsburg in a limousine and called on Mike Pihakis. "He picked him up for a ride, and he couldn't believe it," said Frank Sarris, the owner of Sarris Candies and a longtime friend of Como's.

These days, everyone would believe it. Perry Como might have been an internationally acclaimed entertainer, but to his friends and family back home, he forever remained a down-to-earth, humble man who treated everyone with respect.

Canonsburg mayor Anthony Colaizzo called Como an "ordinary guy" who never forgot his roots, even with his fame and stardom. "He was Mr. Canonsburg himself because he never forgot where he came from. He gave inspiration to many people in Canonsburg," Colaizzo said. "He never forgot Canonsburg. When people asked where he was from, he didn't say Pittsburgh. He said he was from Canonsburg."

Friends and family contacted last night repeated the same types of stories over and over, stories about a man who would publicly welcome old friends from Canonsburg when they caught one of his shows in Las Vegas or shoot the breeze about hometown happenings well into his twilight years or take relatives' children to Dairy Queen when he was in town.

"All you had to do was mention Canonsburg, and he greeted you with open arms. He never forgot his roots," Pihakis said.

Como had been ailing for some time, but those close to him said he had never been the same since his wife of 65 years, Roselle, died in 1998. A short time later, Como suffered another blow when his sister, Venzie Jakubetz, passed away.

"We loved him very much. He was a good guy. He was very true to everybody. He missed his wife a lot," said Como's niece, Shirley Liapes, age 67, of Canonsburg. "I talked to his daughter tonight. He had asked for a glass of water, and when they brought it to him he said he didn't want it and he died," Liapes continued. "She said it was very peaceful."

One McKeesport resident who got to know Como was Samuel R. LaRosa, who founded the LaRosa Boys and Girls Club of McKeesport with the singer's help. LaRosa, age 88, said he called Como out of the blue one day nearly 50 years ago to tell him that he liked the way he sang. It started a lifelong friendship.

When LaRosa put together a boxing show in 1956 to raise money for his club, Como lent his support by attending. LaRosa said his presence helped to increase attendance and to raise more money. Como, he said, also sent two autographed photos to the head of the G.C. Murphy Co., whose financial support LaRosa needed for his club. While the help was nice, the thing LaRosa remembers most about Como was his way with people. He last talked to him about a year ago. "He was like a next-door neighbor. He was an easygoing fellow and very congenial. He made you feel as if—well, to me, he made me feel like a relative, to tell you the truth," he said. "Like I say, he was a good man. He was really a good buddy. I don't think they come like him anymore. That's how close he made you feel."

Victor Maffio, age 78, also considered himself part of Como's family.

He said his older brother and Como were inseparable growing up together. As a little boy, he idolized Como. "He came and he ate in our home. He'd come into the house and have old-fashioned Italian dinners with us," Maffio said. "He'd wrap his arms around my neck and give me one of those knuckle rubs. I'd kick him in the shins."

When he grew up and went off to Europe to fight in World War II, Maffio said he looked for any opportunity to hear his friend Como on the radio. "Anytime I got a chance to get to a canteen or a Red Cross setup, if I could catch Perry on the radio, I would," Maffio said. "I loved him. I just thought the world of him."

Around that time, recalled Madaline Mazza, another Como niece in Canonsburg, Como's father went to the movies to see his son act in either *Something for the Boys* or *Doll Face*— she can't remember which. "My grandfather saw Perry kiss the girl in the movie, and he walked out. He said, 'Is that how he's making his money?' He just thought that was terrible. You see, Perry was married."

Como's father needn't have worried. Those close to the singer said his wife meant everything to him. The Reverend Ralph Volpe, age 64, pastor of Central Assembly of God Church in Houston, Pennsylvania, believes Como never recovered from her death. "His memory of his wife was so important. He was grieving. I think he never really did get over that," Volpe said. "His health faded very quickly since her death."

The last time Volpe saw Como was in November during a trip to visit his children. Volpe said he stayed in a mobile home about 300 yards from Como's home. "Perry to me was quite a gentleman. He was never cocky or smart-alecky. He always had a deep respect for whoever he was talking to," Volpe said. "That's what we respected most about him. He was just a Canonsburg hometown guy all the time."

Volpe was one of a number of Canonsburg-area residents who worked to erect a life-size statue of Como in Canonsburg, which was unveiled May 15, 1999. Como couldn't make the trip because of a bronchial ailment. He never saw the statue in person, but watched a videotape of the celebration. In the end, however, Como struggled even with the video.

"You could see that he would not remember much. We would show him the video of the dedication of the statue, and he just would say humbly, 'My, oh my, they did that for me,'" Volpe said.

The statue wasn't the only honor Canonsburg bestowed upon Como. Third Street was renamed Perry Como Avenue on August 24, 1977.

Ask anybody from Canonsburg, though, and they'll likely tell you that it was Como who bestowed honor on the town, not just by putting it on the map, but by merely being himself. "He was just like an ordinary guy," said Colaizzo, the mayor. "He was a gentleman. His stardom never went to his head."

SUNDAY, SEPTEMBER 30, 2001

Nicholas P. Lomakin, 84
Dean of Dixieland Jazz
By Jeffrey Cohan, *Pittsburgh Post-Gazette*

As he has done many times before, local musician Denny Kurzawski will sub for his mentor, Nicholas P. Lomakin, at a gig today. But this will be the last time Kurzawski ever fills in for the man who pushed him to succeed in music and in life. Mr. Lomakin, long regarded as the dean of Dixieland jazz musicians in Pittsburgh, died Friday after a 12-year fight with prostate cancer. He was 84.

Still performing until his last days, Mr. Lomakin was booked for a private party at PNC Park today. In taking his place, Kurzawski will perform with the same clarinet that Mr. Lomakin played as a Carnegie Institute of Technology student in the 1930s. "He would want me to do a good, happy job," Kurzawski said. "It's very difficult to do."

For Mr. Lomakin, the party at PNC Park would have added another line to a musical resume that spans eight decades. A tenor saxophonist who also excelled on the flute and clarinet, he played in bands backing Frank Sinatra, Henry Mancini, and Judy Garland. He also led his own bands, including Nick

Lomakin and his Riverboat Six and Nick Lomakin and the Dixie Flyers. In the 1940s he arranged the music for KDKA radio's weekly *Memories Show*.

"He was a great musician," said drummer Bobby Rawsthorne, who played on *Mr. Rogers' Neighborhood* for 30 years.

Vince Lascheid, longtime organist for the Penguins and Pirates, played piano in a band with Mr. Lomakin in the Westin William Penn's Terrace Room during the 1980s and 1990s. "He loved to play. Music was his profession. That's it," Lascheid said. "I don't think he could drive a nail."

Mr. Lomakin, of Glenshaw, was as well-known for his music stores as for his concert performances. He ran stores in the Pittsburgh area for more than 40 years, finally closing his signature location at 633 Liberty Avenue Downtown in 1984. "We used to go there almost every week [in the 1940s] to purchase 78s," said Danny Kohn, a trumpet player. "He had all of the latest records. One week it would be Dizzy Gillespie, next week it would be Charlie Parker."

Mr. Lomakin hired young musicians to work as clerks in his stores, giving them the means to support themselves as they honed their skills. "He'd go out of his way to help anyone he felt was a talented player," Kurzawski said.

Kurzawski was a South Side kid with a bleak future when he first walked into one of Mr. Lomakin's stores in 1967. Mr. Lomakin recognized the youth's musical ability and prodded him to try out for the Tamburitzans, Duquesne University's renowned folk ensemble. Kurzawski not only made the cut, he received a full scholarship, without which he could not have afforded college.

"Nick was my life," Kurzawski said. "If not for him, nothing would have ever happened to me."

The son of a Russian Orthodox priest, Mr. Lomakin grew up on Pittsburgh's north side playing the violin, pushed by his mother to practice and practice.

In college he switched to wind instruments and studied teaching and music at the Carnegie Institute of Technology. While still in college he taught music at the old Fifth Avenue High School. One of his students, Erroll Garner, would grow up to be a legendary jazz pianist.

In 1938, a year before he graduated, he played in a college band on a trans-Atlantic cruise ship. When they arrived in Europe, he and some fellow band members bicycled across France, Germany, and Italy. "He remembered seeing that everyone was in denial over there," said Judith Dodd, of Allison Park, one of his two daughters. "Nobody seemed concerned about what was going on in Nazi Germany."

After college, Mr. Lomakin played in bands but supported his family by teaching music, briefly in West Virginia and then for a few years at Avonworth High School. He eventually left teaching to devote more of his time to his music stores, opening his first at 422 Wood Street Downtown.

Running the stores allowed Mr. Lomakin to keep current with musical trends. In 1987, during the era of New Wave music, he told the *Pittsburgh Press*, "I like the new beats and the brass lines and the synthesizer. The sounds of some of the new rock tunes are terrific."

But more recently, rap and hip-hop music, with their ultra-simple or even nonexistent melodies, did not appeal to him. "He would have told you that there is not much [in today's music] that is going to live on," Dodd said. "He was glad he went out of the [music store] business before he had to see that."

Mr. Lomakin was preceded in death by his wife, Vi Burger Lomakin. Besides his daughter Judith Dodd, he is survived by another daughter, Patricia Lomakin of Glenshaw; a brother, Michael Lomakin of Green Tree; two grandchildren; and two great-grandchildren.

FRIDAY, AUGUST 2, 2002

Leonard Litman, 88
Colorful Nightclub Owner

By Christopher Rawson, *Pittsburgh Post-Gazette*. *Post-Gazette* staff writer Nate Guidry contributed to this report.

Leonard Litman, age 88, one of the most influential and colorful figures of the 20th-century Pittsburgh entertainment scene, died Wednesday of Parkinson's disease.

Best known as owner-producer of Lenny Litman's Copa, the high profile nightclub that flourished here between 1948 and 1959, the man almost everyone called Lenny spent most of his life producing, promoting, or writing about show biz. As local correspondent for *Variety*, he kept Pittsburgh on the national entertainment map, and he even made a brief foray into professional sports.

"He was a Damon Runyon character," said his longtime friend Jason Shapiro, who copromoted concerts with him. "He was up all night and slept most of the day. He was totally involved in show business."

"Lenny was a friend to entertainers,"

said trumpeter Danny Conn. "Between the Copa and the Encore, I think he brought every major act to Pittsburgh, from Miles Davis to Billie Holiday."

Mr. Litman shared his own professional summary in 1985 with the *Post-Gazette Dossier*, saying, "I had the most success promoting rock shows and the roller derby. The biggest bombs were the Pittsburgh Rens and Charles Laughton."

Born Norman Leonard Litman on May 15, 1914, in North Braddock, the son of immigrants from Eastern Europe, he began his career in 1931 covering high school sports for the *Braddock Daily News Herald*, the *Pittsburgh Press*, and *Pittsburgh Sun Telegraph*.

After graduating from Braddock High School in 1932, he went on to Shenandoah College and the University of Richmond before graduating from the University of Pittsburgh in 1937.

A story he wrote about cowboy entertainer Hoot Gibson led to a long, sometimes uproarious relationship as Gibson's press agent, promoter, trouble-shooter, and pal. It took him to Hollywood, where he worked as press agent and promoter for boxers, several small circuses, and a donkeyball troupe. Mr. Litman was signed to a boxing contract himself, but returned his $1,000 retainer when he was knocked out in the first round of his first fight.

In the midst of all this, he put in one year at the University of Pittsburgh Law School, then produced the Hoot Gibson Rodeo and Thrill Circus. It folded after playing Homestead and North Braddock. Mr. Litman's brother Archie paid off the cowboys and Indians and Gibson's hotel bill at Webster Hall.

His show business career was interrupted in 1941, when Mr. Litman enlisted in the navy, serving until 1945. He returned to Pittsburgh and, with the help of his brothers Archie and Eugene, bought Mercur's Music Bar. From 1945 to 1948, Mercur's presented the most important jazz in Pittsburgh. Among the performers were Art Tatum, Erroll Garner, Ethel Waters, Reid Jaynes, George Shearing, Mary Lou Williams, and Walt Harper.

But it was the Copa, at 818 Liberty Avenue, just down from the Nixon Theater, and right across from its competitor, the Carousel, that became the acme of Pittsburgh's nightlife.

Mr. Litman and his brothers bought the old Villa Madrid in 1948 and turned it into the Copa. Almost by accident, it opened with Frankie Laine, a big recording star, but not known as a nightclub act. He did huge business, so Mr. Litman took a chance on Vic Damone and then Ella Fitzgerald. Their success convinced him to follow the pop charts, a policy new to nightclubs.

He also had an eye for unknowns, and he was nicknamed "Options" for signing newcomers to contracts that gave him the right to bring them back repeatedly at low rates after they became famous.

The Copa's seating capacity was 287, but it could squeeze in a lot more when the fire marshal wasn't looking. There were three shows a night, Monday through Saturday.

Among the Copa's headliners: Johnny Mathis, Ella Fitzgerald, Cab Calloway, Mel Torme, Conway Twitty, Patti Page, Andy Williams, Count Basie, Duke Ellington, Woody Herman, Henny Youngman, Pearl Bailey, Johnnie Ray, Rudy Vallee, Artie Shaw, Bela Lugosi, Marty Allen, Lili St. Cyr, Buck & Bubbles, Bill Haley's Comets, Al Hibbler, and Miles Davis.

Mr. Litman wouldn't book Lenny Bruce because he thought Bruce's act was too dirty (although Bruce's mother, comic Sally Marr, played the club). He did help Bruce get other local work, though, when he was stuck in Pittsburgh during his wife's convalescence from a car accident.

Litman wasn't infallible: he passed on Elvis back when Presley still was affordable.

At midnight on New Year's Eve, 1959, the Copa closed its doors forever. The times they were a-changing. Acts that previously had played for $1,000 a week were now getting fees in five figures, and Mr. Litman's options were running out.

Over the years, he also shared ownership of a half-dozen more clubs and lounges.

"When I met him it was in the late 1950s, and he was at the pinnacle of his career," said 83-year-old drummer William Condeluci. "It's funny now, but I remember one day he had a fistfight with a drummer named Billy Marracano at the old musicians union on Penn Avenue. I don't believe any punches that landed were of any consequence."

In 1960 Mr. Litman and his brothers tried to get a Pittsburgh franchise in the National Basketball Association. Rebuffed, they applied to Abe Saperstein's fledgling American Basketball League, where the three-point line was born. They named their team the Rens after the Pittsburgh Renaissance. Their chief asset was Connie Hawkins, who was a skinny, wide-eyed 19-year-old when Mr. Litman signed him in 1961.

Hawkins had been implicated in a point-shaving scandal a year earlier as a freshman at Iowa State University and returned in disgrace to his home in the Bedford-Stuyvesant section of Brooklyn. Although he has always insisted he was innocent, he had been barred from college athletics and the NBA.

Mr. Litman showed up at Hawkins's home unannounced but armed with a contract and came back to Pittsburgh with Hawkins, a 6'9" forward with the peripheral vision of an eagle and hands the size of serving plates. The Hawk immediately became one of the short-lived league's dominant players. Some ABL club-owners protested that his signing violated league rules because his college class had not yet graduated and because of his alleged role in rigging games.

But Saperstein ruled Hawkins eligible. Hawkins went on to star in the American Basketball Association and then, after the ban on him was overturned in court, in the NBA.

Hawkins was one of the few Pittsburghers who didn't call him Lenny. He called him Dad. Hawkins said yesterday from Phoenix, where he now works in the front office of the NBA's Suns, "Lenny [and his family] took me under their wings. I've gone to all their funerals and bar mitzvahs. I'm family."

Mr. Litman had started promoting concert attractions in the 1950s. After the Copa closed, he started using every available space to present new talent in concert: West View Park (the Rolling Stones); Syria Mosque (Peter, Paul, and Mary; Bob Dylan; the Band; The Kingston Trio; Mort Sahl); Soldiers & Sailors Memorial Hall (Newport Jazz Festival); Carnegie Music Hall (Brenda Lee); Civic Arena (Harry Belafonte, Sammy Davis Jr.); Loews Penn Theater (Joan Baez, Jefferson Airplane, Ann Corio in *This Is Burlesque*). He continued to produce concerts through the 1970s.

"All through that period we were doing different things," Shapiro recalled. "We brought the Bolshoi Ballet to the Civic Arena and the event was black-tie, first class."

With the national tour of *Hello, Dolly!* starring Carol Channing at the Stanley, Shapiro said, "We played a full month, and it was the biggest hit to come to Pittsburgh."

Working with various other partners, he also produced concerts in a number of other cities, from Cleveland westward to St. Louis and as far afield as Albuquerque, New Mexico.

Shows Inc., which he started with Hy Kotofsky in 1958, built Valley Cable TV Co. in Turtle Creek, the first cable company in Allegheny County. Mr. Litman sold his share of the company in 1978.

Although his journalistic experience helped him as a promoter and publicist, the reverse was also true. Mr. Litman developed a high-profile career as a show-biz reporter. He was the Pittsburgh correspondent for *Billboard* magazine from 1948 until 1960. Then Harold V. Cohen, columnist and critic for the *Post-Gazette*, picked Mr. Litman to succeed him as the correspondent for *Variety*, where for 30 years Litman covered the Pittsburgh entertainment scene, reviewing everyone from Ben Vereen to Philip Glass.

His taste was eclectic. Although he loved the music of Chet Baker and Miles Davis, he also appreciated and reviewed Glass's abstract modern music. His daughter, Rebecca Litman, remembers going to a *Saturday Night Live* taping where Glass was featured and meeting comedian Dennis Miller, who told her that her father had authored his first review in *Variety*.

"I've known him for more than 40 years," said 74-year-old trombonist Harold Betters. "He helped contribute to the careers of probably every artist of my generation, both local and national. When an artist came to Pittsburgh, Lenny was the man making it happen."

From 1970 to 1984 Mr. Litman wrote a nightlife column for the *Pittsburgh Press*, giving support to smaller clubs and new talent. He was passionate about the entertainment scene which he had helped to build and was proud that he never wrote a mean word about anyone in his column.

He is survived by his wife of 55 years, Rosslyn Leiber Litman; his daughter; his sister, Ruth Litman; and his brother, Eugene. A son, David, died in 1993.

On the Air, Stage, and Screen

The life of this city is not played out only on its Downtown streets, in its Oakland classrooms, in its Shadyside boutiques, in its South Side tattoo parlors. The life of this city is also played out on its stages—Downtown, Uptown, all around the town. It's no surprise that Pittsburgh, a city of drama, has produced dramas and actors and performances well out of proportion to its population. All the world, or at least our world, is a stage.

SATURDAY, FEBRUARY 3, 1996

Gene Kelly, 83
A Life of Amazing Grace

By Christopher Rawson, *Pittsburgh Post-Gazette*. *Post-Gazette* staff writers Barbara Vancheri, Mike Pellegrini, and Jane Crawford contributed to this report.

Gene Kelly. *Photo by V.W.H Campbell Jr.*

"I've gone through four deaths in a year," said Gene Kelly's "baby brother" Fred, age 79, from his home in Tucson, Arizona. Sister Louise's husband Bill Bailey died last May in Pittsburgh, Fred's wife Dorothy died last March, and sister J's husband died last year. Brother James had already died a couple of years ago. And now Gene.

"I'm at that age when I hate to open the mail," Fred said. But Louise is well in Dothan, Alabama, near her daughter, and J (really Harriet) is doing fine in Fort Lauderdale, Florida—"she swims, in-line roller skates, plays bridge, and she's seven years older than me. But don't call her—she'll break up."

Fred himself is a flowing fount of memory: "All you have to do is say hello to me, and I'm off."

His own career followed closely behind Gene's. They all started as the Five Little Kellys in imitation of the Seven Little Foys. Of the five, James went to Carnegie Tech and the others to Pitt. Fred followed Gene as director of Tech's Scotch and Soda Show and at the Pittsburgh Playhouse.

Fred even took over Gene's Broadway role in *The Time of Your Life* and did the tour—"I played the Nixon, but everyone thinks they saw Gene because they used his picture with my name!" The balance was righted when Gene's *For Me and My Gal* played Pittsburgh, and for a week the movie marquee mistakenly listed Judy Garland and Fred Kelly.

Jeanne Coyne, Gene's second wife, had been Fred's dance student in Pittsburgh. Fred's New York apartment "was where she first met Gene as a grownup," he said. "*Deep in My Heart* in 1955 was the only picture where we danced together," he mused.

The memories of Gene Kelly are thick throughout his hometown, where he is memorialized many times. In 1981 he became honorary chairman of the Civic Light Opera. South Whitfield Street in his home neighborhood of East Liberty was named Gene Kelly Square in 1987. That same year he was given a bicentennial medal by Pitt. But his living memorial is the Gene Kelly Awards, started by the CLO in 1991 to honor excellence in high school musicals.

At the Pitt ceremony, Kelly spoke to those who asked why he "wasted" four dancing years in college: "It not only made me more of a person, but it aided me in everything I did as a creative artist." He quipped that his economics degree allowed him "to discuss intelligently certain things with the IRS."

At the East Liberty dedication, Mayor Caliguiri filled in for the absent Kelly by opening an umbrella and imitating the famous routine from *Singin' in the Rain*.

In 1981 he came to accept his honors from the CLO at a ceremony in Mellon Square presided over by Bob Prince. Bill Copeland, CLO board member, recalls Kelly's one stipulation was that he not be asked to dance with anyone, "because I hate to say no, but then I have to dance with everyone."

Nonetheless, he did dance with a slight, white-haired woman at that noontime rally. Anne Greenberg beamed at him, holding tight to a thin blue program from a children's dance recital held on April 13, 1932, by Beth Shalom Temple.

Roz Litman, wife of longtime local club owner and *Variety* correspondent Lenny Litman, remembers Greenberg, now age 98, had been in charge of hiring a dancing teacher for Beth Shalom and she chose Kelly. She didn't know she was making a lifetime friend. "He sent her a birthday card every year and he also wrote a beautiful letter on her 90th birthday, when her daughter gave her a big party at the Hilton," Litman said.

Litman has her own story of crossing paths with Kelly. About eight years ago she was visiting a friend in California, and they were en route to the Friars Club for lunch. They came upon a parade of vintage cars with Kelly as grand marshal. No wallflower, Litman waved and called out, "I'm the delegation from Squirrel Hill. Mrs. Greenberg sends her love." Litman said Kelly stopped the car and got out. "He was so sweet—just a darling man."

The CLO's Bill Thunhurst has an earlier Kelly story. When he was a chorus boy in *South Pacific* he met Kelly to audition for *On the Town*. "No, you're too good-looking," Kelly told him. "That was the nicest and swiftest brush-off I've ever had," Thunhurst laughed.

Al Checco, a fellow East Liberty native a decade Kelly's junior, remembers playing amateur contests in movie houses. "Gene, Fred, and his sister had a wonderful act where they did a dance on roller skates, going up and down steps. I had to follow that act as a four- or five-year-old kid, singing 'Brother Can You Spare a Dime!' He taught me how to take a bow. There was an ovation,

and I wanted to run out, but he said, 'Hold it, kid. Let 'em want you more.'"

Presented a 1985 Life Achievement Award by the American Film Institute, Gene Kelly said, "All I wanted was to play shortstop for the Pittsburgh Pirates." Instead, he went "screaming and kicking" to dance lessons. Then at 14, "I discovered the girls liked the fellows who were good dancers."

Kelly once told the *Post-Gazette*'s George Anderson, "I don't like social dancing because it was a form of courtship in my day.… It was the only time a fellow could put his arm around a girl's waist. Now if I get up on the floor to dance, people move away to watch. Forget it. If you want to watch, pay me."

Bob Miller remembered meeting Kelly at age 10 at a camp near Ashtabula, Ohio, where Kelly, 20, was a counselor. "I came back and had two years at his dancing school. I danced with Gene and Fred in one of the kermisses they gave each year at Taylor Allderdice.… He took me under his wing—it's like losing an older brother."

Leslie Brockett also studied tap with Kelly. She recalls one school show at the old Nixon Theater. "The number was 'The Parade of the Wooden Soldiers.' The curtain closed, and I got stuck in the middle of the curtain"—rear toward the audience. Kelly was in the wings whispering, "Leslie, this way."

Like so many Pittsburghers who never watched Kelly dance in person, she said, "I thought he was so wonderful. He's such a legend. I'm so proud he's from Pittsburgh."

THURSDAY, JULY 3, 1997

Jimmy Stewart, 89
A Wonderful Life

By Marylynn Uricchio, *Pittsburgh Post-Gazette*. *Post-Gazette* staff writer Barbara Vancheri contributed to this report.

Actor Jimmy Stewart visits his hometown of Indiana, Pennsylvania on May 20, 1983. *Photo by Mark Murphy.*

Jimmy Stewart had the knack of looking rumpled even when his shirt was starched. There was something supremely comfortable about the lanky actor from Indiana, Pennsylvania, who died yesterday from a blood clot in his lung at his Beverly Hills home. He was 89 and had been ill in recent years with a heart condition and a bout of skin cancer.

Friends said Stewart never really recovered from the loss of his beloved wife of 45 years, Gloria, who died in 1994. He just seemed to retreat quietly into his home and family. But Stewart was never much of a gadabout, even though he was considered Hollywood royalty for almost 60 years.

He was a family man, a decorated war veteran whose eldest son, Ronald, was killed in action in Vietnam, and a grandfather who said there wasn't much point "in getting myself fixed up, so I don't look like that."

Apple pie, the Fourth of July— if John Wayne became the image of this country at war, Stewart came to symbolize America at peace. It was no accident that so many of his screen roles seemed a reflection of his personal life. He didn't choose them because of that. In fact, Stewart bragged that he didn't choose them, period. A lifelong proponent of the studio system he knew would never again exist, Stewart often praised the workmanlike atmosphere that kept the roles coming his way.

"The main thing was that you were busy all the time when you were working at a studio. People today don't realize that you didn't sit around and wait for somebody to call you and send you a script you liked," Stewart told *The New York Times* in 1990. "You went to work every morning at 8 and left at 6:30, and you had big parts in little pictures and little parts in big pictures."

Some parts were better than others, but many of the more than 75 films he made have become screen classics.

For millions of Americans, Stewart will be forever associated with the Christmas classic *It's a Wonderful Life*, a heartwarming fantasy about a small-town banker so overwhelmed by problems that he considers suicide. He finds himself rescuing an angel who, in turn, rescues him. Stewart's George Bailey of Bedford Falls learns that a man with friends and family is rich, indeed.

Stewart once told film critic Leonard Maltin that fans who wrote to him often mentioned they had seen the story of hope and redemption 15 or 20 times. "They make it sort of like putting up the Christmas tree.… It's part of the annual ritual now. That means a great deal to me."

The slow-talking actor embodied the American values of decency and moral courage in movies such as *Mr. Smith Goes to Washington*. He never seemed to lose the aw-shucks friendliness that came from hanging around his dad's hardware store in Indiana.

Academy Award

In 1941 he won an Academy Award for playing opposite Katharine Hepburn in the sophisticated comedy *The Philadelphia Story*. After accepting the statuette in front of a raucous, approving audience at the Biltmore Hotel, he spoke with his father in Indiana, who instructed him to send the Oscar home. For years it sat in the hardware store case that had once displayed knives.

Later it was on display at the Jimmy Stewart Museum in Indiana, in a room surrounded by movie memorabilia. Down the hall is a theater where Stewart is alternately western hero, average man, aviator, musician, and friend to an invisible 6' rabbit named Harvey. When nearly 30,000 people—double Indiana's population—attended the bash the town threw for Stewart's 75th birthday, a rabbit topped his birthday cake.

The museum yesterday issued this statement:

> For nearly a century, Jimmy Stewart has been a surrogate brother, father, and friend to fans of American film. He made his projections on the silver screen so much more than the words in his scripts. He made them friends. And, as all good friends, he helped us learn how to live and how to appreciate living....
>
> In the news you may hear that he has left us. Don't you believe it. Like all stars, he'll be shining down on us for years to come.

Tall, thin, and boyish, without the conventional handsomeness of Robert Taylor and Ronald Colman, Stewart seemed a method actor ahead of his time. He had the ability to play both comedy and drama and was not afraid to show raw emotions—the despair of George Bailey, the dangerous obsession of the neurotic detective in Alfred Hitchcock's *Vertigo*—which was not the case for most leading men of the era.

Frank Capra, who directed *Mr. Smith* and *It's a Wonderful Life*, once said that even better than a great performance was "a level of no acting at all, when the actor disappears and a real live person appears on the screen, a person the audience cares about immediately." Stewart was one of the few to reach that level, Capra said.

Reserved and self-effacing, he was more likely to credit his directors than his own talent. A former amateur magician, Stewart conjured up some of the most memorable performances in cinema history. He specialized in playing earnest, sometimes shy heroes, slow to anger but with endless reserves of perseverance. He excelled in righteous tales such as *The Man Who Shot Liberty Valance*, *Destry Rides Again*, and *The Flight of the Phoenix*. Later he turned to darker roles, especially for Hitchcock in films like *Rear Window* and for Anthony Mann in a series of revenge-themed Westerns including *Winchester '73* and *The Man from Laramie*.

The Everyman

But in all his best roles, no matter how outlandish or far apart on the surface, there remained a strong quality of the everyman. Stewart struck a chord with audiences because he always remained what he was—a small-town boy whose religious upbringing in a happy, stable home had imbued him with impeccable values.

"Hollywood dishes out too much praise for small things," Stewart once said. "I won't let it get me, but too much praise can turn a fellow's head if he doesn't watch his step."

James Maitland Stewart was born on May 20, 1908, the eldest child of Alexander and Elizabeth Stewart. Two sisters, Virginia and Mary, followed. He attended Mercersburg Academy, where he began acting in student plays, and then he graduated with honors and a degree in architecture from Princeton University. It was there that he met the future movie producer Joshua Logan, who invited Stewart to join him as a member of the Falmouth Players in Massachusetts the summer after graduation.

Henry Fonda was also a member of the acting troupe, and the two became friends and roommates both in New York, where they worked on Broadway, and later when they moved to Los Angeles. Stewart was a lifelong conservative Republican, Fonda a New Deal Democrat, and their political differences became so heated they stopped talking to each other. Finally, they agreed never to discuss politics again, and they remained close until Fonda's death.

Stewart made his feature film debut in 1935's *The Murder Man* as a newspaper reporter named Shorty, opposite Spencer Tracy. "I was all hands and feet, and didn't know what to do with either," he once said.

But in his first five years in Hollywood he made 24 films, including *You Can't Take It with You*, *No Time for Comedy*, and *Destry Rides Again*, with Marlene Dietrich. He even played a bad guy, just once, in 1936's "*After the Thin Man*"—his second movie role.

Stewart joined the air force nine months before Pearl Harbor, flew 20 missions over Germany, and rose to the rank of full colonel. When he retired from the Air Force Reserve in 1968 he was a brigadier general and the highest-ranking entertainer in the military. He was shot down during the war in *The Glenn Miller Story* and played pilot Charles Lindbergh in *Spirit of St. Louis*.

After the war, both Stewart and Fonda, who had served in the navy, suffered professional lulls. After being away from Hollywood almost five years, Stewart's first picture was *It's a Wonderful Life*, which lost money at the box office and threatened to derail the careers of both Stewart and Capra.

A Family Man

It was at a dinner party in 1948 at Gary Cooper's house that Stewart, age 41 and one of the most eligible bachelors in Hollywood, met model Gloria McLean. They married a year later, and she brought her two young sons, Ronald, age five, and Michael, age two, into the marriage. In 1951 twin daughters named Judy and Kelly were born to the Stewarts. Stewart is survived by Michael, the twins, and his grandchildren.

In the course of his career Stewart received four other Academy Award nominations: for the idealistic young senator in *Mr. Smith Goes to Washington* in 1939, for the depressed businessman whose guardian angel gives him new hope in *It's a Wonderful Life* in 1946, for the eccentric whose best pal is an imaginary 6′ rabbit in *Harvey* in 1950, and for the defense lawyer for an army officer in *Anatomy of a Murder* in 1959.

In 1980 he was honored with the American Film Institute Lifetime Achievement Award, and in 1984 he received an honorary Oscar for 50 years of performances. His last movie credit was for lending his folksy voice to Sheriff Wylie Burp in the 1991 animated film *An American Tail: Fievel Goes West*.

An astute businessman, Stewart was one of the first actors to work for a percentage of his films' profits, a very rare deal at the time. He became a multimillionaire with diversified investments including real estate, oil wells, a charter-plane company, and membership on major corporate boards.

In his spare time Stewart played the accordion and wrote poetry. He published a best-selling collection in 1989 titled *Jimmy Stewart and His Poems*. An ode to one of his dogs read in part:

"He'd dig up a rosebush just to spite me, and when I'd grab him, he'd turn and bite me."

Stewart once said, "I don't act; I react.... I'm the inarticulate man who tries. I don't really have all the answers, but for some reason, somehow, I make it."

FRIDAY, FEBRUARY 28, 2003

Fred Rogers, 74
Liked Us Just the Way We Are

By Rob Owen and Barbara Vancheri, *Pittsburgh Post-Gazette*. Staff writers Andrew Druckenbrod and Dennis Roddy contributed to this report.

The first time Marc Brown, creator of the animated PBS series *Arthur*, met Fred Rogers, they talked about loss. "He never used the word *death*, he always used the words 'going to heaven.' Boy, if anyone deserves to be in heaven, it's Fred Rogers," Brown said yesterday. "Gosh, when you die, the one thing you want is to feel that your life is worth something. Think of the millions of families and children he's touched and made their lives better and easier in some way."

Like one of his signature zippered cardigans, Mr. Rogers symbolized warmth, comfort, and reassurance for TV viewers in Pittsburgh and beyond. And yesterday, the world felt just a little colder, emptier, and less gentle after Mr. Rogers's distinctive voice was silenced by a brief, lethal bout with cancer.

Mr. Rogers was diagnosed with stomach cancer in December, underwent surgery January 6 and ultimately chose to die at his Squirrel Hill home. At his side was his wife of 50 years, Joanne.

The 74-year-old icon, mimicked with affection and showered with awards, had a polished star on the Hollywood Walk of Fame and instant international name recognition, but he never failed to greet a stranger with the same warmth he would offer a Barbara Bush or a Bill Cosby.

"In real life, as in the *Neighborhood*, Mister Rogers was an extraordinary man," Yo-Yo Ma, the cellist and some-time guest on *Neighborhood* said yesterday in a faxed statement. "Through music and stories, his caring and wisdom transcended every barrier; his advocacy for children was truly an advocacy for the human race. My family and I are incredibly grateful to have enjoyed his friendship, and we will miss him."

Mr. Rogers worked in broadcasting for more than 50 years, but he's best

Fred Rogers at the 10th-annual Presley Ridge Ice Cream Sunday. Also on hand is Mr. McFeely (David Newell). *Photo by Bill Wade.*

known for the 33 years he spent writing and starring in PBS's *Mister Rogers' Neighborhood.*

Children Always Came First

In a world where children's TV has increasingly become a noisy, commercial, product-driven place, Mr. Rogers represented a haven of old-fashioned values and a philosophy that put children first. Always.

"It's been a privilege to pass on the good stuff that was given to me, and television has really been a fine vehicle for that," Mr. Rogers said before recording his last episode of the *Neighborhood* in the fall of 2000. He pointed to a framed reminder on his office wall: Life Is for Service. "Those of us in broadcasting have a special calling to give whatever we feel is the most nourishing that we can for our audience," Mr. Rogers said. "We are servants of those who watch and listen."

On television he was ever tolerant and always understanding, and that carried over to his humble real-life demeanor. His persona was no act.

There are no stories of him turning into a raging tyrant behind the scenes. By all accounts, he was the same soft-spoken person on the air and off.

Yesterday Mr. Rogers's close colleagues, David Newell and Hedda Sharapan, stepped into the chilly morning air outside WQED's headquarters to do what Mr. Rogers himself had done so well: look into the TV camera and celebrate the best in life. They talked about Mr. Rogers's legacy, his friendship, sly sense of humor, and ever-more-timely message about liking children "just the way you are."

Off camera, Sharapan said, "One of the most beautiful things about Fred's work is his courage to be himself on camera."

Inside the Oakland offices of Family Communications Inc. the phones were jammed with calls of shock and condolence and respectful requests from reporters for interviews. Friends and strangers alike turned the radio and TV airwaves into a communal forum for mourning and remembrance. WQED-FM, located in the same building where the *Neighborhood* castle set always delighted visitors, concluded a news story about his death with Mr. Rogers singing, "It's You I Like."

Mayor Tom Murphy called it a "sad day for all of us as our country lost a national treasure, and Pittsburgh lost a close friend and neighbor. Pittsburgh was Mister Rogers's neighborhood, making our sense of loss today all the more profound. He will be missed but certainly not forgotten."

Last night, WQED preempted its lineup for four hours of remembrance devoted to Mr. Rogers. PBS stations nationwide had the option to carry part or all of the tribute.

Actor Michael Keaton, a Pittsburgh native who once worked on the *Neighborhood*, said Mr. Rogers was "one of the truly great guys, a really, really good person. And the thing about Fred…was how consistently decent he was. He was a nice man, and if it were only that, at the end of the day, that would be enough. But he was a lot more than that."

Brown, creator of the books and TV series *Arthur*, which once featured an animated Mr. Rogers, acknowledged in a call from Boston yesterday, "I think I'm just feeling very helpless, like a lot of people," and he thought talking might help. It sounded like something Mr. Rogers would say as he ushered a visitor into his surprisingly small but cozy office and invited them to take the chair to his left as he sank into the couch.

Knack for Respecting Children

Nancy Curry, a former professor and director of child development at the University of Pittsburgh, met Mr. Rogers in the early 1960s at the Arsenal Family and Children's Center in Lawrenceville. He came to the center during his years in Pittsburgh Theological Seminary to practice face-to-face interaction with children.

Curry recalled the way young people reacted to Mr. Rogers's puppets, talking to the puppets directly, ignoring the man who was controlling them.

"He had a way of encouraging them while still respecting them," she said. "One little girl had a pet bird that had died, and she had to tell every one of Fred's puppets. Each one had its own individuality in her eyes. He was always very respectful with children and didn't make fun of children. Some performers have their tongue in cheek. He did not have that."

She said children embraced him because he put up no facade. "They responded to him so quickly," Curry said. "He tried out his songs with us and had the children dancing and participating with him. His creativity was breathtaking."

Fred McFeely Rogers was born on March 20, 1928, in Latrobe. He spent a year at Dartmouth College before transferring to Rollins College in Winter Park, Florida, where he graduated with a degree in music in 1951. Instead of going on to seminary as he had planned, he landed a series of positions in the brand-new medium of television, with *NBC Opera Theater, The Voice of Firestone, Lucky-Strike Hit Parade,* and *The Kate Smith Hour.* He did any number of jobs, from fetching coffee to serving as a floor manager and orchestrating action behind the cameras.

It was the fledgling WQED and *The Children's Corner,* which debuted in April 1954 with host Josie Carey, that brought him to Pittsburgh. He produced the program, performed the music, and gave life to the puppets—including Daniel S. Tiger and King Friday XIII.

Carey said she and Mr. Rogers asked to work together after realizing they shared a mutual interest in children's television. "He was probably the most creative person I ever worked with,"

Carey said yesterday. And just as Mr. Rogers taught children to accept feelings, their feelings of affection for him could not be extinguished, even as they grew.

"You didn't stay a fan for all your childhood. Once you passed the years when you really loved him, you pretended you didn't watch. All of sudden you were too sophisticated—too grown up for Mr. Rogers. But there was a point in every child's life where he was the nicest person on television," said Carey, who had learned Mr. Rogers was near death in a phone call Wednesday.

After moving to Canada to create a 15-minute children's show called *Misterogers,* he returned to WQED to develop a new half-hour format of *Mister Rogers' Neighborhood.* PBS began distributing it nationally February 19, 1968.

In that landmark inaugural episode Mr. Rogers walked through the front door of his television house, doffed his raincoat and suit jacket, and donned a sweater—button-down, not zippered like the red one he would donate to the Smithsonian Institution.

The routine established that day was designed to give children a sense of security. Rituals help them know what to expect and to settle in for Mr. Rogers's "television visit," as he called it. Songs composed by Mr. Rogers also allowed him to connect with children and were a clever way to deliver messages about, for instance, "What do you do with the mad that you feel when you feel so mad you could bite?"

Robert Thompson, director of the Center for the Study of Popular Television at Syracuse University, said

Mr. Rogers is among those who shaped the medium, and educational children's television in particular. "Along with a very small group of people—Steve Allen from late night, Irna Phillips with soap operas, Ernie Kovacs with video art—Fred Rogers really understood what the medium of television was all about, what it could do, how it was this intimate forum that talked to you in the privacy of your own living room, and he grasped that very early on," Thompson said.

"There's something about [Mr. Rogers's] program, when you're in your little pajamas with feet attached to them and you're home in the comfort of your living room on the couch, that was so extraordinarily comforting and quiet. It went down like a nice hot bowl of soup."

Mr. Rogers, who was ordained a Presbyterian minister in 1963, saw his PBS program as a form of ministry to children.

In 2000, the Religion Communicators Council gave him the Lifetime Wilbur Award for supporting religious values in the public media. The Reverend Dennis C. Benson accepted the honor on his behalf and recalled how a friend and Mr. Rogers were walking together in a Pittsburgh neighborhood when the TV host spotted an infant's pacifier on the sidewalk.

"He said, 'Someone lost something very important.' He walked up to a nearby house and knocked on the door. When a woman answered the door, Fred asked, 'Did someone here lose this?' She said, 'Why, yes, thank you.'"

It was classic Mr. Rogers.

Pittsburgh Theological Seminary yesterday mourned its most well-known graduate and recalled what he said during the 1994 commencement: "You know, it's not the honors and the prizes and the fancy outsides of life which ultimately nourish our souls. It's the knowing that we can be trusted, that we never have to fear the truth, that ultimately there is someone who loves our very being."

Production of the *Neighborhood* ceased in December 2000, and the last week of original episodes aired in August 2001. Since then, PBS has had *Mister Rogers' Neighborhood* on a continuous loop of about 260 shows culled from more than 1,000 taped during Rogers's 33 years in national production.

Nancy Polinsky, who cohosts WQED's cooking marathons, recalled standing in New York's Times Square in December 2000 when an image of Fred Rogers flickered onto a JumboTron. The news ticker announced that he had taped his last episode of the PBS series. Polinsky, husband David Johnson of WPXI-TV, and their two sons were suddenly surrounded by a babble of languages from around the world. The only recognizable phrase was "Mister Rogers," she recalled yesterday.

"And in this rather spontaneous display, somebody started singing 'It's a beautiful day in the neighborhood' and everybody within earshot of that joined in.… I turned to my children and said, 'Look at the international impact this man has had.'"

In that same spirit, a kindergarten teacher in the Bronx told a friend in Pittsburgh that she led her charges yesterday in a rousing round of "Won't You Be My Neighbor?"

After production of the program ceased, Mr. Rogers devoted his time to working on the *Mister Rogers' Neighborhood* website, writing books, and fulfilling long-booked speaking engagements. Even then Mr. Rogers often spent his mornings at his "writing office" away from the hustle and bustle of his Family Communications office. The older he got, the more he cherished silence, he said in spring 2001.

"You're able to be much more mindful of what is deep and simple and how essential that is, in order to keep on growing," he said. "And whatever our expression of care might be, whether it be television or the Internet or all of these books that the people want us to write—whatever that expression is—it must come out of the depth of understanding that we continue to nourish. Otherwise, you know it could get superficial. That's not going to happen with us."

Calming Voice in Stormy Lives

Grateful viewers came from happy, secure households and ones where Mr. Rogers was a port in the storm. Talking about the volume of mail that poured into the Oakland office, he said, "It's the quality of the letters, it's the quality of the reaching out that is even more important than the quantity. The things that people want to share with you are just stunning.... They knew we were a safe place to go."

Mr. Rogers's message was so simple and yet so life-affirming—"to say that you can be lovable just the way you are.

The overriding theme that people long to hear is that they're acceptable as they are. And as they grow, they will be capable of loving themselves."

Like other residents of Mr. Rogers's real-life neighborhood, the executive director of the Pittsburgh Children's Museum got choked up yesterday while trying to explain how important Mr. Rogers was to children—and the world at large. "He was our moral compass, our guiding force," Jane Werner said. "He teaches everyone how to talk to children, how to listen to children, how to love one another.... He teaches kindness, and to be kind to one another is one of the most amazing things, one of the most important lessons you can teach children."

The museum has the original puppets on display and will feature the 2,500-square-foot *Mister Rogers' Neighborhood* exhibit in its new expanded space when it opens in September. Werner last saw Mr. Rogers in the fall, when she stopped into his office at WQED to say hello and fondly recalled spending time with him at the Family Communications picnic at Idlewild Park, where the *Neighborhood* has been re-created as a children's attraction.

As the Children's Museum staff considered ways to honor Mr. Rogers's legacy yesterday, they decided on a plan that would have pleased the TV icon: they will open their doors to the public, for free, on what would have been Mr. Rogers's birthday on March 20. And they will try to maintain a sense of normalcy for their young visitors.

Over the years, Mr. Rogers's program hosted many celebrity guests, including Yo-Yo Ma, LeVar Burton, David Copperfield, Tony Bennett, Lynn Swann, Wynton Marsalis, Stomp, Margaret Hamilton, Julia Child, and locals like Bill Strickland of the Manchester Craftsmen's Guild.

"Fred Rogers is as sweet a man as they come," Dennis Miller, comedian and Pittsburgh native, once said. "In the world gone mad with what kids get to see nowadays, those calmative rhythms.... He's one of the best things to come out of Pittsburgh. That and Bobby Clemente's arm."

Yet for all the celebrities, Mr. Rogers also remembered visits from unknowns. A disabled child who could hardly speak visited the *Neighborhood* in fall 2000 and sang with Mr. Rogers.

"I was walking this far off the ground," Mr. Rogers said, holding his hand a foot above the floor. "You know, there are special times and there are extra special times. I feel that the real drama of life is never center stage, it's always in the wings. It's never with the spotlight on, it's usually something that you don't expect at all."

He never sought the spotlight, but the list of awards presented to Mr. Rogers ran more than 25 single-spaced, typed pages and included the Presidential Medal of Freedom, two Peabody Awards, four Emmys, and a Lifetime Achievement Award from the National Academy of Television Arts and Sciences. He was named one of the "50 greatest TV stars of all time" by *TV Guide* in 1996, got a star on the Hollywood Walk of Fame in 1998, and was inducted into the Television Hall of Fame in 1999.

Mr. Rogers, a man of great modesty, once acknowledged his contribution to the next generation of children's programs, such as *Arthur* and *Reading Rainbow*, by repeating the words of LeVar Burton: "Fred, you launched the ship that carried us all."

And Mister Rogers steered it with a steady hand and a generous heart.

He is survived by his wife, Joanne Rogers; their two sons, John Rogers of Winter Park, Florida, and James Rogers of Edgewood; and two grand-sons. He also has a sister, Elaine Crozier of Latrobe.

MONDAY, OCTOBER 3, 2005

August Wilson, 60
Playwright Who Chronicled Black Experience

By Christopher Rawson, *Pittsburgh Post-Gazette*. Staff writers Nate Guidry and Bob Hoover contributed to this report.

Last December, Pittsburgh-born play-wright August Wilson's thoughts turned to mortality. With his 60th birthday approaching, he said, "There's more [life] behind me than ahead. I think of dying every day.... At a certain age, you should be prepared to go at any time."

August Wilson at the Copacabana after the opening of his play *King Hedley II* on Broadway in New York City on April 29, 2001. *Photo by Bill Wade.*

In May he was diagnosed with liver cancer, and the next month his doctors determined it was inoperable. But he showed that he was indeed prepared, telling the *Post-Gazette* in August, "I've lived a blessed life. I'm ready."

The end came yesterday morning when Mr. Wilson, age 60, died in Swedish Medical Center in Seattle, "surrounded by his loved ones," said Dena Levitin, his assistant.

Mr. Wilson took a characteristically wry look at his fate, saying, "It's not like poker; you can't throw your hand in." He also noted that when his long-time friend and producer, Benjamin Mordecai, the only person to work with him on all 10 of his major plays, died this spring, the obituary in *The New York Times* included a picture of him and Mordecai together. "That's what gave God this idea," Wilson said.

The fierce poignancy of his eulogy for Mr. Mordecai in a recent *American Theatre* magazine sounds self-reflexive: "How do we transform loss?... Time's healing balm is essentially a hoax.... Haunted by the specter of my own death, I find solace in Ben's life."

Mr. Wilson also told the *Post-Gazette* in August, "I'm glad I finished the cycle," referring to the unprecedented series of 10 plays with which he conquered the American theater. In the process, he opened new avenues for black artists, changed the way theater approaches race, and changed the business of theater, too.

Often called the *Pittsburgh Cycle* because all but one play is set in the Hill

District of Pittsburgh, where Mr. Wilson spent his youth and early adulthood, this unequaled epic chronicles the tragedies and aspirations of African Americans in a play set in each decade of the 20th century.

In dramatizing the glory, anger, promise, and frustration of being black in America, he created a world of the imagination—August Wilson's Hill District—to rank with such other transformational fictional worlds as Faulkner's Yoknapatawpha, Hardy's Wessex, or Friel's Donegal. Critics from Manhattan to Los Angeles now speak knowingly of "Pittsburgh's Hill District," not just the Hill, as it is now or was when Mr. Wilson grew up in the 1950s, but August Wilson Country—the archetypal northern, urban black neighborhood, a construct of frustration, nostalgia, anger, and dream. Mr. Wilson's plays present this world as a crucible in which the identity of black America has been shaped.

The final play in the cycle—the last written, set in the final decade—is *Radio Golf*. It premiered in March at New Haven's Yale Repertory Theatre, where the earlier plays in the cycle were first produced in the 1980s. Even while suffering from cancer and recovering from a small stroke, Mr. Wilson kept rewriting for the play's second production at Los Angeles's Mark Taper Forum, from July 31 to September 18.

There is talk of staging *Radio Golf* later this season on Broadway, where it would be a living memorial along with the August Wilson Theatre, formerly the Virginia, which will be formally renamed on October 17. That is just one of many honors extended to Mr. Wilson since it was learned he was dying. Many have been testimonies to the personal impact the dramatic resonance he has found in the African American life has had on black and white alike.

"While his death was not unexpected, it's a serious blow to the entire theatrical community in the United States and Pittsburgh in particular," said Ted Pappas, artistic and executive director of the Pittsburgh Public Theater, which has staged most of Wilson's work. "August Wilson is one of the seminal figures of 20th-century dramatic art. When we speak of Eugene O'Neill, Tennessee Williams, and Arthur Miller, we will now add the name of August Wilson to that pantheon."

August Wilson was born Frederick August Kittel on April 27, 1945; his family long called him Freddy. His mother, Daisy Wilson, whose own mother had walked north from North Carolina, raised her six children in a cold-water flat behind Bella's grocery on Bedford Avenue in the Hill. She died of lung cancer in March 1983, just before her son's first great success on Broadway.

His father, also Frederick Kittel, was a German baker who died in 1965. "My father very rarely came around," Mr. Wilson said. "I grew up in my mother's household in a cultural environment which was black." He also had a stepfather, David Bedford, who died in 1969.

There were seven children: his older sisters, Freda, Linda Jean, and Donna, and his younger brothers, Edwin and Richard, all of whom survive him. His brothers kept their father's name, but at age 20, Wilson signaled his cultural loyalty by taking his mother's name, becoming August Wilson.

His sister Freda Ellis was attending St. Benedict, the Moor Roman Catholic Church in the Hill District, early yesterday afternoon when she learned of her brother's death. "I knew he died in peace, and that's some relief for me," Mrs. Ellis said. "They told me he just couldn't hold on any longer.

"Because our family was so poor, you had to work for anything you wanted, and August worked so hard to become a writer. He deserves the success and the notice because he did work so hard."

Although Mr. Wilson was not the oldest sibling, he was "the patriarch of the family," Mrs. Ellis said.

Mr. Wilson remembered that his mother "had a very hard time feeding us all. But I had a wonderful childhood.... As a family, we did things together. We said the rosary every night at 7:00. We all sat down and had dinner at a certain time.... We didn't have a TV, so we listened to the radio."

One of his mother's enduring gifts was to teach him to read when he was four. Mr. Wilson called it transforming: "You can unlock information, and you're better able to understand the forces that are oppressing you."

Years later he told a library celebration, "When I was five years old, I got my first library card from the Hill District branch on Wylie Avenue. Labor Historians do not speak well of Andrew Carnegie...[but he] will forever be for me that man who made it all possible for me to be standing here today.... I wore out my library card and cried when I lost it."

His mother also valued education, sending him to St. Richard's parochial school in the Hill, then to Central Catholic High School in Oakland. As the only black student in the school, he was constantly taunted and harassed, so he left just before the end of his freshman year.

He started the next year at Connelley Vo-Tech, which he found pointless, so he switched to Gladstone High School, just across the street from the Hazelwood home the family had moved to when he was 12 years old. He was supposedly in the 10th grade, but because he hadn't graduated from the ninth at Central, they had him taking ninth-grade subjects. The work was well behind what he had already done, so he was bored and didn't work at it until he decided he wanted to get into the after-school college club run by one of the teachers.

It was that teacher who, in an often-told story, doubted he'd written a 20-page paper on Napoleon he submitted. Insulted, the future August Wilson dropped out of school at age 15 and for a while didn't tell his mother.

"I dropped out of school, but I didn't drop out of life," he recalled. "I would leave the house each morning and go to the main branch of the Carnegie Library in Oakland, where they had all the books in the world.... I felt suddenly liberated from the constraints of a prearranged curriculum that labored through one book in eight months."

The other important part of his education came on the streets of the Hill. He once told an interviewer, "Pittsburgh is a very hard city, especially if you're black." And another, "When I was 22 years old, each day had to be continually negotiated. It was rough." As he memorably put it, "I grew up without a father. When I was 20, I went down onto Centre Avenue to learn from the community how to be a man."

That community provided many fathers—the old men chatting in Pat's Place or on street corners, the inhabitants of the diners where Wilson sat and listened, like-minded friends with artistic inclinations. His true father was both the small community that nurtured him and the larger Pittsburgh that, by opposing, stimulated and defined.

He rented a room and worked at many jobs. He discovered the blues. He followed various black identity movements and fought for social justice. And he featured himself a poet, sitting in diners, scribbling on napkins.

"The exact day I became a poet was April 1, 1965, the day I bought my first typewriter," using $20 his sister Freda paid him for writing a term paper for her on Robert Frost and Carl Sandburg.

Many years later he recalled, "The first time I became aware of theater was Pearl Bailey in *Hello, Dolly*, around 1958, 1959. My mother was in New York and brought back the program, her first and only Broadway show."

In the late 1960s Mr. Wilson became part of a talented group of poets, educators, and artists of the future, young men such as Rob Penny, Nick Flournoy, and Chawley Williams, with regular haunts at the Halfway Art Gallery and the Hill Arts Society. Mr. Wilson remembered that "I always had a napkin and a pencil. That's one of the things about writing—the tools are so simple."

He was involved in the debates of the 1960s and continued to consider himself "a black nationalist and a cultural nationalist." He and his friends formed the Centre Avenue Poets Theater Workshop. Later, he and Mr. Penny started the Black Horizon Theater, which toured, and they were involved in the Kuntu Repertory Theater.

But Mr. Wilson's first brushes with theater had been off-putting. In 1965 he saw a 30-minute excerpt of *The Rhinoceros* at Fifth Avenue High School. "That was the first theater I recall, and I wasn't impressed." He met some of the actors in John Hancock's 1966 Pittsburgh Playhouse company, but he stayed for only 20 minutes of Bertolt Brecht's *A Man's a Man*. It was 1976 before Mr. Wilson saw a whole, professional play: Athol Fugard's *Sizwe Bansi Is Dead*, a comi-tragic account of life under apartheid at the Pittsburgh Public Theater.

But in 1968 Mr. Penny wrote a play, and the *Tulane Drama Review* had a special issue on black theater. "That was the first time I'd seen black plays in print—there hadn't been any plays on the negro shelf at the library. So we did them all."

Mr. Wilson's first staged play was *Recycle*, which drew on the unhappy 1972 termination of his 1969 marriage to Brenda Burton. (A happy result was their daughter, Sakina Ansari, born in 1970.) Two other one-act plays from this time are *Homecoming* and *The Coldest Day of the Year*. Soon thereafter, his friend Claude Purdy moved to St.

Paul to work with its black theater group, Penumbra, and he invited Mr. Wilson to join him.

In 1978 he went, taking with him a satirical play *Black Bart* and the *Sacred Hills*, adapted from his poems at Mr. Purdy's suggestion. They did a workshop of *Black Bart* in St. Paul, and Mr. Wilson stayed. In 1981 he was married for the second time, to Judy Oliver, a friend of Mr. Purdy's wife.

Mr. Wilson once explained that St. Paul and Seattle—cool, northern, Scandinavian cities—appealed to him precisely because of their unlikeness to Pittsburgh, allowing him to look back more intently at the true material of August Wilson Country, source of his rich stream of stories, characters, images, and conflicts.

He called *Jitney*, written in St. Paul in 1979, his first real play. He submitted it twice unsuccessfully to the Eugene O'Neill Theater Center's National Playwrights Conference, and it was staged in Pittsburgh by the small Allegheny Repertory Theater in 1982. He unsuccessfully submitted three other early plays to the O'Neill before *Ma Rainey's Black Bottom* was accepted.

At the O'Neill, Wilson met the artistic director Lloyd Richards, dean of the Yale Drama School, head of the professional Yale Repertory Theater, and director of the breakthrough Broadway staging 25 years earlier of the most influential modern black American play, Lorraine Hansberry's *A Raisin in the Sun.*

It was a turning point in both lives. Mr. Richards was the artistic father and collaborator Mr. Wilson needed, an experienced director who taught him stagecraft and helped him learn to rewrite. Mr. Wilson's plays were a gift to Mr. Richards, who went on to direct the first six from workshop to Broadway.

Ma Rainey went quickly from the O'Neill to its premiere at Yale Rep to Broadway. Then time sped up, often with one play in initial workshop, another on Broadway, and a third midway from one point to the other, simultaneously.

In 1990 Mr. Wilson's second marriage ended, and he moved to Seattle. In 1994 he married Constanza Romero, a costume designer—his third marriage, one in each of his three home cities— and together they had a daughter, Azula Carmen Wilson, in 1997.

Even as a nonresident, Mr. Wilson remained a good Pittsburgh citizen, visiting frequently to see his family and friends. On several occasions, such as the 1988 Carnegie Institute Man and Ideas series, 1992 University of Pittsburgh Honors Convocation, and 2000 Heinz Lecture Series, he delivered uplifting but accusatory addresses about the black position in American history and culture, talking across the great national racial divide with prophetic force.

He also came to praise, as at the 1998 Affirmation of the Blues, a benefit for Community Media at the Carnegie Lecture Hall. Woven out of a love of African American community and art, it was shot through with threads of reminiscence over shared early struggles and joys. Honored with him that night were such "elders" as Billy Jackson of Community Media and Kuntu Repertory founder Vernell Lillie, who remembered Mr. Wilson yesterday as "a brilliant director and poet—a gentle, creative man who loved the arts."

He also came back to Pittsburgh to work. He was resident at the Pittsburgh Public Theater in 1996 to revise *Jitney* for its professional debut, and again in 1999 to prepare the premiere of *King Hedley II*, which had the honor of opening the new $20 million O'Reilly Theater in the Cultural District.

In 1994 he was here to coproduce the filming of *The Piano Lesson* for television, the only one of his plays so far to make it to the screen. He even came to speak of the beauty of this city which he had not always loved. In 1994 he said, "Like most people, I have this sort of love-hate relationship with Pittsburgh. This is my home, and at times I miss it and find it tremendously exciting, and other times I want to catch the first thing out that has wheels."

He had come back for six weeks earlier that year, he said, "to reconnect with Pittsburgh, do some writing here—this is fertile ground." The city remained the deep well of memory into which he kept dipping the ladle of his art.

His most popular play, *Fences*, was long ago optioned for film, but Mr. Wilson insisted on a black director of his choice, and although he wrote several screenplays, the project is still in the offing.

But on stage, his clout is great. With his one Tony, two Pulitzers, three American Theatre Critics awards, and seven New York Drama Critics Circle Awards, he has become the flagship of contemporary black theater. In a roundtable discussion among four black playwrights in 1999, Marion McClinton said, "When theaters make money on August Wilson they might say, 'Let's do two [black plays] next year.'"

In 1996 he took on a spokesman role, proclaiming his protest against the marginalization of black theater in a keynote address at the annual convention of professional regional theaters. This led to his very public dispute with critic and producer Robert Brustein, culminating in their January 1997 public debate in New York City that put theater back at the center of the national debate about race and culture.

He was surprised to be called "rich" in a New Yorker profile, but agreed he was not poor. If you invested $1 in August Wilson in 1984, when *Ma Rainey* hit Broadway, he said, "You'd have gotten it back and maybe 40 cents more."

His awards were many, including more than two dozen honorary doctorates (from the University of Pittsburgh, among others), Rockefeller and Guggenheim Fellowships, a National Humanities Medal, the 2003 Heinz Award in Humanities and Arts, and the only high school diploma issued by the Carnegie Library of Pittsburgh. He was a member of both the American Academy of Arts and Sciences and the American Academy of Arts and Letters.

He also anchored his own achievements in his heritage. At the Pittsburgher of the Year ceremony in 1990, he said:

I was born in Pittsburgh in 1945 and for 33 years stumbled through its streets, small, narrow, crooked, cobbled, with the weight of the buildings pressing in on me and my spirit pushed into terrifying contractions. That I would stand before you today in this guise was beyond comprehension.... I am standing here in my grandfather's shoes.... They are the shoes of a whole generation of men who left a life of unspeakable horror in the South and came North...searching for jobs, for the opportunity to live a life with dignity and whatever eloquence the heart could call upon.... The cities were not then, and are not now, hospitable. There is a struggle to maintain one's dignity. But that generation of men and women stands as a testament to the resiliency of the human spirit. And they have passed on to us, their grandchildren, the greatest of gifts, the gift of hope refreshed.

Asked for his own greatest accomplishment, he said he would like to be known as "the guy who wrote these 10 plays."

More specifically, "after I wrote Loomis's speech [in *Joe Turner*] about seeing the bones" on the track of the Atlantic route of the slaver-traders, "I thought, as an artist, right there, I'd be satisfied."

SECTION

X

On the Stump

Pittsburgh has several sports. There is football, where the Steelers are king. Baseball, presided over by the Pirates. Hockey, ruled by the Penguins. Basketball, dominated by the Duquesne teams of yore and the Pitt teams of today. And politics. Politics may be the greatest indigenous sport of this area, which produced a powerful giant like David L. Lawrence, a gentle giant like John Heinz III, and a pioneering giant like K. Leroy Irvis.

TUESDAY, NOVEMBER 22, 1966

David L. Lawrence, 77
"Born Into Politics"

By the *Pittsburgh Post-Gazette*

Governor David L. Lawrence reacts to the Pittsburgh Pirates victory. *Photo courtesy of the* Pittsburgh Post-Gazette.

David L. Lawrence, who once said, "I was born into politics," would have preferred meeting his destiny where he did, in the arena. The former Pennsylvania governor, Pittsburgh mayor, and intimate of Democratic presidents, was stricken with a heart attack at a political rally November 4. Lawrence was lambasting Republican opponents of the Democratic state tickets when the heart stoppage came.

In his 77 years he had spent more than 50 years in politics. He had tasted the bitterness of defeat and political contumely and the heady wine of success.

First Taste in 1912

His political career, which started as a page boy at the 1912 Democratic National Convention, also included offices of national committeeman, state chairman, and secretary of the commonwealth.

As four-time mayor of Pittsburgh, from 1946 to 1958, Lawrence was instrumental in helping mold the city's famed Rennaissance.

Although he disliked being called "boss," Lawrence had held the Democrats together despite feuds that had ripped the party over the years. His death undoubtedly will cause a hard-to-fill void in the Democratic Party, although the party has its share of ambitious men willing to become leader.

Lawrence's ability—some called it a genius—which made him different from the old-time Democratic bosses, was that he could see that a political party must move with the times. It was this quality which impressed upon him the need to cooperate with such Republican industrial giants as Richard King Mellon in rebuilding Pittsburgh. He also could see when he became governor in 1959 that the Democratic Party must shed its role, which had emphasized pasting the wealthy, and adjust to the times.

He Forced the Changes

As a result, with the continuation of the sales tax—once anathema to Democrats—and other concessions to industry, Pennsylvania's business climate improved. Continuing the sales tax brought some grumbling from organized labor members on Lawrence's Tax Advisory Committee in 1959, but he lived up to his "tough old pro" reputation by saying: "The sales tax is here to stay."

The ability to roll with a punch was demonstrated by Lawrence in other head-on brushes with labor leaders and with members of his party who, too, would be the king.

In 1946 during the strike of Duquesne Light Co. workers, the city administration of Lawrence sought an injunction against the union to prevent a crippling stoppage of power. Later the injunction was dropped after the late county commissioners' chairman John

J. Kane reportedly prevailed upon labor leaders to try to stop the strike.

He Won His Fight

In 1949 Lawrence was pushed into a mayoralty primary fight with then–city councilman Edward J. Leonard, a plasterers' union official, which brought about a split in labor support.

Lawrence was victor in another intraparty fight in 1954, when he supported George M. Leader, the organization choice for governor, in a primary battle against former Coroner William D. McClelland. The 1954 defeat, which left McClelland embittered, was forgotten by Lawrence when he supported McClelland for county commissioner in 1959.

In 1958 Lawrence easily survived another party split when he defeated former lieutenant governor Roy E. Furman for the Democratic gubernatorial nomination.

The ability to think quickly in a political crisis helped Lawrence avert what could have been damaging blows to his standing as Pennsylvania's "Mr. Democrat."

Tiffed with Kennedys

Early in 1960 Lawrence reportedly was earning the displeasure of the Kennedys over his opposition to the late President John F. Kennedy's campaign. Lawrence publicly denied he was opposed to Kennedy's campaign, and at the Democratic National Convention that year he got on the Kennedy presidential bandwagon.

The future mayor and governor got his training in politics early in the office of William J. "Billy" Brennen, then Allegheny County Democratic chairman.

Lawrence was born June 18, 1889, in Pittsburgh, only 75 feet from where the old Blockhouse stands, the son of Charles and Catherine Conwell Lawrence.

He was one of four children. A sister, Mary, whom he called "my favorite," died at an early age. He had two brothers.

He graduated from eighth grade of the old St. Mary's Parochial School on Penn Avenue, and attended St. Mary's High School on Webster Avenue, where he took a two-year commercial course. As a typist in Attorney Brennen's office, Lawrence learned the rudiments of politics at the age of 14.

Years later, while being interviewed in the governor's office, Lawrence was asked: "What got you into politics?" His answer: "I was born into it."

The then-governor explained that his father and grandfather had been in politics in minor ways, adding: "As far back as I can remember hearing anything, it would be about politics."

It was in Brennen's office that Lawrence first met city treasurer James P. Kirk. The two became inseparable friends and political allies, and Kirk could truly be said to be one man for whom Lawrence had a deep affection and respect.

In 1920 Lawrence's political ambition began to bear fruit. He became Democratic county chairman. The period from 1920 to 1921 also was memorable for Lawrence in that he married an attractive North Side girl, Alyce Golden, and got his first political job as Pittsburgh registration commissioner.

Lawrence had seen service in World War I, but defective vision prevented him from going overseas. He was discharged as a first lieutenant.

Joined Harris Firm

Shortly after the war Lawrence formed a business alliance which wasn't dictated along political lines. He went into the insurance business with a rising young Republican, Frank J. Harris. Lawrence was still a partner in the Harris-Lawrence Co. at the time of his death, although he had not been active in the business.

In the early 1920s the Democratic Party at the state and local level was in the minority in Pennsylvania and lived on crumbs from the Republican table.

He Once Got the Crumbs

For more than a decade Lawrence had to be content with picking jobs which belonged to the minority party by law, such as county commissioners and jury commissioners.

Lawrence had failed to land a federal job during the administration of Woodrow Wilson because "Billy" Brennen had backed the wrong candidate at the Baltimore convention, Champ Clark.

The 1912 convention also marked the first time that Lawrence had a brush with Joseph F. Guffey, who later became U.S. Senator and a participant in the celebrated 1938 party split.

Lawrence suffered his only personal defeat at an election when he ran for county commissioner in 1931 in a coalition front with the late Republican state senator James J. Coyne.

Star Rose with FDR

His star began to ascend with the advent of President Franklin D. Roosevelt and the New Deal on the political scene. After the Roosevelt sweep in Allegheny County in 1932, Lawrence was appointed collector of internal revenue.

In 1934 Lawrence began to earn wider recognition when he was named Democratic state chairman, a post he held until 1940, when he became national committeeman from Pennsylvania.

When George H. Earle, son of a multimillionaire sugar processor, was elected governor in 1934, he rewarded Lawrence, who had managed his campaign, with a cabinet job. Lawrence became commonwealth secretary, and with his helping hand, much of the Little New Deal legislation was enacted during the Earle Administration.

In 1933 Lawrence had a bittersweet taste of more success locally when William N. McNair was elected Pittsburgh's first Democratic mayor in 23 years. McNair, who launched an eccentric career in city hall, highlighted by his selling apples and appearing on an amateur-hour radio program, would have none of Lawrence.

He Was Taboo Then

For three years Lawrence and job-hungry Democrats were taboo in McNair's office until, in 1936, McNair resigned suddenly after a series of clashes with city council. From then until his death, Lawrence was the guiding hand in succeeding city administrations, beginning with the late Mayor Cornelius D. Scully and

extending through his own and into the present.

At the state level, however, serious trouble for Lawrence developed. A forerunner of the Democratic Party split took place in 1937 when the Earle Administration, with Lawrence's support, pressed for passage of the railroad full-crew bill.

Guffey opposed the legislation, which the Railroad Brotherhood unions wanted, and wired state senators to vote against it. That was the second—but not final—Lawrence-Guffey encounter.

In 1938 Guffey obeyed President Roosevelt, who had been asked to intervene, but told Guffey to stay out of the race for Pennsylvania governor.

Guffey obeyed the president, but the Guffey-Lawrence split got bigger despite their protestations of friendship, supposedly sealed with the pledge "only the grave will part us."

Guffey backed a gubernatorial ticket headed by Thomas Kennedy, Earle's lieutenant governor, who had United Mine Workers support. Against Kennedy, Lawrence backed Charles Alvin Jones, who later became a state supreme court justice.

Feud with Margiotti

The 1938 primary campaign took on a deadly aspect when attorney Charles J. Margiotti, who said Lawrence had promised to support him for governor when Margiotti became attorney general, released his fury. Margiotti, in a series of preprimary speeches, charged graft and corruption pervaded the Little New Deal. He charged scandals in buying gravel, "bought" legislation, payroll macing, and kickbacks. Most of Margiotti's angry denunciation was leveled at Lawrence.

Lawrence was vindicated during the 1939 and 1940 trials of the "Erie Gravel Scandal" charges, and in 1940 he went back to the political war with Guffey.

Guffey won the party's nomination for the U.S. Senate, and Lawrence stepped down as state chairman and came back to devote his time to leading the party in Allegheny County.

Tragedy struck the Lawrence family in 1942 with the deaths in an auto crash of two sons, David Jr., age 13, and Brennen, age 16.

Lawrence submerged his grief in more vigorous political activity and a renewal of the Guffey feud. In 1942 he backed F. Clair Ross for governor against Guffey's candidate, the late Judge Ralph H. Smith. Ross won the Democratic nomination, and Lawrence again became state chairman. In the general election, however, Ross was defeated, and Lawrence came back to the county again to shore up the local political house.

Takes Over as Mayor

The Scully Administration, which had been slipping in public esteem, was the immediate problem. Lawrence decided in 1945 to rebuild the party's prestige by running for mayor.

He won the mayoralty election by 14,000 votes and was reelected in 1949 by 56,000 votes, by 55,000 in 1953, and by 59,000 in 1957—the highest majority ever recorded up to then in a Pittsburgh mayoralty election.

As mayor, Lawrence approached the crest of his long political career. He lent his support to the city's Renaissance, including smoke control, the Parking Authority, the Penn-Lincoln Parkway, and a broader tax base to take some of the burden off real estate.

He practically stole the political ball from Republican county leaders by going to Harrisburg and urging legislative support of the "Pittsburgh Package," bills necessary for the city's renewal.

During these years, Lawrence's associates found, he appeared happy and relaxed. In the late afternoon, when the city's business was finished for the day, he would hold a kind of informal session. Trusted lieutenants from the city and legislature might drift in to sit around and talk. They never, however, gave the mayor any advice on how to play a gin rummy hand, which might be going at the time with a city hall reporter.

Has Other Hide

During these brief moments the mayor would excel as a storyteller and sometimes display a side of his nature, which many people, who thought him "cold," did not see. Like his remark after a pay-roller had done something especially outrageous: "If it weren't for his wife and children, I would have fired him long ago."

Lawrence reached the pinnacle of his career in 1958 when, in a surprise move, he accepted the party's nomination for governor. He was the first Roman Catholic to win the office.

As the state's chief executive, Lawrence backed funds for more school buildings, hospital care for indigents, workmen's and occupational disease benefits, and the anti–skid row bill limiting the concentration of taprooms.

A National Figure

Lawrence's political shadow extended beyond the state's borders. He helped in the first nomination of President Roosevelt and was instrumental in Truman's nomination for vice president over Henry Wallace in 1944.

In 1960 Lawrence was accorded the honor of nominating Lyndon B. Johnson for vice president.

At the time of his death Lawrence was chairman of the President's Committee on Equal Opportunity in Housing and a confidant of President Johnson, whom he had known since the New Deal days.

His Washington job, however, didn't stop Lawrence's activities in state and local Democratic politics.

Fought, Then Backed Shapp

He had opposed the unsuccessful Democratic candidate for governor, Milton Shapp, but when Shapp won the nomination in the primary, Lawrence supported him.

There was considerable speculation in Democratic circles that Lawrence might issue orders to cut Shapp in the general election because Shapp had indicated after the primary Lawrence should step down from the party's councils. Lawrence not only resented being called a Democratic "boss," but his eyes would quickly turn frosty at a hint he had cut a party candidate.

Lawrence is survived by his wife, Alyce; two daughters, Mrs. Thomas K. Donahoe, of Mt. Lebanon, and Mrs. Joseph Gannon, of Bethel Park; a son, Gerald, of Willow Grove, Pennsylvania; and five grandchildren.

SATURDAY, MAY 7, 1988

Richard S. Caliguiri, 56
Architect of Renaissance II
By Tom Barnes, *Pittsburgh Post-Gazette*

Mayor Richard Sylvester Caliguiri, age 56, who died early yesterday of heart failure brought on by a rare disease, was the architect of the Renaissance II urban renewal program and leader of the effort to keep Major League baseball in Pittsburgh.

Caliguiri, who first became mayor in April 1977 and then was elected three times, began his public career in 1956 in the city Parks Department. He rose to become city parks director, then a city councilman, and, finally, mayor.

Caliguiri became mayor when, as city council president, he was named to replace Pete Flaherty after Flaherty went to Washington, D.C., to become U.S. deputy attorney general in the administration of President Jimmy Carter.

Many Democrats thought Caliguiri would merely serve out the remainder of Flaherty's term, until January 1978.

Pittsburgh mayor Richard Caliguiri reads a proclamation on November 14, 1983, to mark the reopening of Sixth and Liberty Avenues. The streets had been closed to two-way traffic since January 1982 for subway construction. *Photo by Harry Coughanour.*

But he caught the Pittsburgh Democratic organization off guard in July 1977 when he announced that he would run as an independent for a full four-year term.

"Many people inside the party were shocked by his candidacy," county controller Frank Lucchino said late last year. "They thought they had struck a deal back in the spring" of 1977 for Caliguiri to serve only as a caretaker mayor for the remainder of that year.

In the November 1977 election, Caliguiri overcame the city's strong Democratic Party structure and defeated county commissioner Tom Foerster, the Democratic candidate for mayor, and Republican candidate Joseph Cosetti.

Caliguiri went on to become one of the most popular mayors in city history.

Running as a Democrat, he easily won reelection in 1981 and 1985. Voters responded well to his low-key, non-flamboyant style of governing. "There are some things the people of Pittsburgh do not want in their government," he said three years ago. "They do not want confrontation for confrontation's sake, or name-calling, or publicity-grabbing. They don't want razzle-dazzle, phony charges, and phony promises. The people of Pittsburgh know this is not, and never will be, my style of government."

There was no question about Caliguiri's enduring love for his native city. When he disclosed his incurable disease, some wondered whether he should step down as mayor and turn the responsibilities over to someone else. But Caliguiri said no one would have to tell him when it was time to go. "The day that I can't put in a full day's work is the day I will leave this office," he said in October. "I don't intend in any way to jeopardize this city. I love this city too much. I respect it too much."

In December 1987, when *U.S. News & World Report* magazine named him as one of the 20 best mayors in the United States, Caliguiri said he was happy for himself but happier for Pittsburgh, which finally was getting some long-overdue recognition after decades of being branded the "smoky city." "There is a good, positive future for Pittsburgh," he said.

Although he was a Democrat, Caliguiri's conservative stands on political and social issues endeared him to the city's business community, many of whose members are Republicans. The top corporations and law firms in the city consistently lined up to contribute to his political campaigns.

He said that as mayor, he had tried to be "serious, sensible, hard-working, earnest, and honest."

When Caliguiri became mayor in the late 1970s, development and urban renewal efforts had slowed considerably from the days of Pittsburgh's first renaissance under David L. Lawrence, who was mayor from 1946 to 1959. While Lawrence had overseen such major projects as the development of the Gateway Center office complex, the clearing of land for Point State Park, and the passage of laws to control smoke from steel mills, renaissance efforts had dwindled under his successors, Mayor Joseph Barr in the 1960s and Pete Flaherty in the 1970s.

Caliguiri got urban development back on track, overseeing the effort to create several distinctive new Downtown buildings in the early 1980s, including PPG Place, One Mellon Bank Center, and Oxford Centre.

In the mid-1980s came the second phase of Renaissance II, with the opening of the Vista International Hotel and Liberty Center office building and the construction of two other major Downtown office buildings, the CNG office tower and Fifth Avenue Place.

The late 1980s saw progress on several other developments, including the conversion of the Stanley Theater into the Benedum Center for the Performing Arts, the rebirth of the Pennsylvania Railroad station into apartments and shops, and construction of light manufacturing buildings on the long-abandoned Herrs Island, now Washington's Landing, in the Allegheny River.

During his reelection campaign in 1985, one of his opponents, city controller Tom Flaherty, derided Caliguiri as merely a "cheerleader" and a "ribbon cutter," rather than someone who deserved credit for Pittsburgh's redevelopment.

Caliguiri turned the insults into compliments. "I want to continue to be the biggest cheerleader this city ever had," he said. "I think we've got a hell of a lot to cheer about. I wish I could cut a ribbon every week because that means progress in this city, and that means jobs."

Although the glamorous projects built Downtown attracted the most attention, Caliguiri repeatedly insisted that he devoted equal time and financial resources to improving the city's housing stock and to upgrading many neighborhood business districts in Pittsburgh. "Renaissance II is, of course, the golden triangle, but it's also the neighborhoods' renaissance," he said in 1985, adding that "these [Downtown] glamour projects get the headlines" in the newspapers and obscure the more mundane improvements, such as street paving, sewer lines, and new storefronts.

Besides his urban renewal efforts, Caliguiri was best known for his aggressive campaign in 1985 and 1986 to prevent the Pirates from leaving Pittsburgh. He was determined not to go down in history as "the mayor who lost the Pirates." The John Galbreath family put the team up for sale in November 1984, saying it no longer could afford the multimillion-dollar losses that the team was incurring.

Caliguiri waited on the sidelines for several months as various individuals in private industry talked about putting together a coalition to buy the team. When their efforts failed, Caliguiri jumped in and, by October 1985, had put together a "public-private partnership" that raised $45 million to buy the team from the Galbreaths.

Half of that amount came from city government in the form of a loan to a group of private corporations that was buying the team. To raise the money, Caliguiri and his advisors designed a novel plan to sell Three Rivers Stadium to a private investor and use the proceeds to loan to the Pirates.

The sale still hasn't taken place, and the city had to use a more customary fund-raising method, a bond sale, to raise the public share of the money for the Pirates.

Caliguiri, who lived in Squirrel Hill with his second wife and two sons, was a 1950 graduate of Allderdice High School. Anita Rosenberg Neaman was his first wife.

After serving in the air force, he got a job in the city Parks Department in 1956, his first step up the ladder of city politics. He went on to become an assistant executive secretary to Mayor Barr in 1968–1969 and then served as director of the Parks Department in 1969–1970.

In 1970 he was appointed to fill a vacancy on City Council. The next year, after being denied the Democratic Party endorsement, he ran successfully for a full term on council as an independent—the same strategy he was to use six years later in the mayor's race. He stayed on the council until 1977, becoming council president in March 1977, just a few weeks before taking over as mayor when Flaherty departed for Washington.

He rarely went out of his way to pick a fight. He made an exception in 1984 when he became embroiled in a controversy over pornography involving *Hustler* magazine. Caliguiri, a Catholic, urged news dealers in Pittsburgh to remove the May 1984 issue from their shelves voluntarily because it contained a pictorial parody of Holy Week containing nude women. Caliguiri called the magazine "offensive and distasteful."

Unlike many big-city mayors, Caliguiri didn't have an enormous ego or a relish for the public spotlight. He didn't hold regular news conferences,

On September 10, 1986, Pittsburgh mayor Richard Caliguiri, a speaker at an ecumenical memorial service, prays for the victims of recent terrorism in Turkey (a synagogue attack) and Pakistan (a hijacking). *Photo courtesy of the* Pittsburgh Post-Gazette

and he met with reporters only when making major announcements, such as in 1985 when he said the Pirates would remain in Pittsburgh.

He sometimes was perceived as inaccessible, and his critics claimed he was afraid to face reporters. He usually let his aides do the talking, especially David Matter, a longtime friend and confidant who served as his executive secretary from 1977 until early 1986. After Matter left to work for a private firm, Caliguiri used David Donahoe, Matter's replacement, and Mark Zabierek, another aide, to make most of the administration's statements to news media.

Caliguiri's success in winning reelection led many Democrats to think he would run some day for governor. Associates said privately that Caliguiri felt happy and satisfied being the mayor of Pittsburgh and never longed for a move to Harrisburg.

He stunned the city October 2 when he disclosed that he suffered from amyloidosis. He had become aware that something was wrong in March 1987, when he became dizzy while playing a round of golf. After tests were done at Shadyside Hospital and later at the Mayo Clinic in Rochester, Minnesota, doctors determined the cause of his problem, but nothing was said publicly for several months.

Over the summer, friends and political acquaintances began noticing that Caliguiri looked pale and even thinner than his normal weight of 140 pounds. For a while, he dismissed concern by saying it was only an intestinal ailment. But he finally revealed the truth.

The disease left harmful deposits of protein in his heart, which made the heart still and interfered with his heartbeat and blood pressure. In late December, doctors implanted a pacemaker to keep his heartbeat regular.

In January, he began taking drugs to regulate his heartbeat further. But by April, his condition was deteriorating as fluid built up in his chest and his energy level decreased. At the time of his death, doctors had become convinced that

Caliguiri needed a heart transplant to have a chance to survive. He was said to be enthusiastic about the idea because he hoped it would restore his energy.

Surviving are his wife, Jeanne; two sons, David J. and Gregg R.; his father, Cris; a sister, Virginia; and 15 nieces and nephews.

FRIDAY, APRIL 5, 1991

John Heinz III, 52
Heir to a Vast Fortune, Won Respect as a Legislator
By Ernie Hoffman, *Pittsburgh Post-Gazette*

Handsome, wealthy, a Republican power in a Democratic stronghold, Senator John Heinz of Fox Chapel was killed along with six others yesterday when the small plane in which he was a passenger collided with a helicopter outside Philadelphia.

Senator Heinz, age 52, was one of the top-ranking Republicans in the senate as he entered the middle of his third term. He also was one of its wealthiest members, heir to an international food corporation founded by his great-grandfather and possessor of a personal fortune estimated by *Forbes* magazine at more than $500 million.

First elected to the senate in 1976, he would have been up for reelection in 1994.

Active in legislation involving the elderly, the steel industry, and financial matters, Senator Heinz was the ranking Republican of the Special Committee on Aging; a member of the Banking, Housing, and Urban Affairs Committee and chairman of its international finance and monetary policy subcommittee; a member of the Finance Committee and chairman of

John Heinz III. *Photo by Harry Coughanour.*

its economic growth, employment, and revenue-sharing subcommittee; a member of the Energy and Natural Resources Committee; chairman of the coal and steel caucuses; and a member of caucuses on tourism, Vietnam-era veterans, and exports.

He was best known recently for his advocacy of legislation that would have barred the military from deploying married couples or single parents in combat zones. The proposal, introduced after the start of Operation Desert Storm and staunchly opposed by the Pentagon, did not pass.

Senator Heinz used the resources of his wealth, political savvy, and business skills to promote the economic and cultural development of Pittsburgh and Allegheny County.

"John Heinz was one of the investors of the original group that brought the Pittsburgh Penguins franchise to Pittsburgh in 1966. He saw an opportunity to enhance Pittsburgh with another major-league sports franchise, and obviously, while he was very young, his involvement was crucial in bringing the franchise to Pittsburgh," said Tad Potter, who bought the club several years later.

Senator Heinz, who resided with his wife, Teresa, in an imposing white mansion on Squaw Run Road in Fox Chapel, first attained political office in 1971, when he won the 18th Congressional District seat vacated at the death of Robert J. Corbett, who had held the post for 14 terms.

Despite a 14,000-Democratic majority in the 18th district, Heinz defeated Democrat John E. Connelly, owner of the Gateway Clipper fleet by a 2-1 vote to become the youngest Republican member of the House at the age of 33.

Scholarly and genteel, he quickly became one of Pennsylvania's most popular politicians. In its July 15, 1974, edition, *Time* magazine featured him in a list of rising American leaders in an article titled "200 Faces for the Future."

Senator Heinz remained a member of the House until 1976, when he was elected to the senate, replacing one of his political mentors, the retiring Hugh Scott. Heinz received 52.4 percent of the vote that year, defeating Philadelphia Democrat William J. Green, also a member of Congress, and several other candidates.

The senator spent $2.9 million of his personal fortune to finance the 1976 election campaign. He later rebuked some who criticized him for that: "I used some of my own money to fund my campaign, and the news media thought it was scandalous. But Jay Rockefeller spent $15 million to become governor of West Virginia, a state one-quarter the size of Pennsylvania, and somehow it wasn't [scandalous]. I guess that's the difference between being a rich Republican and a rich Democrat."

Still, after entering the senate, he stopped using his full name—Henry John Heinz III—and adopted the informal John Heinz in a move to soften his patrician image.

He was reelected in 1982 with 59.3 percent of the vote, defeating Democrat Dr. Cyril H. Wecht, then a county commissioner, and other minor party candidates.

He was reelected again in 1988 with an overwhelming 67 percent of the vote, defeating Democrat Joseph Vignola, a former Philadelphia city controller.

Senator Heinz was born October 23, 1938, in Pittsburgh, the son of Henry

John Heinz II and the former Joan Diehl. His great-grandfather, H.J. Heinz, had founded the food-processing company of the same name in 1869 in Sharpsburg and had developed it into an international business.

After his parents divorced, Heinz went to live in San Francisco, where he was raised by his mother and his stepfather, navy captain Clayton C. McCauley.

Senator Heinz graduated with honors from Phillips Exeter Academy in New Hampshire in 1956, then received a bachelor's degree in history and letters from Yale University in 1960. He received a master's degree in business administration from the Harvard Graduate School of Business Administration, graduating near the top of his class in 1963.

He was in the Air Force Reserve, stationed at Lackland Air Force Base in San Antonio, Texas, and he served with what is now the 911th Military Airlift Group at Greater Pittsburgh International Airport. He was honorably discharged with the rank of staff sergeant in 1969.

During his school years, he worked at various times as a ranch hand in Montana, hauling pickle crates on a production line at the Heinz factory in Holland, Michigan, and as a trust manager for a bank in Geneva, Switzerland. He was also a special representative to the Far East for the International Association of Students in the Economic and Commercial Sciences and a truck salesman for International Harvester Ltd. in Sydney, Australia.

After graduating from Harvard, Heinz was offered and accepted a job with the marketing division of H.J.

Henry John Heinz III signals victory to his supporters at the Vista International Hotel in Downtown Pittsburgh on November 8, 2006. *Photo by Joyce Mendelsohn.*

Heinz Co. without the knowledge of his father, the president. "When my father found out I was hired, he wasn't happy. He didn't want to be surprised that way," he recalled years later.

In 1964 he became an office aide and political advance man for Senator Scott, the man he would replace in the senate 12 years later.

From 1965 until 1970, he worked for the family company in the financial and marketing divisions. He then spent one year as a lecturer at Carnegie Mellon University's Graduate School of Industrial Administration before entering politics.

He married Teresa Simoes-Ferreira, a Portuguese woman who became a naturalized U.S. citizen in October 1971. She is a former resident of

Mozambique in eastern Africa. The couple had three sons, 24-year-old H. John IV, 21-year-old Andre, and 18-year-old Christopher.

Besides his wife and children, Senator Heinz is survived by his mother, Joan Diehl McCauley. Mrs. McCauley, a San Francisco socialite once known for her prowess as a pilot, told reporters last night that she was "greatly shocked" at the news of her son's death and declined further comment.

Senator Heinz was a fellow of the Carnegie Institute Museum of Art; a board member of Children's Hospital and of Yale University Art Gallery; a member of the National Association for the Advancement of Colored People, the Pennsylvania Society, the Air Force Association, and the World Affairs Council of Pittsburgh; a trustee of the Howard Heinz Endowment; and chairman of the H.J. Heinz II Charitable and Family Trust. He was a member of the American Legion, the Polish National Alliance and the Italian Sons & Daughters of America.

In other political activities, Heinz was a founder and member of the Northeast-Midwest Coalition and a member of the Republican Policy Committee in the senate.

He was chairman of the national Republican Senatorial Committee in 1978–80; chairman of the Pennsylvania Republican State Platform Committee in 1970; and a delegate to the GOP national party conventions in 1968, 1972, 1976, and 1980.

WEDNESDAY, JANUARY 12, 2000

Thomas J. Foerster, 71
Seven-Term Commissioner
By James O'Toole, *Pittsburgh Post-Gazette*

Thomas J. Foerster, the soft-spoken ex–football coach who rose from the political back benches to dominate Allegheny County government through the last quarter of the 20th century, died yesterday.

Mr. Foerster, age 71, was elected to a record seven terms in the courthouse before being rebuffed in the 1995 Democratic primary. In the last months of his life, Mr. Foerster made what would remain a figurative return to the courthouse with his election to the County Council, the legislative arm of the new form of government he had helped to create.

His physician, Dr. Bruce Dixon, said Foerster's death, at 4:32 PM, was caused by complications of the cardiac arrest he suffered last Wednesday and the diabetes that he had suffered for years. He had been in a coma since last Wednesday when he suffered the heart attack in the midst of tests in the hospital.

At his death, in UPMC Montefiore Hospital, Foerster was accompanied by his wife, Georgeann, as well as his two brothers and sisters and their children.

Mr. Foerster was an unabashed liberal, unafraid to raise taxes for the public works projects and social programs at the center of his view of government. He was proudest of his work in nurturing the community college system and seeing through the development of the new Pittsburgh International Airport.

During his 28 years in office he also presided over the expansions of a wide variety of human service programs and the construction of four Kane Regional Centers to replace the old Kane Hospital for the elderly. At the prodding of a federal judge, his administration built the massive new jail along the banks of the Monongahela.

On his way to those accomplishments, he was an easy person to underestimate. He entered the legislature in the years when the word *charisma* first became associated with success in politics. It was a word never associated with Mr. Foerster. He had a plain, stolid, untelegenic face. He fought a lifelong battle with his weight. But through mastery of detail, perseverance, and an innate understanding of politics and coalition-building, he put together a record as perhaps the greatest builder in the history of Allegheny County government.

While he amassed—and, critics said, jealously guarded—power as a political leader, he dismissed accounts of his influence as more perception than reality. And in a post-machine age, he never had the degree of clout that figures such as David Lawrence wielded

in the political generation that preceded him. But he did have power.

In later years, his old-school style and sheer longevity sometimes allowed the perception of a sense of sclerosis about Democratic politics. Republican commissioner Larry Dunn constantly complained of Mr. Foerster's governing style, charging that he was frozen out of decision-making.

But Common Pleas Judge Frank Lucchino, the longtime county controller who once ran against Mr. Foerster then became a close ally, saw him as a benign influence, "a rock of Gibraltar," to his party and his county.

Morton Coleman, the former head of the University of Pittsburgh's Institute for Politics, said, "Others may quarrel with some of the decisions and methods he employed to get things done, but year in and year out for 28 years, he is the guy who kept the party going.... He gave loyalty and expected loyalty in return. And he often used his power for visionary ends.

"The things he did with the community college during the collapse of the steel industry, I thought, were brilliant."

"At a time when most people were in denial about homelessness…he moved almost immediately," said Phil Pappas, executive director of Community Human Services, a settlement house. "His abiding passion was to level the playing field, and he had a sense of the need to move quickly.... He was outcome-driven."

"There would not be a [Senator John Heinz Regional] History Center if it were not for the vision of Tom Foerster," said John Herbst, the strip district institution's former director. "He was the first public official to see the potential of the history center and get behind it in a practical way."

Over his long public life, Mr. Foerster battled, at one time or another, with figures across the political spectrum. But, time and again, he would repair those rifts and go on to work with former enemies—abiding by his oft-repeated adage: "Today is the first day of the rest of your life."

He opposed Pete Flaherty's insurgent campaign for mayor of Pittsburgh but ended up working in tandem with him on the board of commissioners. Years later, he feuded bitterly with Jim Flaherty, Pete's brother, when he joined him on the board of commissioners and froze Mr. Foerster out, forming an alliance with Republican Bob Peirce. By the end of that term, Mr. Foerster and Jim Flaherty were partners again.

Mr. Foerster lost to the late mayor Richard Caliguiri in his only run for mayor but went on to work with his former rival on a variety of political and governmental issues. A split with former commissioner Cyril H. Wecht led to years of acrimony between them, but even they had a rapprochement by the time Wecht ran for county executive last year.

Until his death, Mr. Foerster lived in the same North Side neighborhood in which he had grown up. "He lived such a simple life," said Lucchino. "He had his place in Conneaut, which, if you've ever been there, there's nothing to it.... And he has this nice but very modest house on Troy Hill."

A big kid, he played the line, on offense and defense, on North Catholic's football teams in the early 1940s and later at Slippery Rock College. While still a student at North, he began coaching youth football, an avocation he would continue up to his election to the state legislature.

He and Steelers owner Dan Rooney, who would be a lifelong friend, were rival coaches in a North Side grade-school league—Rooney at St. Peter, Mr. Foerster at Nativity. "He really was a person who thought of the small guy," said Rooney. "He had this great sense of compassion."

Empathy and eagerness to reach out are qualities cited again and again in reminiscences of the former commissioner. "One memory that sticks with me was a Christmas 12 years ago when we couldn't meet our payroll," said Bill Strickland, the acclaimed leader of the now-thriving Manchester Craftsmen's Guild. "We put out a kind of appeal, and [Representative] Leroy Irvis and Tom Foerster were the two people who showed up on this Christmas week evening and said, 'How can I help?'"

For most of his adult life, Mr. Foerster seemed the archetype of the confirmed bachelor. But at age 62 he stunned even his closest friends with the news that he would marry Georgeann Zupancic. "She's just the most wonderful person I've met in my life," he said shortly after their wedding on November 23, 1990. "Not only am I in love with her, she is my best friend." From his wedding day on, Mr. Foerster was quick to volunteer a fond, precise accounting of his nuptial bliss, citing the exact number of days since the end of his bachelorhood, "with never an argument or a fight."

He was an avid antismoking crusader. His ban on smoking in the courthouse was routinely defied, but he seldom hesitated to remind a smoker of the error of his ways. Once, hitching a ride with a reporter, he expressed disgust at the auto's overflowing ashtray. Then, mindful of his steelworker constituents, he upbraided the reporter for driving a foreign car.

Mr. Foerster's first two runs at the General Assembly, in 1954 and 1956, ended in failure. But, characteristically, he persevered. He was finally elected to the state House in 1958, beating former Steelers quarterback John "Harp" Vaughn. He went to Harrisburg at the same time as his political hero, Lawrence, the longtime Pittsburgh mayor who had been elected governor.

In the legislature Mr. Foerster, looking beyond the agenda of his urban district, forged a reputation as "Clean-Streams Tom," the champion of sportsmen and environmentalists.

"I think one of the things that strikes me about him is that he's always been underestimated," said former House speaker K. Leroy Irvis, the Hill District Democrat who entered the General Assembly in the same class as Mr. Foerster and another longtime ally, the late Senator Eugene Scanlon, a Democrat from the north side. "They gave him an assignment on the committee on mines and minerals that had nothing to do with the north side; that's the way they treated us freshmen back then," Irvis recalled. "But he surprised them all. His leadership turned that committee around so that it changed the whole terrain of Western Pennsylvania."

Mr. Foerster was one of the architects of laws curbing abuses in the state's strip-mining industry. He was a prime sponsor of the 1965 Clean Streams Act and the 1966 Mine Subsidence Act.

He would be elected to the legislature five times. One of Mr. Foerster's frequent legislative partners was state senator Leonard Staisey. They were chosen by the still-functioning Lawrence machine to replace the incumbent Democratic commissioners William McClelland and John McGrady.

The challengers styled themselves as the "Action Team," promising to bring more dynamic government to the county. It was a step forward for Mr. Foerster. But he was still very much the junior member of that team, taking a backseat to the brilliant Staisey, who had not allowed blindness to deter him from successful careers in law and politics. There were even rumors then that Staisey had considered replacing his running mate with the late sheriff Eugene Coon for his second term. Few would have predicted then that it would be Mr. Foerster who would go on to make the greater mark on the county.

The Staisey-Foerster administration would pursue expansions of the county park system and its social service network, new antipollution efforts, and the construction of Community College of Allegheny County.

Irvis had written the law creating the state's community college system. His friend Mr. Foerster supported the concept in the legislature and embraced its brick-and-mortar embodiment throughout his long tenure in the courthouse.

"When people talk about his record, you always hear about the airport, and that was important," said Bob Nelkin, a close advisor on human service issues. "But to Tom, it was the community college and human services that were closest to his heart."

The Staisey-Foerster years also saw an expansion of rapid transit, an area that included the controversial Skybus proposal that would contribute to the end of their partnership. Skybus was to be a pioneering rubber-wheeled train running on separate, sometimes overhead, rights of way.

The plan was hailed as visionary by some but denounced as expensive and untested by others, including Pete Flaherty, then the popular mayor of Pittsburgh. In the face of the widespread opposition, Mr. Foerster would eventually back away from the proposal, while Staisey remained steadfast in his support. In the 1975 primary, Staisey was ousted by Jim Flaherty. Mr. Foerster survived, but the Democrats' partnership didn't last much beyond the general election. Flaherty formed a coalition with Peirce. Mr. Foerster was still in office, but not in power.

In 1977 he turned his sights across Forbes Avenue, to the city county building where Caliguiri had succeeded Pete Flaherty as mayor after Flaherty went to Washington in the Carter administration. Mr. Foerster won the Democratic nomination over a multicandidate field that included Lucchino and James Simms, now a county councilman. Mr. Foerster thought he also had received assurance from Caliguiri that he would not seek a full term and would instead

support Mr. Foerster. But Caliguiri, after staying out of the Democratic primary, ran as an independent and defeated Mr. Foerster by 5,000 votes.

After that disappointment, Mr. Foerster got some consolation with the breakup of the Flaherty-Peirce alliance. Mr. Foerster and Flaherty mended their rift, restoring Mr. Foerster's share of county power.

While Flaherty stepped down after a single term, Mr. Foerster won reelection in 1979 teamed with Wecht. Environmental issues were again a preoccupation. County government tried to balance air quality against the interests of the steel industry—then on the verge of a decade-long collapse—as it implemented new federal clean air laws.

The Democrats also joined in taking the first steps toward the financing and construction of the midfield terminal project at the airport. And they struggled to craft a response to a civil rights suit protesting inhumane conditions at the county jail.

Wecht was serving as chairman of the county Democratic Party at the time, and his term, for a variety of reasons, was a fractious one. Mr. Foerster eventually sided with his former rival, Caliguiri, against Wecht. They opposed Wecht's reelection both to the party post and as a commissioner.

Wecht, along with Coon, won the party endorsement for commissioner in 1983, but Mr. Foerster prevailed, winning nomination in the primary and going on to reelection teamed, warily at first, with Pete Flaherty. Some doubted the durability of that alliance of very different political personalities, but it proved a productive partnership, with accomplishments including the completion of the airport project and the massive new jail.

Every other week the commissioners and their aides would pile into buses, traveling to the far corners of the county to get a first-hand view of its projects and problems. From Aleppo to Wall, from Pine to Moon, Mr. Foerster boasted that he had been in every one of the county's 130 municipalities more than five times.

"I would assert that his legacy is more than any particular project," said Lucchino. "It was his quiet but firm willingness to move ahead on issues before they were popular. There were the obvious things—the airport, the community college, the Kanes—but there were many other things that people don't know anything about."

Echoing Herbst, he mentioned Mr. Foerster's role in supporting the Heinz history center. Lucchino said Foerster played a similar role in committing the county to a countywide computer system for libraries and the the Carnegie's development of the Andy Warhol Museum. "He was no arts devotee, but he saw the advantage of this unique institution," said Lucchino. "He was the perfect example of the saying, 'It's amazing how much you can get done if you don't care who gets the credit.'"

With his reelection in 1991, Mr. Foerster became the first commissioner in the century to serve seven terms, eclipsing the record held by the late commissioner John Kane. But it would prove to be Mr. Foerster's last term and one that would be buffeted with personal and political controversy.

In the Democratic primary that year, Mr. Foerster had supported Michael Coyne against an old protege and former aide, Joseph Brimmeier. The race caused a lasting intraparty rift. Four county employees who had supported Brimmeier later sued the county, charging that their subsequent firings were acts of political retribution by Mr. Foerster. The commissioners who succeeded Mr. Foerster settled the suit in 1997 with a payment of $475,000. But Mr. Foerster opposed the settlement, insisting that there was nothing to the charges. He said that if he had fired everyone who disagreed with him over the years, "There probably wouldn't be anyone left working for the county."

Mr. Foerster was indisputably a champion of social programs, constantly importuning the state and federal governments for more money for human services. But his administration faced sharp criticism even in those areas in the early 1990s. Children and Youth Services was the subject of frequent complaints and eventually of a scathing report citing its inadequate procedures and overflowing caseloads. The county Housing Authority was officially designated "troubled" by the U.S. Department of Housing and Urban Development.

In 1993 a major round of reassessments brought howls of suburban outrage, spotlighting an antiquated and frequently inequitable tax system—one that Mr. Foerster himself had often complained of. Newspapers were filled with reports of symptoms of government bloat such as the provision of rent-free housing in county parks to a few favored employees and lack of control and accountability in the distribution of county cars.

Cutting closer to home, Mr. Foerster's stepson, just months before the primary, was indicted and, after pleading guilty, sentenced to eight years in jail for trafficking in cocaine. Mr. Foerster's own actions were scrutinized in connection with the case, with questions raised over whether he had intervened with law enforcement officials on his stepson's behalf. But federal prosecutors later said there was no evidence that Mr. Foerster had done anything improper.

As the 1995 primary approached, all of those factors reinforced an aura of vulnerability about the incumbents. A big field lined up to exploit that opportunity, led by state senator Michael Dawida and his running mate, Coleen Vuono. With all their baggage, Mr. Foerster and Flaherty were still favored, but Dawida and Vuono rolled to upsets for the Democratic nominations. The voters who had reelected him again and again apparently felt that Mr. Foerster had stayed too long at the party. He trailed in fourth place.

If they didn't agree with the premise that there was something wrong with their administration, Mr. Foerster and Flaherty had endorsed and encouraged a growing view that there was something wrong with the structure of county government itself. Enlisting Duquesne University president John Murray as its chairman, they appointed a committee, Compac 21, to study how a mode of government more than two centuries old should be tailored for a new century.

"Tom called me one afternoon and invited me to meet with him without telling me what it was about," Murray recalled. He traveled down the Bluff from Duquesne to the courthouse and sat down with Mr. Foerster and Flaherty in Mr. Foerster's office. "Tom did most of the talking," he said. "He told me to take a very copious look at the structure of county government. He told me there would be no interference, and he lived up to that completely.... In my experience, it's fair to say what he cared about was making this county a lot better regardless of how it had to be changed. He was interested not in his own legacy, but in the future of Allegheny County."

After the 1995 defeat, Mr. Foerster settled, with surprising enthusiasm, into senior-statesman status. Foundations supported a distinguished fellow chair that allowed him to teach at Pitt, Carnegie Mellon, and Duquesne universities. "He was a really outstanding teacher," said Coleman. "It was a hard period for him. He had lost the election. He had his health problems, but he jumped into his work and he did it so well. I never heard him complain."

The recommendations devised by the Compac 21 panel were the seeds of the home-rule government and, indirectly, of Mr. Foerster's return to public life.

Staying with his North Side roots, he declared his candidacy last year for the new District 13 seat on County Council. Not for the first time, he was denied his party's endorsement. But Mr. Foerster cruised to easy victories in the primary and general elections. He promised to take a nonpartisan approach to the new council, saying, for instance, that he would avoid party caucuses if they were formed. Mr. Foerster actively campaigned for the council presidency, but his new colleagues preferred to go in another direction.

In his hospital room, he was sworn in by an old county government colleague, state supreme court justice Stephen A. Zappala Sr. Without Mr. Foerster, the County Council might very well not have existed, but he was never able to attend one of its sessions.

"Just a couple of weeks ago we were talking and I know he would have loved being president of council, but his real concern was that the job be done the way it should be done," said Elsie Hillman, the former Republican national committeewoman. "It's just a shame he didn't get to play a part in it."

Nelkin said, even as his health was failing, Mr. Foerster was working the phones on issues he hoped to tackle on the new council—harnessing the city's universities in a new center to address racial understanding and increasing funding for the community college's

work in developing skills for the changing workplace.

"I worked with Tom on a lot of government things, but when I think of him, I think of the impact he's had on many lives—and mine personally," said Mayor Murphy. "My daughter graduated from high school not knowing what she wanted to do. She started at the community college, and she ended up getting a master's from CMU.... We had an aunt in Kane Hospital a number of years ago. Kane used to be a terrible place. But, really with Tom's leadership, the mini-Kanes are excellent. I think there are families he's touched like that all over Allegheny County."

In addition to his wife, Mr. Foerster is survived by two sisters, Mary McLaughlin of the North Side and Virginia Muth of McCandless; two brothers, John of Point Breeze and William of Zelienople; and five stepchildren.

County executive James C. Roddey ordered flags at county facilities placed at half-staff to commemorate Foerster's death.

TUESDAY, APRIL 19, 2005

Peter F. Flaherty, 80
Former Mayor
By James O'Toole, *Pittsburgh Post-Gazette*

Peter F. Flaherty, a pivotal figure in Pittsburgh politics who brought reform and charisma to city hall while challenging the city's party and business establishments, has died. His longtime adviser, Bruce Campbell, said Mr. Flaherty died of cancer yesterday at

his home in Mt. Lebanon, surrounded by family.

In a public career that spanned four decades, Mr. Flaherty, age 80, was three times the Democratic nominee for statewide office, served as deputy U.S. Attorney General, and was a county commissioner for 12 years. But by far his most profound impact came as mayor of Pittsburgh, an office he captured in 1969 proclaiming himself "Nobody's Boy," distancing himself from the Democratic organization that had produced every Pittsburgh mayor since the Great Depression.

Mr. Flaherty's 1970 inauguration was bracketed by the deaths of David L. Lawrence, the former mayor and governor, and Richard King Mellon, the powerful business leader who, in a unique and productive partnership with Lawrence, helped to remake Pittsburgh in the years after World War II.

Mr. Flaherty's maverick candidacy and administration recognized and exploited dissatisfaction with the top-down civic structure those men had created. His rise also reflected larger national political currents in an era marked by the increasing assertiveness of civil rights and community groups outside the traditional political order.

As mayor, Mr. Flaherty won overwhelming public popularity but continued to antagonize established interests as he emphasized a streamlined and reformed approach to government. He trimmed the city payroll and repeatedly cut taxes while shifting development priorities toward neighborhoods beyond the Downtown core.

"He was a very significant figure," said Joel Tarr, a Carnegie Mellon University historian. "He capitalized on the waves of unhappiness with the Pittsburgh Renaissance and, I think, also the fact that the 1960s were such a traumatic decade...he was a breath of fresh air at a time that it was required."

Morton Coleman, of the University of Pittsburgh's Institute of Politics, called Mr. Flaherty "a leader in understanding that the traditional organization was weakening and a new kind of personal politics was strengthening."

"He was a brilliant pioneer in the new fiscal populist mayoral style," said Terry Nichols Clark, a scholar on urban issues at the University of Chicago, who studied Mr. Flaherty's administration. "He invented a whole style of politics...he came from a left Democratic Party background, and he combined it with fiscal conservatism, fighting business, fighting labor unions, fighting interests groups of all sorts."

Mr. Flaherty traveled a bumpier political road in the years after his successes as mayor. He was unable to transfer his Pittsburgh popularity statewide, losing two elections for the U.S. Senate and one for governor. In a brief tour in President Carter's Justice Department, he never established a rapport with the Georgia network that came to Washington with Carter.

Mr. Flaherty ended his public career with three productive but, by the standards of his dynamic tenure as mayor, relatively low-key terms as county commissioner, where he served as junior partner to veteran commissioner Tom Foerster.

Entry to Politics

Mr. Flaherty was the child of Irish immigrants. His father, also named Peter, emigrated from County Galway in 1909 and settled in San Francisco. After serving in World War I, the elder Flaherty returned to California but was called to

Pittsburgh in 1919 after his brother, Coleman, and his wife died in the flu pandemic that swept the globe after World War I, leaving their children orphans.

In Pittsburgh Peter met and married another Galway native Anne O'Toole. The elder Flaherty worked as a streetcar conductor and operator. The couple also operated a small grocery store about a block from their home on the North Side, then a polyglot community of Irish, Italians, Germans, and African Americans. The future mayor was born in their home on Alpine Avenue on June 24, 1924.

He attended St. Peter's, a Catholic elementary school, went on to Latimer Middle School, and graduated from Allegheny High School in the first year of World War II.

In an interview for the University of Pittsburgh's oral history archives, Mr. Flaherty recalled that they were a typically, for the time, devout Irish Catholic family. The two brothers and five sisters knelt together to say the rosary every night. Mr. Flaherty was an altar boy at St. Peter's. Throughout their school years, the children helped out in what for them was literally a mom-and-pop grocery store.

After high school, in the middle of World War II, Mr. Flaherty joined the Army Air Corps and was trained as a navigator. He shipped out to the Pacific in the last summer of the war, joining a B-29 squadron based in Guam. His unit concentrated on Japanese oil refineries in 15-hour missions across the Pacific.

After the war, Mr. Flaherty returned to Pittsburgh and, like thousands of his contemporaries, went to college on the GI Bill. He attended Carlow University, then known as Mount Mercy College, for two years and then enrolled at Notre Dame Law School.

Mr. Flaherty's parents had moved to Mt. Lebanon during the war, and he moved in with them after his return from the Pacific. He got his political baptism shortly thereafter, running unsuccessfully for Mt. Lebanon school board as a Republican.

After graduating from Notre Dame and passing the bar exam, Mr. Flaherty got a job as an assistant district attorney under Democratic district attorney Edward Boyle.

After laboring through a string of fairly anonymous cases, Mr. Flaherty attracted attention prosecuting what was known as the "free-work" case, in which a handful of city workers were accused of performing private work on city time. That newfound prominence led to Mr. Flaherty's embrace by the organization that he would later spurn.

Joseph Barr, successor to the legendary Lawrence, was mayor at the time. Mr. Flaherty recalled that, at one point in the early 1960s, Barr talked to him about the job of city public safety director. Mr. Flaherty wasn't interested in that post, but later leapt when the Barr administration approached him about running for city council.

By then he was wading deeper into politics. In 1964 he had worked as an advance man for Senator Hubert Humphrey, when he was running for vice president with Lyndon Johnson. Mr. Flaherty had developed ties with Barr's chief aide, Aldo Colautti, during the free-work case. And the council seat he was tapped for was held by an Irishman. During that soon-to-end era, the committee of Democratic insiders who anointed candidates followed what was known as Balkan succession, with council seats apportioned to preserve an ethnic mix among the officeholders.

Mr. Flaherty was elected in 1965 and sworn in in 1966. The next year, some members of the Democratic organization were determined to replace the two Democratic incumbents on the Allegheny County Board of Commissioners, largely because of the incumbents' reluctance to work with the city on development projects. In a recent interview Mr. Flaherty recalled that Barr called him at home one evening and asked him to run on a ticket with Leonard Staisey. Mr. Flaherty refused. "I got the feeling that I was just window dressing, that Staisey was the man," Mr. Flaherty said. "It hit me between the eyes, and I just rejected it out of hand."

The second spot on that ticket went to Foerster, then a state representative. Mr. Flaherty would soon run for a more prominent office, but the offer is noteworthy given the intersection of Mr. Flaherty's and Foerster's careers years later.

In 1968, again as a lieutenant for Humphrey, Mr. Flaherty attended the ill-fated Democratic convention in Chicago, where demonstrators battled police in Grant Park. As a Humphrey partisan, Mr. Flaherty was working for the party establishment against the insurgent candidacy of Senator Eugene McCarthy. But his experience there, after a year of assassinations and urban riots, prodded his political evolution.

"I think it made me realize that the party's divided," Mr. Flaherty told an interviewer. "There's room in the party for dissent, which there never was before, or which there was very little of. So, in that sense, it had an effect on me."

As that year continued in Pittsburgh, there was uncertainty over whether Barr would seek another term as mayor. There also was widespread speculation that if he did step down, he and the party organization would anoint Mr. Flaherty as his successor. In an interview last year, however, Mr. Flaherty said that he never got that assurance or even that impression from Barr himself. Mr. Flaherty, feeling increasingly estranged from the party organization, instead embarked on the campaign that would remake the political map of Pittsburgh.

"Nobody's Boy"

Through the latter part of 1968, Mr. Flaherty became an increasingly vocal critic of the Barr administration, calling his budget unbalanced and opposing an administration proposal for the taxation of hospitals and other nonprofit institutions. Finally, Mr. Flaherty declared his candidacy for the Democratic nomination. With the trademark slogan "Nobody's Boy," he flaunted his independence from the party organization.

Barr announced that he would leave office, so the organization turned to Harry Kramer, then a judge on common pleas court. Mr. Flaherty's candidacy embodied and capitalized on the rising independent spirit of the late 1960s. Kramer attacked him, telling one rally, "There is a strange pattern when you analyze it—the Students for a Democratic Society, the New Left, and my most vocal opponent."

That caricature would prove far from the truth about the fiscally prudent policy maker that emerged over Mr. Flaherty's career.

"In many ways, he was a populist, but a cautious and conservative populist," said Coleman. "He was not a big-government person."

Mr. Flaherty trounced Kramer and the organization with 62 percent of the Democratic vote. Republicans, who had courted Mr. Flaherty for their own ticket, saw in the divided party an opportunity to capture an office that they hadn't held in four decades. The GOP ran the respected John Tabor and poured more than $400,000 into his campaign, an enormous sum for the times.

Mr. Flaherty continued to defy the Democratic establishment. As a peace offering, the party organization printed thousands of Flaherty stickers and sent them to his headquarters. The next day the newspapers ran photographs of Mr. Flaherty and his wife, Nancy, throwing the stickers into the trash.

The local papers were filled with pictures of the couple that year. The repeated images of Mr. Flaherty, tall, broad-shouldered and handsome, and Nancy, a former homecoming queen, reinforced the youthful, energetic image that bolstered Mr. Flaherty's political appeal. Years later the couple would divorce. In 1998 Mr. Flaherty married Charlene Flaherty, with whom he lived in their Mt. Lebanon home at the time of his death.

Mr. Flaherty, though outspent by a margin of more than 4-to-1, nonetheless cruised to a landslide victory in the 1969 election, launching an administration that would permanently transform Pittsburgh government.

"We weren't afraid of getting things done," recalled Campbell, a key adviser who was one of a team of young people, most new to government, whom Mr. Flaherty brought into the City-County Building.

In an interview last year, Mr. Flaherty saw that personnel roster as his greatest legacy. In addition to Campbell, it included Louise Brown, later a president of Chatham College; David O'Laughlin, developer and member of the city's fiscal oversight board; Robert Paternoster, a respected urban planner; and Robert Colville, his public safety director, later Allegheny County district attorney and now a judge of common pleas court.

Campbell's first job was director of lands and buildings.

"When I took over there were spittoons in city hall," he said. "There was a job in city council called spittoon cleaner."

During the Flaherty administration, the city's payroll dropped from roughly 7,000 to less than 5,000, while Mr. Flaherty repeatedly cut property and wage taxes in a city that had been losing population for two decades.

"Pete's great strength was that he was the first mayor to recognize the changing demographics of the city and the need to hone it back to reflect that reality," said David Donahoe, executive director of the Allegheny Regional Asset District, who was a senior aide to Mr. Flaherty's successor, the late Mayor Richard Caliguiri. "That's the kind of thing that stirs a lot of resentment, but it was an important step that someone had to take."

Mr. Flaherty was portrayed as hard-hearted for cutting the number of cleaning ladies in city hall. He insisted, however, that they were only working four hours a day while being paid for eight.

The administration attracted much better publicity in a crucial face-off with the Teamsters Union. A project to replace the city's water meters employed two-man crews: a plumber to do the actual work and a Teamster to drive the truck. "I'd gotten rid of my own chauffeur, so I didn't see any reason why they needed drivers," Mr. Flaherty said.

The Teamsters struck citywide, halting, among other things, garbage collection. Mr. Flaherty and some of his department heads went out and collected trash themselves. Television pictures of their labors were broadcast nationwide, enhancing Mr. Flaherty's public support and political leverage.

"I would go out into the community and they would say, 'Stand your ground,'" Mr. Flaherty recalled.

"Pete had a genius at getting coverage," said Campbell.

No Business as Usual

Mr. Flaherty's independence from a business elite that was accustomed to a strong working relationship with city government was exemplified in the bitter, protracted fight over Skybus, an ambitious proposal for automated, rubber-wheeled trains on concrete guideways.

With an eye to making Pittsburgh "the Detroit of transit," the county transportation agency and Allegheny Conference—the business group that was heir to the longtime Lawrence-Mellon partnership—united behind Skybus.

Mr. Flaherty was most prominent among critics who assailed the cost, unmanned concept, and route of the plan.

In their study, *Four Decades of Public-Private Partnerships in Pittsburgh*, CMU's Tarr and Shelby Stewman observed, "The position that had worked well with his predecessors—'Mr. Mayor, here's what we think you ought to do'—did not work with Flaherty."

For a time, the Port Authority attempted to press ahead with work on Skybus, but Mr. Flaherty opposed it at every point.

Mr. Flaherty called the Port Authority board a creature of the business community. "The tone of the board toward public suggestions was to look upon such suggestions as minor intrusions," he said in one interview. "In my own case, it was as though I were interrupting the usual order of business...their tone is not one of 'The public be damned,' but rather 'We know best.'" Eventually, after years of conflict, a compromise was struck that spawned the light-rail system that now serves the South Hills.

Then and in recent interviews, Mr. Flaherty insisted that his position was not antibusiness. He noted that he had made a point of visiting Richard King Mellon shortly before his death in 1970 to convey that message. Mr. Flaherty conceded, however, "It didn't go that well. [The reception] was kind of lukewarm."

In his second term, Mr. Flaherty was able to compromise with a new Allegheny Conference chairman, Robert Dickey, on issues including construction of a new convention center Downtown. He noted that he worked with community and business interests on the development of Station Square.

Running for reelection in 1973, Mr. Flaherty easily defeated his Democratic primary opponent, then-Councilman Caliguiri, as Democrats heeded his call to "Re-Pete." Mr. Flaherty captured the Republican nomination as well with a sticker-based write-in campaign in which GOP voters agreed to "Stick with Pete."

During Mr. Flaherty's years in office, the Pittsburgh school board was struggling to craft a desegregation plan. At one hearing, Mr. Flaherty spoke out against busing as an element of the plan. In interviews, he said he strongly favored desegregation but opposed widespread busing as a tool to accomplish it. He later would say that his views were distorted in some contemporary accounts.

"The newspapers basically portrayed me as an anti-buser," he said. "The whole issue to them was busing, whether you were for school busing or against it. I was against massive school busing, not all school busing."

Mr. Flaherty boasted of his civil rights record. Campbell noted, for example,

that he had been innovative in increasing minority representation on boards and commissions. His administration disbanded the police "tactical squads" that stirred resentment in the black community with aggressive methods. Flaherty personally intervened to peacefully defuse an incendiary confrontation on the North Side after an elderly white woman shot a black youth. "Pete drove over there himself, and he had the cops pull back and he walked the streets of Manchester," Campbell recalled.

Mr. Flaherty's busing statements sparked lingering resentment among some black leaders and other partisans of the desegregation plan, feelings that would be hurdles in Flaherty's political future.

Three Statewide Losses

After his smashing reelection in 1973, the mayor tried to transfer his popularity statewide in a race that he later recalled as "probably a mistake." He scored a narrow victory in the primary for the Democratic nomination to challenge Republican senator Richard Schweiker. Schweiker easily defeated the Pittsburgh mayor in the general election at the same time that Democratic governor Milton Shapp won a comfortable reelection.

In the 1976 presidential race Mr. Flaherty was the first Northeastern mayor to endorse Jimmy Carter, another Democrat who emphasized fiscal discipline while challenging traditional party power brokers. He was rewarded with the post of deputy attorney general, one that seemed an attractive new challenge to the former prosecutor. But attorney general Griffin Bell split the duties of the office with a new post—associate attorney general—which reduced its power.

Mr. Flaherty recalled that prior to his confirmation hearing, "[Senator] Ted Kennedy invited me over to his office for lunch, and he told me not to take the job. 'You're going to be just a figurehead,' he said, because Georgians were installed in all the responsible positions. And he was right, and I wish I had listened to him."

It proved a short, frustrating assignment for Mr. Flaherty. One indelible memory from the period came on March 9, shortly after Mr. Flaherty took office, when members of the Hanafi Muslim sect took 134 hostages and occupied three buildings, including the District Building—the equivalent of city hall—in the center of Washington. Mr. Flaherty was at the center of the tense negotiations that led to the release of the hostages and the surrender of their captors after a siege of 39 hours.

Mr. Flaherty, who never established a rapport with Carter insiders, was relieved to leave Washington behind as he returned to Pennsylvania to enter the 1978 governor's race. He finished first among four Democrats in the primary, among them Robert P. Casey, the former auditor general who would go on to win two terms as governor years later.

Mr. Flaherty entered the general election much better-known than the GOP nominee, Dick Thornburgh. Flaherty had a huge lead in early polls, but a variety of factors helped Thornburgh whittle away at it.

In one bit of bad luck, Mr. Flaherty was saddled as a running mate with another Robert Casey, an Allderdice High School teacher who won on name confusion with the gubernatorial candidate from Scranton.

Mr. Flaherty had nothing to do with the homonym candidate, but the result didn't help his popularity in Casey's Democratic base in Northeastern Pennsylvania. Mr. Flaherty also had to overcome a cloud of scandal that hung over Pennsylvania due to multiple prosecutions of members of the Shapp administration.

Another intraparty hurdle presented itself in Philadelphia, where the controversial Mayor Frank Rizzo was seeking a change in the city charter to allow himself to run for a third term. Mr. Flaherty announced that he was opposed to the charter change, bringing the opposition of Rizzo's Democratic supporters. Rizzo was a racially polarizing figure, and his attempt to stay in office catalyzed an unprecedented turnout among black voters.

Thornburgh, through the intercession of Pittsburgh civil rights activist Nate Smith, managed to bask in an endorsement from the Reverend Jesse Jackson that was trumpeted widely in Philadelphia. Thornburgh, in a stunning showing for a Republican, carried the majority of Philadelphia's predominantly black wards, a result that held down Mr. Flaherty's lead in the Democratic stronghold. Overall, Thornburgh, who outspent Mr. Flaherty by a wide margin, won the state by roughly 230,000 votes.

Hoping that the third statewide run would be the charm, Mr. Flaherty won the Democratic nomination for U.S. Senate two years later and faced Arlen Specter, another former prosecutor with a track record of statewide losses. It was Mr. Flaherty's strongest statewide showing, but it was not enough to overcome the GOP tide that rolled in with Ronald Reagan's 1980 victory over Mr. Flaherty's former boss, Carter.

Mr. Flaherty practiced law in Pittsburgh after that defeat but decided in 1983 to run for Allegheny County commissioner. "Oh, I missed it, I missed public service," Mr. Flaherty said of the decision. "It's been my life, basically."

Mr. Flaherty hoped to lead the ticket but, while he won one of the three seats, his vote total was second to that of the veteran Foerster.

Foerster's more traditional political style offered a contrast to Mr. Flaherty's track record of disdain for organization insiders. The pair's initial partnership was tentative, but it evolved into a productive one, with achievements over their three shared terms including the completion of the new Pittsburgh International Airport terminals, the building of the four Kane centers for the elderly, and the massive jail complex along the Monongahela River.

Over the years, their professional collaboration became easier, but it never translated into a close personal relationship. "We never had dinner together the whole time I was there," Mr. Flaherty recalled. "We spoke. We got along. But we never became close associates."

Mr. Flaherty and Foerster, the two very different North Side natives, were ousted from power in the Democratic primary of 1995, one that set the stage for a stunning Republican victory in the general election, ending six decades of Democratic control of county government.

With Charlene, Mr. Flaherty settled into retirement in Mt. Lebanon, just blocks from the house where his parents had moved during World War II. He battled cancer over the last months of his life, but still could be seen frequently striding the streets of Virginia Manor, nodding to acquaintances and strangers who invariably hailed him as "Pete."

Last summer, Mr. Flaherty spoke of the impact of his struggle with cancer. "Of course it changes you," he said. "It makes you realize how unimportant you are and how important other people are, so there's a good side."

Asked his most important accomplishment, he said, "Oh, I think we changed the scene in city hall, from the old guard to a new, wide-open kind of administration. We put the city on a sound fiscal basis; we brought in new people."

In addition to his wife, Mr. Flaherty is survived by a daughter, Dr. Maggie Gurtner of Mt. Lebanon; four sons, Shawn, Peter, and Brian of Pittsburgh, and Gregory of Los Angeles; a brother, commonwealth court judge James Flaherty; five sisters, Sister Rita Flaherty of Pittsburgh, Margaret Moretti of Mt. Lebanon, Catherine Flaherty of Delray Beach, Florida, Helen Smith of Mt. Lebanon, and Patrice Mahon of Boynton Beach, Florida; and eight grandchildren.

FRIDAY, MARCH 17, 2006

K. Leroy Irvis, 89
Former Speaker of State House
By James O'Toole, *Pittsburgh Post-Gazette*

Henry John Heinz III signals victory to his supporters at the Vista International Hotel in Downtown Pittsburgh on November 8, 2006. *Photo by Joyce Mendelsohn.*

K. Leroy Irvis has died. The first African American speaker of the Pennsylvania House of Representatives, a poet, orator, civil rights leader, and champion of education was 89.

Mr. Irvis spent more than three decades at the pinnacle of politics, in the Hill District, Harrisburg, and Pennsylvania. The first black speaker of any state legislature since Reconstruction, he shaped legislation that reformed the state's fiscal system, promoted health care, and expanded access to education.

As a young civil rights leader, he challenged his adopted city's business and political leadership, battling for job opportunities. Though he paid a price for activism in the short term, he would be embraced by the establishment he had confronted, emerging as a towering figure in Pennsylvania politics.

"He was a giant, no doubt," said former governor Dick Thornburgh.

"Leroy Irvis was, by any definition, a great man," said Governor Ed Rendell, who ordered state flags to be flown at half-staff. "He was a trailblazer...he brought grace, dignity, and a real sense of purpose to Harrisburg."

"I think back to so many groups of freshman members who would encounter him for the first time and just be awed by him, he had such a powerful presence," said former state representative Ron Cowell.

A New York native, Mr. Irvis was the first black graduate of Albany Teachers College, now the State University of New York at Albany. He graduated summa cum laude and went on to earn a master's degree. In the midst of the Depression, he began his career teaching in the public schools of Baltimore.

From his early years growing up outside Albany, Mr. Irvis had nurtured an interest in aviation, often pedaling out to a small airfield to watch biplanes take off and land. When World War II broke out, he recalled a few years ago, his first impulse was to sign up for the Army Air Corps.

"We're not recruiting any colored boys," an officer told him.

"That angered me more than anything else," he recalled. "That anyone would judge me by the color of my skin.... My father and mother raised me to judge people based on what they do."

Instead of flying airplanes as he'd hoped, the future politician spent the war years as an aircraft-assembly instructor in a defense plant.

After V-J Day, Mr. Irvis moved to Pittsburgh to take a job with the Urban League. In that position, he organized demonstrations against the city's department stores, protesting their segregated hiring policies. It was an audacious move on more than one level, as some of the major department store owners were significant contributors to the Urban League.

Laurence Glasco, an assistant professor of history at the University of Pittsburgh who is working on an Irvis biography, noted that the late Mayor David L. Lawrence was among those who tried to dissuade Mr. Irvis from the protests, arguing that they hurt the city's image. Mr. Irvis responded that it was the stores' hiring practices, not the protests, that posed a threat to Pittsburgh's reputation.

After a stormy few years, the Urban League let Mr. Irvis go. For a few years, he moved from job to job, including working for a while in a steel mill. Mr. Irvis eventually entered Pitt Law School, graduating fourth in his class in 1954.

He worked as a law clerk for Judges Anne X. Alpern and Loran L. Lewis and was among the first African Americans to serve as an assistant district attorney in Allegheny County. By 1958 Mr. Lawrence, despite their earlier clash, recognized Mr. Irvis's talent and supported him as a candidate for a state legislative seat representing the Hill District.

The victory and initiation into the profession he was born for was tempered, however, by the death of his first wife, Katharyne Jones Irvis.

Mr. Irvis, a Democrat, would be elected to 15 terms, rising quickly through the ranks of the fractious chamber. Within a decade, in one of the litany of firsts that marked his career, he became the state's first black House majority leader. In 1977, after a scandal forced the resignation of

Representative Herbert Fineman, Mr. Irvis was chosen by acclamation to wield the speaker's gavel.

The only previous House speaker to be elected by acclamation was Benjamin Franklin.

Mr. Irvis's stature quickly rose above the criticisms of the controversial chamber he would lead. A Republican leader quoted in Paul Beers's history, *Pennsylvania Politics Today and Yesterday,* described the new speaker as "absolutely honest, intellectually and morally."

In contrast to his fiercely partisan predecessor, Mr. Irvis prided himself on his ability to work with lawmakers on both sides of the aisle. One of his strongest friendships in Harrisburg was forged with Republican leader Matthew Ryan, who also would serve as speaker.

Irvis's leadership of the House was enhanced by a productive partnership with the late Representative James Manderino, a brilliant legislative strategist who, as majority leader, patrolled the chamber's aisles corralling votes, allowing Mr. Irvis, his deep, sonorous voice echoing from the speaker's rostrum, to strike a more statesmanlike stance.

"There are different models for being a speaker," Mr. Cowell said. "It can be a very partisan position or it can rise above partisan politics, and that's the example he set."

The former teacher was a key architect of landmark education initiatives, including the establishment of the state's community college system, creation of the Pennsylvania Higher Education Assistance Agency, and the measure that conferred state-related status on the University of Pittsburgh, Temple University, and Lincoln University, a shift that addressed chronic financial problems at the three schools.

Mr. Irvis told his biographer, Dr. Glasco, that the piece of legislation of which he was most proud was a measure that mandated PKU tests for newborns in the state, a test now used across the nation that detects an enzyme imbalance that can cause brain damage.

In an often uneasy alliance with then-governor Milton Shapp, Mr. Irvis was one of the key architects of the state's income tax, which, while much criticized, helped to repair the state's budget after years of chronic shortfalls. He was frustrated, however, in his support of a constitutional change needed to replace the flat tax with a graduated income tax, an approach that he believed would be more progressive.

Mr. Irvis was a champion of the state's Human Relations Commission, fighting to grant it subpoena power against widespread opposition. He opposed the death penalty, and as a delegate to the state's 1968 Constitutional Convention, sponsored, along with Mr. Thornburgh, the mandate for public defender offices across the state.

In 1971, Mr. Beers recounted, when a prison reform bill was in jeopardy, Irvis reminded his colleagues that William Penn had been a prison inmate, saying with his trademark eloquence, "We have to make up our minds whether we consider the people we put behind bars as animals or human beings. We must not put them behind walls so high that they cannot see daylight and we can't hear their cries."

In 20th-century America, the respect that Mr. Irvis was universally accorded within the capitol was not guaranteed beyond its walls. After one late-night session of the House in 1969, Mr. Irvis, as a guest of some legislative colleagues, was denied service at a Harrisburg Moose lodge. He challenged the denial in court and won at the trial level.

In a bitter disappointment to Mr. Irvis, however, the U.S. Supreme Court would later uphold the lodge's position that it was entitled, as a private club, to enforce its discriminatory rules. "The irony was that while he lost the case in court, within a year of the court case, the Moose quietly dropped race from their membership criteria at a national level," Dr. Glasco noted.

Mr. Irvis resisted racial categorization. "You have not elected a black man to be speaker, but…you have elected a man who happens to be black," he said on the day he rose to the post.

On another occasion, while emphasizing that his first loyalty was simply as an American, he told the Associated Press, "You have to think of yourself as a black man first and a Democrat second. Any black man that says he doesn't is either a fool or a liar."

Visible from the windows of Mr. Irvis's office suite in the capitol is the large state office building that would be renamed for him in 2003. Another tangible tribute to his career, the K. Leroy Irvis Reading Room at Pitt's Hillman Library, displays evidence of the varied interests he pursued beyond politics and government. On its walls are several African-styled masks crafted by Mr. Irvis, an accomplished painter and sculptor.

In addition to official documents, the archives include examples of his poetry and many of the journals in which he recorded, in clear, upward-sloping handwriting, observations and notes ranging from literary excerpts to the phrases and inflections of young men he heard hawking the *Pittsburgh Courier* on Hill District corners.

Mr. Irvis owned an extensive private library of his own. "He was very scholarly," Dr. Glasco said. "There are thousands of volumes: art history, church history. He was a really devoted reader of Shakespeare—the histories and the tragedies more than the comedies."

Mr. Irvis's early fascination with aviation, frustrated by the Army Air Corps recruiter after Pearl Harbor, evolved into a passion for building and flying model airplanes. He spent countless days and weekends flying the model craft and forging friendships with other enthusiasts at the K. Leroy Irvis Airfield at Hillman State Park in Washington County.

"He loved going out there as often as he could," Dr. Glasco said. "Later in life, he couldn't fly anymore because his eyesight wasn't good enough; he'd crash the planes. But he still loved going out there, kibitzing and talking."

Mr. Irvis is survived by his wife, Cathryn L. Irvis; son Reginald Irvis of Harrisburg; daughter Sherri Irvis-Hill of Philadelphia; and four grandchildren.

SEPTEMBER 2, 2006

Robert E. O'Connor Jr., 61
His Enthusiasm for City Was Unbounded
By Rich Lord, *Pittsburgh Post-Gazette*

O'Connor at his swearing-in ceremony in January 2006. *Photo courtesy of the* Pittsburgh Post-Gazette.

R obert E. O'Connor Jr. so naturally attracted people and so readily dispensed firm handshakes, pecks on the cheek, warm words, and pledges of help, that it sometimes seemed a minor miracle that he could walk a city block with all of that human need and affection heaped upon him.

The early July day he was hospitalized with what turned out to be brain cancer was no exception. He moved through the sweet and sour soup of goodwill and grueling problems that was the Bob O'Connor mayoral administration, ceremonially installing the first antenna in a downtown wireless Internet system and putting the finishing touches on a strike-averting trash collection contract. All the while he carried a burden that no one suspected.

Mr. O'Connor's life was, in many ways, a perfect expression of this biggest of small towns. It featured neither pretension nor strict ideology. A handful of key relationships helped to determine its course. He exercised more willpower and common sense than book learning along the way to an impressive array of achievements. His life featured a steady, determined climb and a wrenching fall.

A child of Greenfield, he was born December 9, 1944, to Bob Sr. and Mary Anne Dever O'Connor. His father was a truck mechanic who carried Pacific theater–shrapnel in his back and died of a heart ailment in 1978. His mother kept the kind of warm, welcoming home that was a magnet for O'Connor's friends and those of his one younger brother, Tim.

They were a car-loving family, going off five nights a week to watch local races, especially those involving Bob Sr.'s brother, Buddy O'Connor. Even as mayor, Mr. O'Connor was once approached by a fan of Buddy's, an old racing program in hand, asking for an autograph. With an unrestrained, boyish enthusiasm rarely seen in politicians, he gathered everyone there for a run-down of Buddy's career.

An unspectacular educational run took him from St. Philomena's grade school to, briefly, Central Catholic High School and then a 1962 graduation from Allderdice High. He spent his savings from summer work at Jones & Laughlin's steel mills not on college but on a Corvette convertible.

The Corvette certainly impressed the younger brother of one Judy Levine. Judy was a fellow Allderdice grad whom O'Connor courted earnestly in those years after commencement.

The car didn't sway Judy's parents, who wanted their Jewish daughter to marry someone of the same faith. She and Bobby eloped to Wheeling, West Virginia, in 1964, where they were married by a pastor they'd never before met, with only Tim O'Connor as a witness.

Her parents later warmed up to their son-in-law when they saw what a good father he was.

From 1972 on they lived in the Squirrel Hill home in which she grew up. They raised three children, Heidy Garth, now of Swissvale and a marketing research manager; Terrence O'Connor, a law-school graduate who went on to become a Catholic priest at St. Alphonsus Parish in Pine; and Corey O'Connor, varsity golf coach at Central Catholic High School.

Even decades later, no one could be near Bob and Judy O'Connor without feeling the warmth of their bond.

Soon after O'Connor became mayor, a maintenance worker shooting at pigeons was mistaken for a sniper, and the search paralyzed downtown. It surprised no one who knew him when Mr. O'Connor put on a bulletproof vest and rushed across the feared line of fire to check on his wife, who was at work at the Highmark Caring Place in the hot zone.

After five years in the mills, Mr. O'Connor took a pay cut—not his last—to join Judy's uncles in a restaurant business. The company was later sold to Beaver County businessman Lou Pappan.

Mr. Pappan, the owner at various times of many Pappans, Roy Rogers, and Wendy's restaurants, took a shine to the friendly but serious young O'Connor. Recognizing management material,

Pappan put O'Connor through leadership training and eventually made him an executive vice president in charge of 1,000 employees in 36 locations.

Mr. Pappan would stick by his protégé long after he left the business, contributing to O'Connor's political campaigns and, in 2005, hiring him as a loosely defined consultant while he ran for mayor.

Mrs. O'Connor worked as a preschool teacher and, later, a children's party organizer. Daughter Heidy, meanwhile, married Richard Garth. The two gave the O'Connors three granddaughters. In the 1990s Mrs. O'Connor and her daughter ran Bobby O's, an Oakland restaurant, and Mr. O'Connor bused tables on football Saturdays.

The bridge between business and politics was community service.

Roy Rogers restaurant outlets in St. Francis Hospital and the University of Pittsburgh's Cathedral of Learning led to Mr. O'Connor's membership on the hospital's board and involvement in the university's charitable campaigns and student organizations.

The death of his niece, Yael Pelled, at six months of age from Sudden Infant Death Syndrome taught O'Connor about the effect the loss of a child can have on a family. He later served on the Sudden Infant Death Syndrome Alliance board, and he and Judy helped found the Highmark Caring Place—a Center for Grieving Children, Adolescents, and Their Families, where Judy worked as a receptionist and a counselor even after her husband's ascent to mayor.

In a time when few have time for neighborliness, making friends was a reflex action for the O'Connors. N. Catherine Bazan-Arias said her family arrived in Pittsburgh from Latin America in 1983. "The mayor was one of several parishioners at St. Philomena's who really opened their arms to us," she said. They were part of a tiny Latino minority in Pittsburgh then, but the O'Connor family took them under its wing and showed them "that this really had the potential to be home."

Thousands of such relationships laid the groundwork for a political career that transcended policy. "I guess, in my mind, he's been a pillar that cannot be shaken," Ms. Bazan-Arias said.

Eventually Mr. O'Connor came to the conclusion that his service to mankind should go beyond food and charity work. He resigned himself to another pay cut, and at age 45, ran for office.

It's one of those only-in-Pittsburgh plot twists that O'Connor's boss at Jones & Laughlin Steel in the 1960s was Thomas Murphy, father and namesake of the city's 57th mayor. Early in his political career, Mr. O'Connor said it was the elder Mr. Murphy who advised him to leave the mills and aim for a management career, though O'Connor later said his memory of that had faded.

The younger Tom Murphy, when he was a state representative in the 1980s, wrote legislation changing city council elections from citywide competitions to by-district races. That change loosened the lock party committees and campaign donors had on council races, giving advantage instead to people with deep community roots.

Murphy's reform made possible the rise of the man who would become his principal rival.

O'Connor was one of the first to take advantage of the change, winning a council seat in 1991. He beat three better-known Democrats, thanks in part to an enthusiastic, hyper-loyal troupe of volunteers and gigantic popularity in Greenfield and Hazelwood.

After the election he did something that, along with his always-perfect silver hair and his cookie-cruise fundraisers, would become a trademark: He stood on a busy street corner with a sign that said, simply, "Thanks."

His political role model was Mayor Richard Caliguiri, whom he knew personally from coaching Caliguiri's sons, David and Gregg, in Little League baseball. By the time O'Connor ran for office, Caliguiri was dead three years from a rare protein disorder, amyloidosis, which felled him in office. His widow, Jeanne Caliguiri, thought enough of her sons' coach to serve as his honorary campaign chairman.

It was one of the great coincidences of his life that the son of his mill boss and the son of his role model teamed up to beat him in the bare-knuckles 2001 mayoral election. Tom Murphy Jr. was the incumbent, and David Caliguiri was his campaign manager.

O'Connor's early city council years set the tone for his career. He was all about beat cops, clean streets, fixed playgrounds, and raw ambition.

In January 1994, with two years on council under his belt, he made a bid for that body's presidency. Just-elected Mayor Murphy, though, exerted his influence and placed Jim Ferlo, now a state senator, in the presidency. There was talk that a deal had been struck in which Mr. Ferlo would serve one year then step down to let O'Connor serve the next.

Never happened.

"When I retaliate," O'Connor said a few years later, "it will be more than the presidency of council" at stake.

In 1997 he challenged Murphy in the Democratic mayoral primary. He campaigned not so much on a platform as on a series of criticisms of the incumbent. He opposed public financing of new stadiums for the Pirates and Steelers, which Mr. Murphy supported. He said Murphy was shortsighted in selling the city water system, trading a steady source of revenue for short-term cash. He predicted financial implosion.

He was badly outspent and undermanned. His campaign vehicle was a beat-up, white-panel truck, supplemented by his aging Oldsmobile. Nonetheless, he pulled in 42 percent of the vote, which was 12 percentage points behind Murphy in a three-candidate field.

In 1998 Mr. O'Connor won the council presidency on the second ballot, in part through brilliant parliamentary moves by Ferlo. That would mark the beginning of an odd political pairing— two Democrats, one conservative and the other liberal, one rooted in business and the other in activism, united by mutual respect and deep suspicion of Murphy.

O'Connor presided over council for four years, during which time he and Ferlo helped defeat Murphy's plan to raze and rebuild downtown's retail core and rewrote the city's property tax system so that land and buildings would be taxed at the same rate.

That led into a tough 2001 mayor's race that some of O'Connor's backers still maintain was stolen. In its closing weeks, Murphy agreed to the outlines of a generous contract with the city's firefighters, who promptly endorsed him. Murphy won by 699 vote—fewer than the number of city firefighters at the time—and Mr. O'Connor conceded only after weeks of scouring the tally for errors.

Murphy's dealings with the firefighters led to a federal probe, though not to prosecution. The firefighters' contract, fiscal woes, and bad relations with state legislators contributed to his decision not to run for a fourth term in 2005.

Mr. O'Connor considered a 2002 run for lieutenant governor but instead left city government in 2003 for an appointed post, running Governor Ed Rendell's southwestern Pennsylvania office. Some thought O'Connor would be content to stay on the political sidelines and build a state pension, but insiders knew better.

His 2005 platform was simple and appealing. He pledged to professionalize city management, fix its distressed finances, and cooperate more with the county and state governments. He would "inspect, not expect," to make sure city workers were doing their jobs and give them the tools to do better.

"If things were booming or great in this town, I wouldn't have even run," O'Connor said in an interview during the 2005 primary campaign. "But this is a time that you need experienced, smart leadership. Put the word 'smart' in there, too, because it takes a smart man, when he has cancer, to call in the doctor."

He faced younger, more eloquent Democratic primary opponents in city councilman William Peduto and county prothonotary Michael Lamb but cruised to victory with 49 percent of the vote. Then O'Connor easily beat Republican Joe Weinroth in the general election.

On January 3, 2006, O'Connor was sworn in as mayor in front of the city-county building, and he spent the afternoon shaking hands and posing for pictures in the mayor's office.

He did not launch national searches for top staffers, as some people had hoped he would. He instead surrounded himself with a mix of longtime loyalists and city veterans, along with a handful of recruits from other sectors, like chief of staff B.J. Leber, who helped to turn around public broadcaster WQED Multimedia.

In his first six months in office O'Connor launched a drive to "redd up" the city in time for the Major League Baseball All-Star Game, and he rewrote the budget and refinanced debt to give his administration some fiscal breathing room.

More subtly, and perhaps more importantly, he ended the psychological isolation that had plagued the mayor's office during Murphy's years. A steady stream of county, state, and school-district officials entered and left his office. He led department heads and reporters on Bob-a-thons through long-neglected neighborhoods, walking block after block, bringing attention to problems and ordering fixes on the spot. In Knoxville he had underlings remove heaps of old carpet and demolish an abandoned home—pronto. The home went down that day.

"He initiated cleanup of all of our alleys, which hasn't been done since 2002," said Mary Ann Flaherty-Bennett, president of the Upper Knoxville Block Watch, not long after. Many neighborhood groups privately rejoiced that basic services, rather than the grand development plans of Murphy's tenure, were city hall's top priority.

On July 6, the 185th day of his administration and five days before the All-Star Game, he was admitted to UPMC Shadyside Hospital for mounting fatigue, nausea, and head and neck pain. He was diagnosed first with a duodenal ulcer, and later with the extremely rare T-cell type of the uncommon primary central nervous system lymphoma.

From the beginning of his illness his administration emphasized that he was still in charge of city governance, making much of equipping him with a laptop computer and his call in to a weekly staff meeting to ask for accounting details.

Pittsburgh, meanwhile, waited anxiously, with civic leaders fretting about the effects of a lengthy illness on regional momentum and fans signing a giant card hung in the lobby of the city-county building. Gift baskets, cards, and letters flooded the family home, the hospital, and the mayor's office.

Worries about the direction of the administration in his absence mounted 17 days into his hospitalization. That's when he phoned in and fired chief of staff B.J. Leber, solicitor Susan Malie, and finance director Paul Leger. They were replaced by loyalist Dennis Regan, longtime city lawyer George Specter, and financial veteran Scott Kunka, resolving a long-festering rift.

Though the firings generated criticism, the situation was drowned out by a tidal wave of affection as the mayor's condition worsened. Giant cards, flower bouquets, prayer vigils, and the quick sale of 10,000 bracelets by the Leukemia & Lymphoma Society showed strong support for the mayor personally and for his family.

Yarone Zober took the reins as deputy mayor on August 6, when the mayor was declared disabled.

O'Connor was treated with an experimental protocol of two chemotherapy drugs then with radiation when the medicines didn't work. In late August seizures and an infection further complicated treatment. Family gathered, and staff tried to keep a brave face.

"Here's a man that worked really hard for a long time to get to be mayor," said city public works director Guy Costa, "and then this happened, and it doesn't seem fair."

SECTION

XI

Philanthropists

A lot of money has been made here. Piles of it. But a lot of money is given away here. Tons of it. Many places—Philadelphia, Boston, New York, Silicon Valley—have lots of rich people. No place has philanthropists like Pittsburgh. These philanthropists support the schools, underwrite the arts, fix the buildings, inspire the young, give boosts to the talented, feed the hungry, and fortify the weak. The principal distinguishing feature of the modern Pittsburgh may not be the arts, the Steelers, or the hospitals. It may be the philanthropists.

SATURDAY, NOVEMBER 10, 1984

Helen Clay Frick, 96
Publicity-Shy Benefactor
By Alvin Rosensweet, *Pittsburgh Post-Gazette*

Helen Clay Frick. *Photo courtesy of the* Pittsburgh Post-Gazette.

Helen Clay Frick, who inherited $38 million from her father and spent much of her lifetime memorializing him by enhancing and administering the family art collection, died yesterday. She was living at Clayton, the family's residence at 7200 Penn Avenue in Point Breeze, where she was born.

Miss Frick, who was publicity shy, almost never granted interviews, and studiously avoided most photographers, was 96 years old.

Miss Frick, who never married, submerged herself in perpetuating the name of her father, Henry Clay Frick, a controversial coal-coke-steel baron whose estate was appraised at $93 million after his death in 1919.

With the money she inherited Miss Frick administered a $50 million collection of art in the museum established by her father in New York City and built two art museums in Pittsburgh.

Like her father, she was frequently a controversial figure. She was involved in at least three lawsuits, losing two of them, and, in a heated controversy with the University of Pittsburgh, withdrew her support from the Henry Clay Frick Fine Arts Building in Schenley Park and built a second museum in Point Breeze adjoining her residence and Frick Park.

A conservative Republican, she contributed generously to Republican candidates and staunchly defended President Richard Nixon during the height of the Watergate scandal. But she once contributed $1,000 to the campaign of former U.S. Representative William Moorhead, a Pittsburgh Democrat whom she described as "a very dear friend of mine."

In 1966 Nixon, who was then a former vice president, chose a number of GOP congressional candidates for her to assist financially, but it was Miss Frick who chose the final 15 to receive financial aid. In 1972 she contributed $10,000 to the Committee to Reelect the President for Nixon's campaign.

Although her home had been in New York since 1904, when her father built a mansion there, Miss Frick maintained strong ties with Pittsburgh. She retained Clayton, her turreted Victorian home, and lived there for most of the last three years. She returned here to vote and made frequent visits for other purposes.

She restored and preserved her father's birthplace in West Overton in Westmoreland County, a property that included the distillery of Abraham Overholt, her father's grandfather, maker of the well-known rye whiskey. In 1927 Miss Frick made the homestead available to the Westmoreland-Fayette Historical Society as a museum of early Pennsylvania Americana.

In 1967 she appeared in court in Carlisle in Cumberland County at a trial resulting from her request for an injunction to prevent distribution of *Pennsylvania: Birthplace of a Nation*, by historian S.K. Stevens. Stevens had described her father as brusque and dealt harshly with his union-busting activities.

Miss Frick contended that her father was an upright and honorable man who treated workingmen fairly and paid reasonable wages.

But Judge Clinton R. Weidner dismissed Miss Frick's suit, holding that the author's observations about her father were true and criticized her for bringing the court action.

At that time Miss Frick, a small, wiry woman with piercing blue eyes, always wearing a hat over her hair, which had turned from reddish to white, gave her age only as "over 50." In later years her associates disclosed her birthdate. But she conceded that at the time of the Homestead steel strike of 1892 she was a baby. Actually, she was 4 years old at the time of that historic event, when her father directed activities of the Carnegie Steel Co.

Historians report that Frick ordered 300 Pinkerton guards to arrive secretly at the Homestead Steel Works, and in a furious battle on July 6, 1892, 10 strikers and three Pinkertons were killed. Only 17 days after that bloody outbreak, on July 23, Alexander Berkman, a 25-year-old revolutionary anarchist, tried to assassinate Mr. Frick.

Miss Frick's dispute with the University of Pittsburgh was an example of her determination. In 1962 she had proposed giving a building to be known as the Henry Clay Frick Fine Arts Building to Pitt. It was to contain the Nicholas Lochoff collection of Italian Renaissance paintings and frescoes donated by her in 1959. It would, said Miss Frick, honor her father's memory and contribute pleasure to "the inhabitants of my hometown."

The museum of gray limestone, with a red Italian tile roof and an open cloister, was dedicated in 1965, but Miss Frick and Pitt parted ways in 1967. She charged through her lawyer that Pitt had welshed on its agreement, and she withdrew annual contributions of $135,000 for maintenance and salaries.

Pitt contended that it must run the building as it saw fit and that a university could not accept domination from the outside. The agreement she referred to called for the collection to be overseen by a special board of directors. But Pitt argued that its own board must control university activities and that there could not be a separate board for the museum.

In the controversy Miss Frick opposed the display of contemporary art.

Subsequently, in 1970, Miss Frick opened the Frick Art Museum at 7227 Reynolds Street in Point Breeze. It contains paintings of Italian and Flemish Renaissance masters, 18th-century French paintings, decorative arts, Chinese ceramics, and Italian bronzes of the 17th and 18th centuries. She thus retained the control Pitt had denied her.

In yet another controversy Miss Frick resigned in 1961 from the board of trustees of the Frick Collection in New York but later returned. She had disagreed with the collection's acceptance of art objects owned by the late John D. Rockefeller Jr., calling them inferior works and in damaged condition.

Miss Frick's greatest interest was the art collection her father had amassed. He left $15 million to maintain it. The collection was opened to the public in the Frick mansion after the death of his widow, Adelaide, in 1931.

The mansion, built at a cost of $5 million in 1904 at 1 East Seventieth Street in New York, became an art museum in 1935. It contained more than 200 works by old masters, including Rembrandt's *Self Portrait* and paintings by Corot, Vermeer, El Greco, Whistler, Hals, and Velasquez.

As trustee of the Frick Collection from its founding until 1961, she displayed a preference for early Italian paintings and those of the French 18th century. This was reflected in the nature of the collection. Among works acquired while she was trustee were major pieces by Gentile Bellini, Boucher, Castagno, Claude Lorrain, Constable,

David, Duccio, van Eyck, Gainsborough, Goya, Greuze, Ingres, La Tour, Fra Filippo Lippi, Monet, Piero della Francesca, Rembrandt, Reynolds, and Paolo and Giovanni Veneziano.

The mansion included a paneled music room with paintings by Boucher done for Madame de Pompadour. The collection included bronzes, an important group of Sevres porcelain, Limoges porcelains, enamels, sculptures, and a group of K'ang Hai porcelains known as Black Hawthorne, which are reputed to be the finest in the world.

In addition to the art museum, another building houses the Frick Art Reference Library, one of the largest libraries of its kind in the world, at 6 East Seventy-first Street, which she founded in 1920. The library opened in 1924 as a memorial to her father.

When the Frick residence was transformed into a museum in 1931–1935, the original library was demolished and replaced by the six-story structure that houses it today. It contains close to 150,000 books, more than 400,000 photographs, and 50,000 art sales catalogs.

During World War II Miss Frick organized the library's facilities and staff as a base to assist the Allies through the American Council of Learned Societies for the Protection of Cultural Treasures in War Areas. The lists of monuments and detailed maps prepared at the library spared many important works of art and monuments from bombing.

The library became the center of Miss Frick's existence. She commissioned photographs of all the significant works of art in this country and in

Europe, and for a time, a half-dozen teams, including a scholar and a cameraman, scoured Europe to photograph works of art. Miss Frick herself extensively toured the South looking for works of art and developed a knowledge of the history of art.

Her art collection in New York is considered one of the great private collections in the world. Miss Frick served as the library's director from its inception until her resignation in 1983. From as early as 1936 Miss Frick and the library made available photographs and funds for scholars working in diverse fields.

Miss Frick devoted considerable scholarly research to one of her favorite artists—the French sculptor Jean-Antoine Houdon (1741–1828)—acquiring a number of his letters and other documents.

Miss Frick's property in Point Breeze, including Clayton, the Frick Art Museum, and the Frick garage containing antique automobiles, are to be combined into a total museum complex.

Miss Frick owned a farm in Westchester County, New York. She established the Westmoreland Sanctuary in Westchester County, New York, for the preservation of native flora and fauna. For many years she retained the family summer home at Pride's Crossing, Massachusetts, where she spent her summers as a child.

Miss Frick graduated from Miss Spence's School in New York. She demonstrated her strong will early when her father wanted her to make her debut in New York at the Vanderbilt mansion where they were then living.

Miss Frick, however, won him over to her desire to make her debut in Pittsburgh, where it took place in 1909.

At her request, her father gave her as a coming-out present 150 acres for a children's park, which became Frick Park in Pittsburgh's East End.

Early in her life Miss Frick became interested in a number of charitable activities. During her summers in Massachusetts she founded the Iron Rail Vacation Home for Working Girls, where they spent their summer vacations. The young women were employed in mill and industrial towns near Boston, where their working conditions were frequently substandard. She laid down strict rules—no smoking, no cosmetics, no bobbed hair, no fibbing, no gossiping, and no male visitors.

In World War I Miss Frick organized and financed a Red Cross hospital unit and spent six months with it in France in 1917. Its purpose was to alleviate the suffering and aid the rehabilitation of war refugees. Miss Frick's knowledge of French helped her in her relations with the people.

During the Depression of the 1930s Miss Frick helped to organize the Forty-Plus Club of Western Pennsylvania to assist older men in finding employment. In a half-dozen years jobs were found for 733 men.

During World War II she gave shelter to seven British girls, looking after their housing and education, and maintained close ties with them after the war.

She was known for her sound business judgment and gave small dinner parties at which she sometimes played practical jokes. Years ago her favorite dogs were a field spaniel and an Irish terrier. She gave no parties for three months after Pat, the terrier, died.

Miss Frick's personal taste ran to Italian art of the 14th and 15th centuries and to French art of the 18th century.

In the late 1920s Miss Frick bought a marble sarcophagus, an Annunciation scene with two figures, the Angel Gabriel and the Virgin Mary, which were reputed to be carvings by one of her favorite artists, Simone Martini. But an investigation by her dealer determined that they were fakes turned out by the Italian contemporary sculptor Andre Dossena. The figures are now in the cloister of the Henry Clay Frick Art Building at Pitt.

Although her father had a reputation as an antilabor industrialist—a reputation she claimed he did not deserve—Miss Frick herself made a contribution in the field of employer-employee relations. She encouraged a pension plan for employees of the Frick Building in Downtown Pittsburgh. The plan, the first of its kind put into effect here, became a model followed or adopted by other office buildings.

Miss Frick's interest in politics led her in 1974 to write three letters to the editor of the *Post-Gazette* defending President Nixon during the Watergate era. In one letter she wrote that she felt the American people would regret it if Congress and the Senate wrongly accused Nixon. She urged that the Senate Judiciary Committee, which was conducting the Watergate investigation, be abolished.

In another letter Miss Frick observed that "the communists and many liberal individuals who have leanings in that direction hate the president and wish to destroy him," because Nixon early in his career showed up Alger Hiss as a communist.

In another letter to the editor Miss Frick wrote that "the honor of our country is at stake if we allow our great president to be impeached by congressmen who cannot offer any proof of his wrongdoing." Miss Frick felt that "the Judiciary Committee has fallen into a trap that has been laid by the communists. President Nixon's name will go down in history as our greatest president."

She bitterly opposed the policies of President Franklin Delano Roosevelt, urged Charles A. Lindbergh to run for president, and was sternly anti-German since World War I.

But her letters to the editor of the *Post-Gazette* did not deal exclusively with politics. In a letter written in 1962, Miss Frick, who scorned contemporary and abstract art, questioned the worth of the Pittsburgh International at the Carnegie Institute Museum of Art. It was, she held, neither beautiful nor educational.

Miss Frick is survived by a niece, Mrs. J. Fife Symington Jr. of Baltimore; a nephew, Dr. Henry Clay Frick II of New York; and 14 grandnieces and nephews.

TUESDAY, FEBRUARY 24, 1987

H.J. Heinz II, 78
Gave Away Millions
By John Golightly, *Pittsburgh Post-Gazette*

H.J. Heinz II, age 78, chairman of the board of the company that bears his name and one of the richest men in the United States, died of cancer yesterday in his winter residence on Jupiter Island in Florida.

Mr. Heinz, father of U.S. Senator H. John Heinz III, a Republican from Fox Chapel, lived in Sewickley Heights. *Forbes* magazine estimated Heinz II's worth at $150 million in 1986 and much higher in earlier years. He gave away millions of dollars.

He was an influential advocate of the redevelopment of Downtown Pittsburgh as long ago as 1943 and supported formation of the Allegheny Conference on Community Development, which led to the undertaking popularly referred to as the Pittsburgh Renaissance, beginning in 1946.

He and his family contributed $10.5 million to purchase the land and buildings and to renovate the Penn Theater, which reopened as Heinz Hall for the Performing Arts in late 1971, a period when several cities in this country were abandoning their downtowns.

"Mr. Heinz worked tirelessly to see that the quality of life in Pittsburgh was unmatched anywhere in this country," Mayor Caliguiri said yesterday. "A quiet man not given to public accolades, his mark has been left on every major institution in this city."

H.J. Heinz Co., founded in Sharpsburg in 1869 by his grandfather, expanded enormously under his leadership. He served as assistant to the president from 1937 until his father's death in 1941, president from 1941 to 1959, and chairman of the board until his death.

Mr. Heinz headed the firm when a large part of the Pittsburgh factory was mobilized immediately after Pearl Harbor for the manufacture of CG-4A military glider wings. Other Heinz facilities turned out K and C rations for the armed forces.

After World War II, the Heinz firm began a steady effort to penetrate the European market. It now has plants in more than 20 countries. Mr. Heinz said then, in what turned out to be a remarkable understatement, that Europeans and others abroad "can be persuaded to eat our product."

The chief hallmark of his tenure was an acquisition program that brought under the Heinz wing Star-Kist Foods Inc. and Ore-Ida Foods Inc., each of which has since moved to the top of its field.

H.J. Heinz Co. sales increased in each of the past 12 years to a record $4.37 billion at the end of the last fiscal year.

Mr. Heinz was a supporter of Republican causes and candidates at every level of government. His political interests paralleled his involvement in business and economic organizations. He was chairman in the early post-war period of the United States Associates, the American affiliate of the International Chamber of Commerce, which had members in about 35 of the principal trading nations. He said, "Trade serves the important role of uniting the peoples of the earth for their common benefit and develops a common understanding throughout the world."

Mr. Heinz had a career-long interest in nutrition, a dedication that he said was part of his inheritance from his grandfather and father. Henry J. Heinz was the only food processor to join with Dr. Harvey Wiley in 1906 to lobby for the enactment of the nation's first pure food and drug legislation, an effort in which his son Howard joined him.

In turn, H.J. Heinz II was a founder in 1940 and continued until his death as a trustee of the Nutrition Foundation, later the International Life Science Institution-Nutrition Foundation, whose purpose was to support basic research and education in the science of human nutrition.

Through the Howard Heinz Endowment, established by his father's will, he supported large-scale nutrition curricula and nutrition education programs at Pennsylvania State University, Jefferson Medical College, and the University of Pennsylvania.

Mr. Heinz was a friend of the late Pittsburgh Renaissance leader, banker, and philanthropist Richard K. Mellon; Mellon's cousin, Paul, also a philanthropist and art lover; and David Rockefeller, retired chairman of the board of the Chase Manhattan Bank. And he served for many years on the board of Mellon National Corp.

Mr. Heinz also had been a friend of Winston Churchill, the late British prime minister and World War II leader, and of members of the British royal family, particularly Queen Elizabeth the Queen Mother and Princess Margaret, who was a house guest in New York in 1977.

Queen Elizabeth II invested him with the insignia of Honorary Knight Commander of the Most Excellent Order of the British Empire in 1979, citing him "for significant contribution in the furtherance of British-American relationships, especially in the cultural, educational, and economic fields." This decoration especially gratified Mr. Heinz, who spent several months each year in the United Kingdom. He was also decorated by Italy, France, and Greece.

Mr. Heinz was a longtime and generous supporter of the Pittsburgh Symphony Society, art museums, community planning, education, health, religion, and welfare. He arranged for many millions of dollars to be granted each year from the Howard Heinz Endowment Fund to more than 50 Pittsburgh institutions. He also gave money in his own name.

Mr. Heinz was regarded as the individual who had done the most for the performing arts here. He, his family, and the fund gave $2.45 million to Carnegie Institute in 1974 for renovation and maintenance of the four Heinz Galleries on the second floor of the Museum of Art. He also served as a trustee of the institute and Carnegie

Mellon University. He also supported the Museum of Modern Art in New York and the Tate and Royal Academy in London.

He was a founding member of the Allegheny Conference on Community Development, on whose executive committee he served. On his initiative, the conference invited the late Richard Llewelyn Davies, the British urban planner, to study a major portion of the Golden Triangle along the Allegheny River for redevelopment.

One such innovative public-private renewal venture, spearheaded by the Howard Heinz Endowment in conjunction with city-county government, was the development of land adjacent to Heinz Hall. This multi-million dollar renewal saw construction started on a new 34-story office complex, to be the home of Consolidated Natural Gas, and renovation of the 2,800-seat Stanley Theater into the Benedum Center for the Performing Arts—home for the Pittsburgh Opera, the Pittsburgh Ballet Theater, Civic Light Opera, and Dance Council.

This complex complements Heinz Hall, a block away, and initiated a new downtown cultural and entertainment district destined eventually to embrace four theaters of different seating capacities funded in part by the commercial office development with local and federal government participation and administered by a new public-private institution, the Pittsburgh Trust for Cultural Resources.

Mr. Heinz, who advanced the concept, said the cultural district "aspires to make Pittsburgh a cultural center for the performing visual arts and to enhance the quality of life in this third-largest corporate headquarters city."

Until construction began on this complex, his most visible gifts in Downtown were Heinz Hall, a two-story addition, and the very popular Garden Plaza. The complex was donated to the Pittsburgh Symphony Society by the Howard Heinz Endowment Fund.

In late 1983 the Allegheny Conference honored Mr. Heinz at its annual dinner for his family's contributions to Pittsburgh. The conference, a nonprofit organization financed by business and industry, had never previously singled out an individual for recognition.

Mr. Heinz in 1968 established the Henry J. Heinz Professor of Development Economics at Yale University, his alma mater. He also endowed the position of art gallery director at Yale in 1982.

He was president of the old Federation of Social Agencies in Allegheny County in 1944. In 1947 he headed the most successful peace-time, fund-raising campaign by the 1,250 Community Chest affiliates in this county. He received the third-annual Red Feather Award for distinguished national service from the Community Chest in 1949.

Mr. Heinz attended Shady Side Academy and Choate School in Connecticut and received his bachelor's degree at Yale in 1931. He then studied for a year at Trinity College of Cambridge University. He trained at the Heinz plant in London before returning to this country to work in the north side plant.

He was a member of the Duquesne Club, Rolling Rock Club, Laurel Valley Golf Club, the River Club in New York City, and Buck's and White's in London.

Surviving, in addition to his son, are his third wife, Drue Mallory Mahler Heinz, and three grandchildren.

WEDNESDAY, FEBRUARY 3, 1999

Paul Mellon, 91
Enriched the Nation's Arts, Parks
By Donald Miller, *Pittsburgh Post-Gazette*

Paul Mellon, age 91, perhaps the most important American philanthropist of the 20th century, died Monday at Oak Spring, his home in Upperville, Virginia, after a few months of illness.

The renowned donor, art collector, patron of the arts, and horse breeder was the only son of Andrew W. Mellon, the Pittsburgh banker, financier, industrialist, secretary of the U.S. Treasury, and ambassador to Great Britain.

"Paul Mellon is unparalleled in his service to the nation, education, and the arts and humanities," said Earl A. Powell III, director of the National Gallery of Art. "His leadership and generosity established the National Gallery of Art in the first rank of the world's museums. Modest and kind, he was one of the greatest philanthropists of our time and a gentleman in every sense. He leaves an extraordinary legacy to future generations."

In his autobiography *Reflections in a Silver Spoon*, written with John Baskett and published in 1992, Mr. Mellon wrote fondly about his mother, Nora McMullen Mellon, an Englishwoman whom his father divorced after she left him for another man, and about his late sister, Ailsa Mellon Bruce.

Mr. Mellon, who listed himself in the 1999 *Who's Who in America* as "retired art gallery executive," was born in Pittsburgh on June 11, 1907, in a house that stood on the site of the Carnegie Mellon University stadium near Forbes Avenue and Margaret Morrison Drive. He later lived in what is now Chatham College's Mellon Hall. Mr. Mellon often visited England as a child and went to the Choate School in Wallingford, Connecticut, before going to Yale University.

Mr. Mellon graduated from Yale in 1929 and took a second bachelor's degree at Cambridge University, England, in 1931 and a master's degree in 1938. He then returned to Pittsburgh.

After working at Mellon Bank and various businesses here, Mr. Mellon determined he wanted a different career, primarily that of a connoisseur, collector, horseman, and philanthropist. However, he served on the board of directors of Mellon Bank from 1933 to 1941 and again from 1960 to 1976.

Paul Mellon. *Photo courtesy of the* Pittsburgh Post-Gazette.

"We are deeply saddened by the passing of Paul Mellon, whose family founded our company 130 years ago," said Martin G. McGuinn, chairman and CEO of Mellon Bank Corp. "He was always very supportive of our efforts and has been an important shareholder. He also was an inspiration for us all through his generous support for the arts and other philanthropic work."

In 1935 Mr. Mellon married his first wife, Mary Conover Brown Mellon, and moved to a farm in northern Virginia. The Mellons spent time in Europe in the late 1930s, chiefly because of their interest in the teachings of famed psychiatrist Carl G. Jung.

In 1945, a year before Mrs. Mellon died, the Mellons founded Bollingen Foundation—named for Jung's town in Switzerland—which published 100 books, including a best-seller, *I Ching*, to advance and preserve learning in the humanities. The foundation supported publication of many other works before closing in 1969.

In his forties, Mr. Mellon began collecting art in earnest with his second wife, Rachel "Bunny" Lambert Lloyd, purchasing works by the French impressionists and post-impressionists as well as English pictures and books.

His favored English artists included John Constable, Joseph Mallord, William Turner, George Stubbs, William Hogarth, Thomas Rowlandson, and Joseph Wright of Derby, as well as lesser known contemporaries. Mr. Mellon had a particular interest in what he called underappreciated genres such as sporting art, informal portraiture, and topographical painting.

He gave some works of art to the Carnegie Museum of Art and oversaw the gift of his sister's antique English and French furniture and ceramics collection, for which the museum created the Ailsa Mellon Bruce Decorative Arts Galleries. Mr. Mellon allocated funds for renovating the galleries.

Mr. Mellon and his family also were responsible for donating Mellon Institute to Carnegie Institute of Technology and giving a $5.5 million gift to its College of Fine Arts in 1967, when Carnegie Tech became Carnegie Mellon University.

Under Mr. Mellon's guidance, many outstanding cultural treasures have been preserved in magnificent structures. He paid for—and virtually filled with rare period paintings—the Yale Center for British Art, which was designed by Philadelphia architect Louis Kahn.

After dedicating his father's gift of the National Gallery of Art's West Building to the nation in 1941, Mr. Mellon would give its East Building, designed by I.M. Pei, to the nation in 1978.

Mr. and Mrs. Mellon also were important continuous donors and lenders to the National Gallery of Art, as well as the Virginia Museum of Arts in Richmond, which Mr. Mellon served as trustee for 40 years.

Since 1964 Mr. and Mrs. Mellon have donated 913 works of art to the National Gallery by such major artists as Edouard Manet, Claude Monet, Pierre-Auguste Renoir, Paul Cezanne, Edgar Degas, Vincent van Gogh, Paul Gauguin, Berthe Morisot, Mary Cassatt, Winslow Homer, George Bellows, and Alexander Calder. In 1965 Mr. Mellon gave 350 paintings of American Indians by George Catlin. In 1983 he gave the gallery 93 outstanding works he and his wife had collected over 30 years. Further gifts of large groups of important works of art followed from 1985 to 1987.

To honor the gallery's 50th anniversary in 1991, Mr. Mellon donated many important works, including Cezanne's masterpiece, *Boy in a Red Waistcoat*, and 69 original wax sculptures modeled by Degas. With 17 waxes given by Mr. Mellon in 1985, the gallery has the largest holding of Degas wax sculptures in the world. In late 1996 Mr. Mellon donated two Pablo Picassos: *The Death of the Harlequin* in 1905 and *Woman Sitting in a Garden* in 1901.

Mr. Mellon was president of the National Gallery of Art until 1979, then chairman of the gallery's board of trustees from 1979 to 1985, and honorary trustee since then.

In addition to art gifts, Mr. Mellon provided essential funding for a number of gallery projects, including generous gifts to the gallery's main fund for acquisitions, the Patrons' Permanent Fund, and, with his sister, funded the East Building construction.

Mr. Mellon also was instrumental in establishing the gallery's Center for Advanced Study in the Visual Arts. Its mandate in his words was: "To increase our understanding of our heritage of the art of the Western world."

In art conservation, Mr. Mellon directed many foundation grants to training programs for prospective conservators and ongoing research aimed at developing new conservation materials and techniques. One of those sites was at Mellon Institute.

He also helped to preserve nature through contributions toward the purchase of Cape Hatteras National Seashore in North Carolina and his gift of Sky Meadows State Park to Virginia. Mr. Mellon wrote, "The saving of these beautiful natural areas has given me the profoundest pleasure and the most heartwarming satisfaction."

But his "one great recreation in life" was horses, said Mr. Mellon, a consistent trophy winner. He enjoyed fox hunting and bred and raced top horses, including many winners from his Rokeby Stables in Virginia. Among champions were: one of the greatest horses of the century, Mill Reef, 1971 winner of the English Derby and the French Prix de L' Arc de Triomphe; Fort Marcy, twice winner of the Washington International and Horse of the Year in 1970; and Sea Hero, 1993 Kentucky Derby winner.

In Pittsburgh, Mr. Mellon oversaw the A.W. Mellon Educational and Charitable Trust, which gave many millions to health, education, and the arts before he dissolved it in 1980. Its board was getting long in the tooth, he said, and it was time for other foundations here to take up the trust's role.

The Andrew W. Mellon Foundation in New York was established by the 1969 merger of Paul Mellon's Old Dominion Foundation, founded in 1941, and his sister's Avalon Foundation. He served as a trustee of the foundation until 1985 and as its only honorary trustee until his death.

William G. Bowen, president of the Andrew W. Mellon Foundation, said, "I have often thought of Mr. Mellon as an exemplar of the ideal of the donor—a thoughtful as well as cheerful giver, never a seeker of the limelight, remarkable for his taste and discernment. His gift for friendship, his impish sense of humor, and his unwillingness to take himself too seriously were evident always."

Among organizations benefiting from his largesse are: Choate Rosemary Hall; Saint John's College in Annapolis, Maryland; the Center for Hellenic Studies; the Conservation Foundation in New York; Virginia Outdoors Foundation; Virginia Polytechnic Institute in Blacksburg; and Royal Veterinary College at the University of London.

He was a trustee of the Mellon Institute of Industrial Research here in 1937–1967 and chairman of its board of trustees in 1960–1967.

Recent awards include: the American Philosophical Society Benjamin Franklin Award, the World Monuments Fund Hadrian Award, and the Thomas Jefferson Memorial Foundation Medal in Architecture. The Yale Medal, awarded

in 1953, was one of his earliest honors.

Near the end of *Reflection in a Silver Spoon*, Mr. Mellon wrote: "I have been an amateur in every phase of my life: an amateur poet, an amateur scholar, an amateur horseman, an amateur farmer, an amateur soldier, an amateur connoisseur of art, an amateur publisher, and an amateur museum executive.

"The root of the word *amateur* is the Latin word for love, and I can honestly say that I've thoroughly enjoyed all the roles I have played."

Mr. Mellon's immediate survivors are: Rachel Lambert Lloyd, his wife of 50 years; a daughter, Catherine Conover; a son, Timothy, from his first marriage to Mary Conover Brown, who died in 1946; and three grandchildren.

TUESDAY, JULY 8, 2003

Frieda Shapira, 89
Committed to Social Reform

By Sally Kalson, *Pittsburgh Post-Gazette*. Staff writer Steve Levin contributed.

Frieda Shapira, matriarch of one of Pittsburgh's most influential families and a former child welfare worker whose commitment to social reform defined her life for more than six decades, died yesterday of a bone marrow disease at her daughter's home near Ligonier. She was 89 years old.

Mrs. Shapira, whose father cofounded the Giant Eagle supermarket empire and whose son now runs the company, was a force on the boards of more than two dozen organizations

dedicated to racial equality, interfaith relations, human services, education, and the arts.

She was a prime mover in establishing one of the country's first nonresidential Job Corps centers for women, and she cofounded a preschool program in the Pittsburgh Public Schools that preceded Head Start.

A lifelong liberal Democrat, she had friends across the political, social, and economic spectrum and worked with many of them for the common good.

"Frieda had her foot in different camps that didn't necessarily communicate with each other formally. She really believed in the rainbow and everyone working together," said David Epperson, retired dean of the University of Pittsburgh School of Social Work, who served with her on the board of the Urban League for many years.

Mrs. Shapira and Republican maven Elsie Hillman bonded instantly when they first met in 1967 as members of the Human Relations Commission. Over the years they worked together on numerous causes. "She was a dominant force in everything that happened in the community in social relations, human relations, and women's interests," Hillman said. "She led us all."

Soft-spoken and unassuming, her petite frame topped by a halo of white hair, Mrs. Shapira was a familiar presence at countless community events and fund-raisers over the years.

She sat on the boards of a wide range of groups, including her favorite, the Pittsburgh Foundation, as well as the United Way of Allegheny County, the United Jewish Federation of Greater Pittsburgh, the YWCA of Greater Pittsburgh, the American Jewish Committee, Beginning with Books, the Center for Victims of Violent Crime, the University of Pittsburgh, and WQED.

She campaigned to establish the city's first free in-school lunch program in 1964. A few years later, she joined with women from Catholic and Protestant national church groups and the national councils of Jewish women and black women to get Job Corps training for women. Initially, Congress had approved the job training only for men.

While frequently honored with humanitarian awards like the Woman of Spirit from Carlow College, Mrs. Shapira had her greatest impact behind the scenes. Colleagues say her training as a social worker helped her zero in on unmet needs and assess programs with a pragmatic eye. She found funding for worthy causes through her vast network of sources. "She was never there for cosmetic purposes," Epperson said. "She was there to change things for the better."

"Sometimes boards were not representative of those they sought to serve," said Alfred W. Wishart Jr., former president and CEO of the Pittsburgh Foundation, where Mrs. Shapira served as a board member for 18 years, including several as vice chairwoman. "Frieda would ask how they could understand the needs if there was no one from the community at the table," he said. "She'd quietly require the diversity issue to be addressed if we were going to help."

Her tenure on the Forbes Fund (now the Copeland Fund) in the 1980s helped to save an array of agencies from extinction, said retired chairman Bill Copeland. The fund's purpose was to salvage groups that were going to die for lack of money because of policies adopted by the Reagan Administration. "She could be ferocious as a lion, and she knew where all the skeletons were," Copeland said. "She told us which groups were redundant and which were serving people well. There are agencies today that are thriving because the Forbes Fund bought them a little time, and she was an integral part of that."

Mrs. Shapira also played an important role in Pitt's research on how the steel industry's collapse was affecting workers and families in the Mon Valley, where a crisis of unemployment, depression, and family dissolution was unfolding. "Frieda recognized the impact on the human condition, not just the economy," Epperson said. "With men not working and housewives entering the labor force, there was an impact on marriages, children, divorce rates, black and white—everything."

The research involved roughly half of the Pitt School of Social Work at one point or another, ran from the late 1970s to the late 1980s, and produced recommendations that were used by United Way and other agencies and foundations in designing programs to help Mon Valley residents.

In many ways, Mrs. Shapira's life reflected the sweep of 20th-century America. Her grandfather, Sam Goldstein, was a Jewish immigrant from Lithuania who peddled dry goods from a horse-drawn carriage on the teeming streets of the Hill District. Her father, Joe Goldstein, worked for a grocery wholesaler on Penn Avenue before joining with two of his customers to form Eagle Grocery Co. They sold that business in 1928 to Kroger, then joined with the OK Grocery chain to form the basis of what became the Giant Eagle empire.

When Mrs. Shapira was three years old, the family moved from Cliff Street in the Hill District to a rental in Point Breeze, then the eastern edge of the suburbs. The oldest of three children, Shapira grew up playing in Frick Woods with her siblings, Morris and Leah, vis-iting the aviary at the Heinz estate on Penn Avenue, and making frequent visits to the Homewood swimming pool and library.

"We'd stand on the Lang Avenue bridge to Homewood when the train passed underneath, breathing in the black smoke," Mrs. Shapira told the *Post-Gazette* in a 1999 interview. "We thought that was great. Now I have emphysema, and I never even smoked."

The family eventually moved to Squirrel Hill on Hobart Street, then the last street before Schenley Park.

Mrs. Shapira graduated from Allderdice High School and, in 1934, earned her undergraduate degree in social work from the University of Pittsburgh. That same year, she married her college sweetheart, Saul Shapira, and together they left for Columbia University in New York City, where he earned a law degree and she got her master's in social work.

Once back in Pittsburgh, her husband went to work for the newly formed Pittsburgh Housing Authority, one of the first in the country to build public housing. That distinction drew President Franklin D. Roosevelt to the groundbreaking for Allequippa Terrace.

"It was very unusual for that time," Mrs. Shapira once recalled. "Black and white professionals worked side by side on equal footing. We made friends with people we never would have met any other way."

Among those friends were Henry Smith, who later became a judge; former Pitt track-star-turned-lawyer named Everett Utterback; Mal Goode, who became the first black network TV newsman; and Billie Brown, mother of pioneer civil rights lawyer Byrd Brown.

Mrs. Shapira made her own inroads, working for several years in the late 1930s teaching neglected and dependent children through the Children's Service Bureau, a forerunner of the county's Office of Children, Youth, and Families. She also supervised children in foster homes.

Saul Shapira eventually joined Giant Eagle in 1945 and was president and CEO from 1968 to 1980. He was succeeded by the couple's oldest son, David, who is chairman and CEO today. Under their leadership, the company expanded to about 200 stores and 35,000 employees in three states. Saul Shapira died in 1981.

The Shapira family's leadership and philanthropy in the Pittsburgh Jewish community is legendary. Four members of the family, including Mrs. Shapira, have been awarded the United Jewish Federation of Pittsburgh's highest volunteer award.

The honors awarded Mrs. Shapira since 1972 fill nearly 1? typed pages. Among them are inclusion as a legend of the Pittsburgh civil rights movement at the Hill District's Freedom Corner Monument, a doctor of humane letters from Point Park College, *Pittsburgh* magazine's recognition as one of the 100 Most Influential Pittsburghers of the Century, and the Florence Reizenstein Award for Advancement of Human Rights & Dignity from the Pittsburgh Commission on Human Relations.

Although she had become increasingly frail in recent months from myelodysplasia, a syndrome that interferes with the bone marrow's production of blood cells, Mrs. Shapira continued to attend public events and reside in the Squirrel Hill home where she had raised her children.

She is survived by a daughter, Dr. Edie Shapira of Squirrel Hill; three sons, Daniel and David of Squirrel Hill and Ralph of Los Angeles; 12 grandchildren; and two great-grandchildren.

THURSDAY, JANUARY 27, 2005

Cordelia Scaife May, 76
Heiress Known for her Generosity

By Johnna A. Pro and Marylynne Pitz, *Pittsburgh Post-Gazette. Post-Gazette* retired senior editor and former art and architecture critic Donald Miller contributed to this report.

Cordelia Scaife May, heiress to the Mellon fortune and a reclusive yet generous philanthropist whose net worth of roughly $800 million put her among the 400 wealthiest people in the country, died yesterday at Cold Comfort, her Ligonier home.

The cause of death was not disclosed, but Mrs. May, who was 76 years old, recently suffered from pain in her spine and had difficulty walking.

She was known simply as Cordy to family and friends, who remembered a warm and giving person who crafted a witty note, told a great story, and kept a keen watch over her charitable interests, which supported conservation groups, Planned Parenthood, and other causes.

Mrs. May was divorced from her first husband, Herbert A. May Jr., but continued to use his name after she married Allegheny County district attorney Robert W. Duggan. Duggan killed himself with a shotgun in 1974, hours before being indicted by a grand jury for income tax evasion and racketeering.

Although his death was ruled a suicide, questions surrounded the circumstances, and his family, including Mrs. May, maintained he had been murdered. The scandal, which rocked the political and the powerful in Allegheny County, reverberated for years afterward.

Even before Duggan's death, Mrs. May eschewed publicity in all forms and guarded her privacy zealously. Early in her life she battled with her family, failed at love, and fought alcohol addiction, according to several sources. She did not like to appear in public, nor did she wish to see her name in print.

Through the Laurel Foundation, which she established in 1951, Mrs. May gave away millions of dollars in grants on the condition that the recipient not disclose her name or that of the foundation. "She often said she had the ability to fund the programs but that it was the special people who were committed to making the programs happen who deserved the attention," said Donna Panazzi, vice president of the Laurel Foundation.

The foundation funds cultural, educational, conservation, and beautification initiatives in the United States. Locally the foundation supports the Montour Trail, the National Aviary in Pittsburgh, the RiverLife Task Force, the Pittsburgh Parks Conservancy, and the Women's Center and Shelter of Greater Pittsburgh.

Panazzi said the foundation's seven-member staff viewed Mrs. May as a sensitive and appreciative boss who also was "a friend and a family member." Each month Mrs. May would insist on closing the foundation offices for a day and would join the staff on an outing to a museum, the National Aviary, or a picnic lunch at the Point in Point State Park. "She was like a child, so excited about showing off this city," Panazzi said.

Mrs. May also was a gifted raconteur, whose vivid description of her stories' settings made listening to her a delight. "She was just so articulate. When she told a story, it was like watching a movie," Panazzi said.

Michael Strueber, an artist and director emeritus of the Southern Alleghenies Museum of Art in Loretto in Cambria County said Mrs. May was "one of the kindest, most generous people I've ever known in my life. She was loyal to a flaw. I'm a better person for having known her. What she did, in most cases, she did anonymously. She wanted no public accolades. That's the rarest kind of philanthropy. She did things because she believed in them."

Among her passions was horticulture, and in particular she supported the Pacific Tropical Botanical Garden in Hawaii, said her longtime friend George A. Griffith, of Johnstown, a horticulturist. "We went there a number of times," he said. "She would come across as if she knew nothing, but she knew so much. She was just so modest. She was so bright, yet so modest. She was the brightest person I've ever known."

Mrs. May lived atop a hill in Ligonier in a home that was neither large nor lavish, according to her personal lawyer, David Armstrong. "It was a lovely place in the woods. She really loved living there," Armstrong said, adding that her

Christmas card for 2004 showed Mrs. May standing in her driveway, dressed casually in blue slacks, a red blouse, and a sweater with puppies on it. Mrs. May's arm was flung around Santa.

Mrs. May, who was born in 1928, was the eldest child of Sarah Cordelia Mellon and Alan Magee Scaife. She was reared by governesses and nurses in the protective confines of Penguin Court, the family's Ligonier estate which she would later describe as palatial, but never happy.

Like other young women of her social class, she was educated at the private, yet progressive Falk School and later at the more conservative Ellis School. By her own admission she was "one of the more contumacious students—I was urged not to return," she told Burton Hersh, author of an extensive Mellon family history.

She later graduated from Foxcroft School in Virginia.

Mrs. May wanted to study languages and attended Carnegie Institute of Technology and the University of Pittsburgh before dropping out to marry. She eventually returned to Pitt and studied British history.

On June 30, 1949, she wed the outgoing Herbert May Jr. at East Liberty Presbyterian in a ceremony that was followed by a lavish reception at the Scaife family home, according to Hersh. Less than a year later, the couple was divorced. "We were just unsuited," Mrs. May told Hersh.

After her family banished her to Palm Beach, Florida, for four years because of the embarrassment of a divorce, Mrs. May returned to Pittsburgh and renewed her friendship with Duggan, according to Hersh.

The two had known and liked each other since childhood, but her family discouraged the relationship because he was of a lower social status and Catholic, according to Hersh.

The two were so much a part of each other's lives that Mrs. May's only sibling, her younger brother Richard Mellon Scaife, the philanthropist and publisher of the *Greensburg Tribune-Review*, treated Duggan like a member of the family.

By the summer of 1973, though, Duggan, who had been elected district attorney three times, was the target of a grand jury investigation that linked him to organized crime, slush funds, and tax evasion. He had lost much of his support, including Scaife's. Despite ever worsening allegations, Mrs. May remained staunchly loyal to Duggan, and in doing so, fractured her relationship with her brother. Their estrangement would last for decades until a recent reconciliation, friends of Mrs. May said.

Mrs. May and Duggan married in Nevada in 1973, just days after Mrs. May was notified by the Internal Revenue Service that she would have to answer questions about Duggan, leading to speculation that the marriage was calculated because a wife cannot be compelled to testify against her husband.

Throughout her life, Mrs. May refused to dignify such speculation. She remained steadfast in her belief that he was innocent, despite mounting evidence. She quietly memorialized her late husband with a plaque at the entrance of the Southern Alleghenies Museum.